The Complete Book of Pies

200 recipes from sweet to savory

Julie Hasson

Robert

For complete cataloguing information, see page 246.

Disclaimer
The recipes in this book have been carefully tested by our kitchen and our tasters. To the best of our knowledge, they are safe and nutritious for ordinary use and users. For those people with food or other allergies, or who have special food requirements or health issues, please read the suggested contents of each recipe carefully and determine whether or not they may create a problem for you. All recipes are used at the risk of the consumer.

We cannot be responsible for any hazards, loss or damage that may occur as a result of any recipe use.

For those with special needs, allergies, requirements or health problems, in the event of any doubt, please contact your medical adviser prior to the use of any recipe.

Design and Production: Kevin Cockburn/PageWave Graphics Inc.
Editor: Carol Sherman
Recipe Tester: Jennifer MacKenzie
Copy Editor: Christina Anson Mine
Photography: Colin Erricson
Food Styling: Kathryn Robertson and Kate Bush
Prop Styling: Charlene Erricson

Cover image: Double-Crust Spiced Apple Pie (see recipe, page 26)

We acknowledge the financial support of the Government of Canada through the Book Publishing Industry Development Program (BPIDP) for our publishing activities.

Published by Robert Rose Inc.
120 Eglinton Avenue East, Suite 800, Toronto, Ontario, Canada M4P 1E2
Tel: (416) 322-6552 Fax: (416) 322-6936

Printed and bound in Canada

1 2 3 4 5 6 7 8 9 CPL 16 15 14 13 12 11 10 09 08

Contents

To Jay

Acknowledgments

Thanks to my incredibly supportive and loving husband, Jay, who so patiently endured a year and a half of endless fruit picking (even when you'd rather have been doing something else), a continually messy kitchen, many nights eating pie for dinner, and taste testing hundreds and hundreds of pies. You rock! And thanks to my awesome children, Sydney and Noah, for all of your taste testing, pie suggestions and patience while I was buried in the kitchen under all of that pie dough.

Thanks also to all of the following: Lisa Ekus-Saffer, for being my über-agent and friend. Bob Dees at Robert Rose — it's always a pleasure working with you. Carol Sherman, for your awesome editing and patience, and for making everything come together so beautifully. Jennifer MacKenzie, for your excellent recipe testing and recommendations. Judith Finlayson, for contributing some of your wonderful savory recipes. Colin Erricson, for your fine photography; and Kathryn Robertson, Kate Bush and Charlene Erricson, for your great food and props styling. Andrew Smith, Kevin Cockburn, Daniella Zanchetta and Joseph Gisini at PageWave Graphics for designing such a beautiful book. Everyone at Robert Rose, for working so hard on this book and doing such a great job!

Thank you, Mom, for truly loving the lumpy lemon pie that I made for you in junior high school (as only a mom could) and encouraging me to go to culinary school. Thanks, Dad and Ellen, for your friendship, love and support. Jon, for being an awesome brother and great chef. Heather, Kim and Michelle, for being such cool sisters. Louie, for sharing my cookbooks with all your friends.

And finally, thanks to my group of recipe testers, who graciously tested and gave me honest feedback on the vegan pie recipes: Thalia Palmer, Julie Farson, Tal Levin, Marleigh Riggins, Webly Bowles, Laura Faye Berry, Shereé Britt, Vicki Hodge, Emilie Hardman, Bahar Zaker, Jamie Garvey and Arine Mentink.

Introduction

What could be better than a fresh summer fruit pie, brimming with sweet ripe fruit? Not much, as far as I'm concerned. I've learned over the years, though, that people say they are either a pie person or a cake person. Period. Well, I can definitely say that I'm a pie person. I'm also a cake person, an ice cream person, a chocolate person and a cupcake person. Do I really have to choose just one dessert?

Although I've always loved eating pies, my passion for baking them goes back to when I was first married. My husband's cousin Jill would bake the most fabulous pies. She always made it seem so easy, casually tossing together sliced apples with cinnamon and sugar, mounding them into a perfectly crimped pastry shell. The thing that was so amazing to me was not that her pies were utterly delicious (which they were) but that she was so easygoing about the whole pie-making process. This became the root of my pie inspiration.

My first homemade pie was a peach one. Our backyard peach tree was so full of fruit that the poor branches were hanging on the ground. I then moved on to apples, buying cases at a time. I dragged my husband (and later, children) to every U-pick farm that I could find. I was ready with buckets in hand as each fruit came into season. What I learned was that a fruit pie is only as good as the fruit that you use. I also discovered that it's so much fun to pick the fruit yourself (and much more economical, too). Pie baking became my therapy.

When the opportunity arose for me to write a book on pies, I jumped at the chance. I wanted to show that pie making is not only fun but easy, too. Threaded throughout this book you will find all sorts of tips and shortcuts for making pies, as well as recipes for ice cream pies and toppings, glazes and sauces, just in case you want to take your pies to a whole new level. There's even a chapter on savory pies, including many created by cookbook author Judith Finlayson. Special features throughout the book include logos highlighting classic pies, from apple to pumpkin, and vegan-friendly ones, too.

After baking literally hundreds and hundreds of pies, I've selected my favorite recipes for this book. I encourage you to go pick some fresh fruit, put on your apron, get out your rolling pin and start baking. And then, just maybe, you will find yourself becoming a pie person, too.

— *Julie Hasson*

Tools and Equipment for Perfect Pies

In the tasty world of pie making, there are definitely some kitchen tools and gadgets that make things easier. You can certainly make do with a large mixing bowl, a pastry blender, a rolling pin, a glass pie plate and a rimmed baking sheet. And, in some cases, I believe that simplicity is better. But once I started experimenting with silicone rolling pins and mats, wooden pie presses, pastry weights and a food processor, I realized that some of these items really did make a big difference. Drawing on my experience in professional kitchens and my great passion for kitchen tools and equipment, here's a list of equipment that I believe will help everyone make delectable pies.

Measuring equipment

Liquid measuring cups: The most accurate way to measure liquid ingredients is in glass or plastic liquid measuring cups with a lip or spout. I like to keep a variety of sizes in my kitchen. Glass measuring cups are also perfect for melting chocolate chips. Just combine the cream and chocolate chips, or chocolate chips and shortening, in a medium or large glass measuring cup and microwave for 30-second intervals, stirring often, until melted.

Dry measuring cups: These are the most accurate tools (with the exception of a digital scale) for measuring dry ingredients. I like to use a good-quality set of metal nesting measuring cups, which come in a variety of measurements. When measuring, always remember to spoon your dry ingredients into the cup, then level the top by scraping across it with the flat side of a knife or a skewer. This will give you an accurate measurement.

Measuring spoons: These are the most accurate tools for measuring small amounts of both liquid and dry ingredients. Look for a metal set that ranges from ⅛ tsp (0.5 mL) to 1 tbsp (15 mL).

Mixing bowls: A nesting set of mixing bowls (or two or three in different sizes) is a must in the dessert kitchen. I like to have both stainless steel and ceramic, depending on the mixing job. Stainless steel works better for whipping cream; both work well for pastry dough.

Cookie or ice cream scoops/dishers: Available in a variety of sizes, these are a blessing in the kitchen. Use scoops to measure out equal portions of batter and dough, which will give you perfectly sized tart shells. Plus, using a scoop will save you quite a bit of time.

Hand tools

Heat-safe rubber spatulas: The new silicone spatulas are heatproof to 600°F (300°C). They are a boon to bakers, as they will scrape a bowl clean with ease. They are dishwasher-safe and can be used for stovetop cooking as well.

Microplane® zester/grater: This tool makes quick work of removing and grating citrus zest. Just rub over the surface of oranges, lemons and limes, carefully removing the colored peel.

Sifter or strainer: This is an important tool for sifting dry ingredients or dusting a dessert with confectioner's (icing) sugar.

Whisk: The most important tool for cream, eggs, batter and anything else that requires air to be incorporated.

Baking equipment

Pie plates: I recommend using 9-inch (23 cm) glass pie plates for most of the pie recipes and 10-inch (25 cm) deep-dish glass pie plates for the deep-dish pies. Although ceramic pie plates are pretty, most of them aren't a standard size (as I learned myself), so you will most likely wind up with an insufficient amount of pastry dough and filling.

Tart tins and pans: You will need a variety of pans to make the desserts in this book. Always invest in heavier, quality pans, as they conduct heat more efficiently. Metal tart pans come in a variety of sizes, often depending on the store where you purchase them. For traditional tarts, look for shallow removable-bottom metal tart pans in 9- and 11-inch (23 and 27.5 cm) diameters. For quiches, look for metal 10-inch (25 cm) deep-dish fluted removable-bottom pans. For little tarts, I use small 2½-inch (6 cm) metal tart pans (not removable-bottom) and shallow miniature muffin pans.

Pie and tart presses: These are something that I never knew existed until I started writing this book. I was intrigued that they were handmade from wood and decided to give them a try. I am now a pie press convert! They help make the pastry/crust process a snap by simply pressing your dough directly into the tin or pan. No muss, no fuss with chilling and rolling dough, and they're perfect for anyone with arthritis. I used the handmade wooden presses from Birds Hill Enterprises in Canada to test out a lot of the recipes in this book. They come in a variety of sizes for both tarts and pies.

Cooling rack: A wire cooling rack elevates a pie pan or hand pies so that air can circulate around them.

Cast-iron skillets: These are ideal for making skillet pies, cobblers and pot pies. They retain heat well and, because they're ovenproof, you can start your pie on the stovetop and finish it up in the oven. I had excellent results with the Lodge brand when testing these pie recipes.

Enameled cast-iron pans and skillets: These gorgeous and versatile pots and pans are oven-safe and do a fabulous job with sauces, fillings and skillet pies. I used the Le Creuset brand with excellent results for the testing of some of these recipes.

Parchment paper: This grease- and heat-resistant paper is used to line baking pans. It keeps your hand pies from sticking and burning (unless you overbake them). This is the number one item on my list of baking equipment. I also like to line my rimmed baking sheet before I place the pie plate on top for baking, because it makes cleanup a breeze.

Rimmed baking sheets: These are key pieces of equipment for making pies. The rimmed sides keep any pie juices from overflowing onto your oven and helps to crisp up the crust. Look for good-quality, heavy-duty construction and feel, as thin pans can warp. They can usually be purchased bundled in groups of two or three in large warehouse stores such as Costco. A good-quality pan is definitely worth the small investment.

Silicone rolling mat: This large silicone baking mat used exclusively for rolling dough is a relatively new invention. Although you can use a standard baking mat for this purpose, a rolling mat is larger and can accommodate the rolled dough more easily.

Silicone rolling pin: I instantly fell in love with this product, especially when combined with a silicone rolling mat. The advantage is that you can use less flour without the dough sticking, resulting in a more tender crust. I used a heavy-duty Sil-Pin™ rolling pin to test the pastry recipes in this book and loved it so much that I have now retired my wooden ones.

Wooden or plastic tart tamper: To make the process go more quickly when scooping dough into prepared mini muffin pans, I use a wooden or plastic tart tamper. The tampers can be found at kitchen stores or online, and work beautifully to press the dough into the mini muffin cups and up the sides.

Electric equipment

Stand mixer: This isn't a must for all recipes but it sure makes life a lot easier. I recommend a heavy, sturdy stand mixer, such as KitchenAid, Cuisinart or Bosch. It will last for years. A stand mixer is great for making pie dough and pastry, and it's your best bet for making batters, whipping cream or beating eggs.

Hand mixer: This is a great tool for quickly whipping cream or egg whites.

Blender: Try to find a blender that has an ice-crushing button; it works well on frozen fruit or chocolate chips.

Immersion/stick blender: I love immersion/stick blenders. They blend quickly with a minimum of mess, making them ideal for sauces and dressings. I even use mine to whip cream, but many of the newer immersion blenders now come with a whip attachment.

Food processor: This machine is essential for making pie dough and pastry. It also does a fabulous job of chopping nuts, chocolate chips, dried fruit and cookies for crumb crusts. I recommend the KitchenAid® or Cuisinart® brands. They will last forever and do a more-consistent job than less-expensive brands.

Ice cream maker: These machines are fun to use, and homemade ice cream and sorbets are nothing short of ethereal! There are several kinds of ice cream machines on the market — from those that use a frozen insulated bowl to ones that have a built-in compressor — and a lot of them are reasonably priced. I tested the ice cream recipes in this book on a Cuisinart® and absolutely loved it.

Fruit and vegetable sanitizing system: This is a relatively new product on the market but one that I used extensively in my recipe testing. There are several brands available now, but the one that I used was the Lotus® Sanitizing System™. With all of the concern these days about bacteria on fruit and veggies, you simply put your produce in a bowl on the machine, fill it with water and the machine infuses the water with ozone, which neutralizes up to 99.9% of bacteria and pesticides on foods. There are no chemicals involved, just oxygen.

Microwave oven: A microwave oven is definitely a plus in the dessert kitchen. I use mine extensively to melt chocolate, heat cream and soften butter. (You can also use a double boiler to melt chocolate.) I have tested the recipes in this book using a 1,000-watt microwave oven.

> **Tip** • To melt chocolate in a microwave oven: In a large microwave-safe bowl (preferably a large glass measuring cup), melt chocolate chips with shortening (or cream or butter) on High, uncovered, stirring every 30 seconds, until chocolate is melted and smooth. Be careful not to overheat or cook the chocolate too long, as it can easily burn.

Oven: It really doesn't matter whether you use a gas or electric oven for baking. But do make sure that the oven is calibrated (precisely adjusted) so that it bakes evenly and at the required temperature. The recipes in this book were tested using a conventional electric oven.

Common Ingredients

I have included a list of many common ingredients used in this book. I recommend stocking your kitchen with many of these items, as it will make pie baking a breeze. If you plan on making pies and crisps year-round, I recommend stocking your freezer with bags of frozen berries. If you like cranberries, I also suggest picking up a few bags to freeze in the late fall, when you see them in grocery stores. Butter, margarine and/or shortening are also good items to have on hand, and are best stored in the refrigerator. That way, if you want to whip together a pastry crust, they're already chilled. With a little planning and a bit of foresight, you will be able to bake up pies, tarts and cobblers that are blue ribbon worthy.

Chocolate

There are many varieties of chocolate. Here are a few that I like to use.

Bittersweet or dark chocolate: This chocolate must have at least 35% chocolate liquor, but many brands now go beyond that up to 90%. When I use dark chocolate in my baking, I often reach for a 70% bar. If you like a sweeter chocolate, use semisweet, which has a less-intense chocolate flavor than bittersweet. For a darker, more intense chocolate flavor, reach for one of the darker, higher percentage bars.

Unsweetened or baking chocolate: Made with 53% cocoa butter, it is excellent for cooking. I like to use unsweetened chocolate in tandem with chocolate chips, as it can deepen and enhance the chocolate flavor.

Semisweet and bittersweet chocolate bars: I like to keep a few on hand because they make a very tasty stand-in if you are out of chocolate chips. Coarsely chop the bars with a sharp chef's knife and use, measure for measure, as you would chocolate chips. Valrhona and Scharffen Berger are two very good brands. They are becoming more readily available at better grocery and health food stores.

> **Tip** • Store chocolate in a cool, dry place for up to one year. Chocolate will sometimes develop a white "bloom," or coating, when it gets too warm, causing the cocoa butter to separate. The chocolate is still fine to use in recipes or for melting.

Chocolate chips: When using chocolate chips in these recipes, use good-quality real semisweet chocolate chips. The better the quality, the better the taste of the final product. I recommend keeping a big bag of chocolate chips in the pantry at all times so you can be ready to go with any of these recipes. Large bags of chocolate chips are available at club stores in most cities.

Unsweetened cocoa powder: I use unsweetened Dutch-process cocoa powder in my baking. It is a dark, rich cocoa powder that has been processed with alkali, which neutralizes its natural acidity.

> **Tip** • Cocoa powder needs to be sifted before use because it can be very lumpy, which makes it difficult to incorporate. Use a fine-mesh sieve to remove any lumps before adding cocoa powder to other dry ingredients.

Coffee

Ground coffee: The recipes in this book were tested using finely ground French roast coffee beans. To make strong brewed coffee, use a ratio of 2 tbsp (25 mL) finely ground coffee to 6 oz (175 mL) water. This ratio will yield a strong yet flavorful brew.

Instant coffee granules: This is an easy way to add coffee flavor without brewing coffee. The crystals dissolve instantly in hot liquid.

Dairy

Butter: I recommend using unsalted butter unless otherwise specified. The quality is better, the flavor purer and you can control the saltiness of your recipe. If you only have salted butter in the house, you can substitute it in most cases; just make sure to omit all other salt called for in the recipe.

> **Tip** • To bring cold butter to room temperature in a hurry, use a microwave oven. I usually set it on Medium (50%) for 10 to 20 seconds, making sure not to melt the butter.

Buttermilk: Buttermilk is made from low-fat or nonfat milk that has had a bacterial culture added (somewhat like yogurt), creating a slightly sour, creamy product. It gives baked goods a delicious, tangy flavor and moist texture.

> **Tip** • If you are out of buttermilk, you can make your own sour milk: Pour 1 tbsp (15 mL) lemon juice or white vinegar into a measuring cup. Add enough milk to make 1 cup (250 mL). Let stand for about 5 minutes before using.

Milk: The recipes in this book were tested using whole milk. Do not substitute nonfat or low-fat varieties.

Soy milk: There are many great-tasting varieties of soy milk in most grocery and natural foods stores. You can use plain or vanilla for brushing on top of pies.

Cream: Look for whipping (35%) cream, also known as heavy cream. It will keep, refrigerated, for quite a while. For better flavor, look for brands from organic dairies. I always have cream on hand, as it is perfect for last-minute desserts from ice cream to truffles.

Cream cheese: This fresh cheese is made from cow's milk. For quality and consistency, you are better off sticking with name brands.

Sour cream: The addition of sour cream, a high-fat version of buttermilk, helps produce rich and tender results.

Sweetened condensed milk: This is made from sweetened nonfat or whole milk that has had all of the water removed. It is not the same as evaporated milk and cannot be used interchangeably.

Eggs

The recipes in this book were tested using large eggs. I generally suggest bringing your eggs to room temperature for baking, but in most of these recipes you can use chilled eggs if need be.

Flavorings

Always use pure extracts in your baking, as they are superior in quality and flavor to artificial flavorings. Imitation vanilla is made from synthetic substances, which imitate only a part of the natural smell and flavor of vanilla.

Flour

All-purpose flour: The recipes in this book were tested using unbleached all-purpose flour, which I feel is a healthier alternative. Bleached flour has been chemically bleached and bromated; I prefer not to use it. You can, however, substitute bleached flour for unbleached flour in these recipes.

Chickpea flour: This flour, also known as garbanzo bean flour, besan or gram flour, is made from ground dried chickpeas. You can find it in some well-stocked supermarkets, health food stores, Southeast Asian, Middle Eastern and Mediterranean markets. It cannot be used interchangeably with wheat flour in baking. It is high in protein, low in fat and gluten-free.

Frozen pastry shells

Although I advocate making pastry from scratch, there are times when you need to take shortcuts. If you want to use a frozen prepared crust, I recommend finding an organic brand that tastes great and doesn't contain hydrogenated oils. I tested some of the recipes in this book using frozen shells from Wholly Wholesome®, and loved both their quality and taste. I also tested recipes using their crumb crusts for ice cream and cream pies, and they worked very well.

Liqueurs and spirits

I love to keep a stash of flavored liqueurs and spirits on hand for cooking and baking. Some key ones are rum, orange-flavored liqueur (such as Triple Sec), kirsch (cherry brandy), coffee-flavored liqueur and brandy. Airline-size bottles work great in a pinch if you don't have full-size bottles on hand.

Nonstick cooking spray

This is a must in the dessert kitchen. Nonstick cooking spray is a quick way to grease your pans and can be more reliable than butter or oil. Choose a spray that is unflavored.

> **Tip** • To make your own nonstick pan release, whip together ⅓ cup (75 mL) vegetable or canola oil, ⅓ cup (75 mL) vegetable shortening and ⅓ cup (75 mL) all-purpose flour. (I use a mini food processor for this.) Store in an airtight container in the refrigerator for up to several months.

Nuts

The recipes in this book use a variety of nuts, such as almonds, walnuts and pecans. Store nuts in the freezer to keep them fresh, as they can become rancid very quickly. Toast them for the fullest flavor. To toast nuts: Preheat oven to 350°F (180°C). Spread nuts on a foil- or parchment paper–lined baking pan and bake for 5 to 10 minutes, stirring occasionally, or until lightly browned and fragrant.

Oats

Oats are a whole grain that is usually purchased "rolled." Buy old-fashioned varieties to use in crisps and crumble toppings.

Oil

The recipes in this book call for vegetable oil. I prefer canola oil, but you can substitute vegetable or soy oil should you desire. You will want to use a light, flavorless oil, which is why olive oil is not a good substitute.

Salt

All of the recipes in this book were tested with plain table salt. Although I like kosher or sea salt on my food, I prefer to use table salt for baking.

Shortening

When a recipe calls for shortening, always use solid white vegetable shortening. Shortening now also comes in organic and non-hydrogenated varieties.

Spices

Certain spices, such as ground cinnamon, ground ginger, ground allspice, ground cloves and ground cardamom, are must-haves in the dessert kitchen. Ground spices tend to go stale quickly, so discard them if they are no longer fragrant.

Sugar

Granulated sugar: A highly refined sugar made from sugar beets or sugar cane.

Confectioner's (icing) sugar: Sugar that has been powdered or pulverized and mixed with a small amount of cornstarch.

Brown sugar: Granulated sugar mixed with molasses.

Superfine or baker's sugar: Ultra-fine granulated sugar that dissolves very quickly in liquid. If you cannot find it in your local grocery store, you can make your own. Process granulated sugar in a food processor until very finely ground.

Corn syrup: This thick, sweet syrup is made from cornstarch. Corn syrup can be purchased in both light (white) and dark (golden) varieties.

Not all sugar is necessarily vegan, but organic sugar and beet sugar generally are.

Vegan margarine

Some of the pastry recipes in this book call for vegan margarine. Look for a brand that is non-hydrogenated and tastes great, such as Earth Balance®.

Vegetarian chicken

Although this sounds like an oxymoron, it definitely isn't. There are several great-tasting brands available now, in refrigerated, frozen and dried forms. My two favorites, which I used for some of the savory recipes in this book, are Gardein, which is available frozen, and Soy Curls, which are available in dried strips.

Tips for better results

Here are a few tips to make you a pie professional.

- Pie baking is fun! Don't look at it as a chore, as this can take away from the experience. Repeat after me: "Baking is fun. Baking is fun. Baking is fun."
- Read through the entire recipe before starting. This way, you know both the steps and ingredients in the recipe before you begin.
- Make sure your oven is properly preheated before baking. It will likely take about 15 minutes to preheat, depending on your oven.
- Line your baking pans with parchment paper for blissful baking. It will keep your baked goods from sticking, making cleanup a snap.
- When measuring dry ingredients, always scoop them into dry measuring cups or spoons, then level the top by scraping across it with the flat side of a knife or a skewer.

- Make sure to bake your pies long enough that the starch has a chance to thicken the juices. Depending on the fruit and your oven, this might take longer than the recipe states. Rely on visual signs, such as thickened juices bubbling up through the lattice or around the edges. Trust me on this one. I learned the hard way by underbaking pies. They just don't cut the mustard after all that work of putting them together.
- Sometimes the juices from the pie will bubble up over the top crust or overflow in your oven. Don't worry, so long as you've made sure to bake your pie on a rimmed baking sheet. Otherwise you'll probably have some oven scrubbing to do. After many exploding pies, I figured this out. As a bonus, the hot baking sheet will help crisp your crust.
- OK — back to the bubbling juices. Don't worry if your pie isn't as picture-perfect as you had hoped. This just adds a homemade, rustic quality — and rustic pies are beautiful!
- If using frozen fruit, don't thaw it before filling the pie. Look for individually quick frozen (IQF) fruit in the freezer section of your supermarket. Remember that frozen fruit might take an additional 15 to 30 minutes to bake.
- For the flakiest pie crusts and shells, measure your shortening and/or butter, cut into pieces and place in the freezer. Using ice-cold fat in your pastry recipe will give you nice, flaky results. If I know that I'll be baking a pie in a couple of days, I will often do this ahead of time, storing the butter and/or shortening in a resealable plastic bag.
- Remember that pie baking takes just a little bit of practice. I find that when I haven't baked a pie for a while I tend to get a little rusty. But once I get back in the groove, my pies start looking much better. So don't despair. Everyone can learn to be a great pie baker — and have fun doing it, too.

Making Perfect Pies

Here's a list of tips and techniques that I've put together to help make you a pie expert. With a little practice, you'll be whipping together perfect pies and tarts, and everyone will want to know your secret.

Perfect pie tips

- Always preheat your oven to the temperature recommended in the recipe. Fruit pies are usually baked at between 350°F (180°C) and 450°F (230°C). Oftentimes, the recipe will instruct you to bake the pie in a 450°F (230°C) oven for the first part of baking, then reduce the heat to about 350°F (180°C). This is important because it helps the crust get nice and brown and crisp on the bottom and sets the shape of the crust.
- I recommend baking your pies in a glass pie plate. This is a great way to ensure that your bottom crust is fully baked, as you can see through the glass. It also conducts heat very well.
- Always place your fruit pies on a rimmed baking sheet. This will prevent messy spillovers in your oven (and trust me when I say messy).
- Before adding the bottom crust, make sure to lightly grease your pie plate or pan. This will keep the pie from sticking and help the pastry to brown.
- When making tarts, always grease the tins, molds or pans before pressing in the dough.
- Use very cold butter and shortening in pie crust and pastry recipes. It will ensure a nice, flaky result. You want little pieces of cold shortening or butter in the pastry. As the fat heats during baking, it creates steam. The steam produces little pockets in the pastry, which make the dough flaky (see next tip).
- It's important to "cut" the butter, margarine or shortening into the flour, not stir it in. "Cutting" means to chop the fat into tiny pieces and coat each with flour; then the little fat globules boil as they heat up, creating steam and making the pastry flaky. This is why I recommend using a food processor, as the blade perfectly cuts the fat into the flour. Alternatively, you can make the dough by hand using a pastry blender, two knives or forks, or a stand mixer to cut the fat into the flour.
- Make sure to chill your dough so that it's easier to roll and shape. If the dough feels too soft to roll out, return it to the refrigerator to chill until it's easy enough to handle.
- Don't overflour your dough when rolling, as too much flour will make the dough tough. I love using a silicone rolling pin and mat for this very reason. You need to use very little flour with these products because of the silicone, which create an almost nonstick surface, resulting in tender crusts.
- Once you press the dough into a pie plate or tart pan, place it in the refrigerator or freezer to chill before baking, or filling and baking. This will prevent the pastry from shrinking too much during baking.
- Patch cracks in the unbaked pastry with scraps before adding the filling when you're going to be baking the pie or tart (this wouldn't work for a prebaked crust). Moisten the underside with a little water to help it stick.
- Before baking, I like to lightly brush the top crust or pastry (not a crumb topping, though) with cream or milk, then sprinkle with coarse or granulated sugar. This helps give the crust a lovely sparkly finish and shine. I learned this trick while working in a fancy restaurant in Los Angeles, where I baked lots and lots of pies. If you want to keep your pies dairy-free, you can brush the crust with soy milk or soy creamer, then sprinkle with sugar.

- When making a double-crust pie, always cut steam vents in the top pastry.
- When baking an apple or pear pie, check to see if your fruit is cooked by inserting a knife into the center of the pie. If it glides right in, the fruit is cooked. If the pie starts to get too brown before it's finished baking, you can cover it loosely with a piece of tented foil.
- One very key way to tell if your fruit pie is done is to check the juices. What you should see is thickened fruit juice bubbling through the vents or around the edges of the pie. If the juices just look juicy (such as in a glass of fruit juice), the pie isn't ready. But if they look more like a shiny fruit pudding, then that means they're thickened. Of course, you want to make sure that the top and bottom crust of the pie are golden brown, too.
- If the recipe calls for just a bottom crust and you don't want to make one from scratch, you can use a frozen store-bought crust. I recommend looking for a good-quality organic brand at a natural food or well-stocked grocery store. Remember that a good pastry crust is only as good as the ingredients used to make it.

Making dough

By hand: In a large bowl, mix together the dry ingredients according to your recipe. Add small pieces of very cold butter, margarine or shortening (depending on the recipe) to the flour mixture. Using a pastry blender, two knives or two forks, cut the butter or shortening into the flour mixture until it resembles coarse meal. There should be some pea-size pieces of fat left. Sprinkle most of the ice water called for in the recipe onto the flour mixture and, using a fork, fold together until the dough just forms a mass. Gently press the dough together with the spatula.

Don't overstir. Test the dough with your fingertips to see if it's moist enough to hold together. If the dough is too dry, gradually add another 1 to 2 tbsp (15 to 25 mL) ice water, or more as needed, and press until dough holds together.

Scoop mixture onto a clean surface and gather into a ball. Divide the dough into two balls, one slightly larger than the other if making a double-crust pie, and flatten them into disks. Wrap disks in plastic wrap or place in a plastic bag and refrigerate until chilled, about 1 hour. Alternatively, you can chill the dough for a shorter time in the freezer.

Food processor: In a food processor fitted with a metal blade, combine dry ingredients, pulsing until mixed. Add pieces of very cold butter, margarine or shortening (depending on the recipe), pulsing just until mixture resembles coarse meal. Add ice water to flour mixture, pulsing until moist clumps form, stopping to test the dough with your fingertips to see if it's just moist enough to hold together. If the dough is too dry, gradually add another 1 to 2 tbsp (15 to 25 mL) ice water, or more as needed, and press until dough holds together. Remove blade and gather dough into a ball, flattening into a disk. Wrap in plastic wrap and chill for at least 1 hour.

Alternatively, follow above directions, but after pulsing the cold butter, margarine or shortening into the flour, scoop the mixture into a large bowl. Sprinkle most of the ice water called for onto the flour mixture. Using a fork, fold together until the dough just forms a mass. Gently press the dough together with a spatula. Don't overstir. Test the dough with your fingertips to see if it's moist enough to hold together. If the dough is too dry, gradually add another 1 to 2 tbsp (15 to 25 mL) ice water, or more as needed, and press until dough holds together.

Tricks and Tips for Rolling Dough

How to roll dough

On a lightly floured surface, a silicone rolling mat or parchment paper, using short, even strokes and rolling from the center of the dough outward, roll dough into a circle. Lift and turn the dough every few strokes, sprinkling the surface with a little bit of flour before putting it back down and dusting rolling pin as necessary. This will help you roll the dough out into a circle and keep it from sticking to the rolling surface. You want the dough to be about 3 inches (7.5 cm) larger than the pie plate or tart tin. The dough should be about ⅛ inch (0.25 cm) thick and fit into the prepared pie plate. If dough is very sticky, you can roll it out between two sheets of waxed or parchment paper.

Press-in pie crust

Here's a quick tip: forget the rolling pin and use your hands. Use the recipe Sweet Oil Pastry Dough or Oil Tart Dough (see pages 185 and 190) and simply press the dough into your pie plate or tart pan.

Pie and tart presses

Here's an amazing invention: the pie press. After lots of dough rolling for these recipes, I was extremely grateful to find a press. They are handmade from wood and generally work very well with any dough (see Sources, page 246).

Fitting dough into pie plate

Use a dough scraper or spatula to loosen the edges of the dough. Fold circle of dough in half, then in half again, being careful not to press the two halves together. Place the folded dough triangle in the prepared pie plate, with the center point in the middle of the plate. Unfold the dough evenly in the plate. Carefully press the dough into place. Make sure not to stretch the dough, as it will shrink during baking. Gently repair any rips, tears or cracks.

You can also roll the dough up around the rolling pin, then unroll it over the top of your prepared pan.

Making a decorative edge

Crimping or fluting the edge of a double-crust pie will keep the pie filling from leaking during baking. It's very easy to do and gets easier with a little practice.

Fluted edge

Place your thumb against the inside edge of the pastry. Using your thumb and index finger on the other hand on the outside edge, press the dough around your thumb toward the inside. Continue around the pie plate until the entire edge is fluted.

Plain edge

For a bottom-only crust, trim the pastry so that it's ½ inch (1 cm) beyond the edge of the pie plate. Fold the edge under, pinching lightly, so that it's even with the rim.

Crimped edge

Follow directions for Plain Edge (above), then press the tines of a lightly floured fork into the dough at a right angle to the edge of the plate all around the edge of the dough.

Leaf edge

Using a small leaf-shaped cookie cutter or a paring knife, cut leaves from scraps of dough. Lightly moisten the edge of the crust with a little water and place the leaves in an overlapping pattern all around the edge. Lightly brush the tops of the leaves with a little cream, milk, soy milk or beaten egg right before baking.

Decorative pie tops

Floating circle: Make a floating top crust to top your pie. This works best for fruit pies, especially berry ones. Roll your top piece of pastry dough. You'll want this to be a little thicker than usual. Using a knife or fluted pastry wheel, trim the pastry into a 7- or 8-inch (17.5 or 20 cm) circle (you can use a round dish as a template). Place the pastry circle over the center of the filling. Brush with cream, milk or soy milk and sprinkle with sugar before baking. Bake pie according to recipe.

Overlapping shapes: I love to top my berry pies with different cutout shapes. Roll out your top pastry, leaving it a little thicker than usual. Using large cookie cutters, cut shapes from pastry dough. This works well with coordinating cookie cutters or the same design over and over. Place the cutouts over the top of your filled pie, just lightly overlapping. Where edges overlap, lift edge and lightly brush with a little water or milk to stick the pieces together. Brush tops of pastry cutouts with cream, milk or soy milk and sprinkle with sugar before baking. Bake pie according to recipe.

Cutouts: For an easy and beautiful top, roll out the second piece of pastry dough for your top crust. Using cookie cutters, stamp out a design in your pastry. Little alphabet cookie cutters work well if you want it to say "Happy Birthday" or someone's name on the pie. Alternatively, you can use a small paring knife in place of the cookie cutters. The cutouts in the pastry will work as steam vents during baking, so there's no need to add additional ones. Right before baking, lightly brush top with cream, milk or soy milk and sprinkle with sugar. Bake pie according to recipe.

Lattice top

Traditional lattice: Roll dough for top crust out into an 11-by 7-inch (27.5 by 17.5 cm) rectangle (or a circle that's 2 to 3 inches/5 to 7.5 cm larger than the diameter of the pan and about ⅛ inch/0.25 cm thick). With a paring knife or crimped pastry roller (also known as a fluted pastry wheel), cut lengthwise into 10 strips, each approximately ½ inch (1 cm) wide. Arrange half of the pastry strips across pie at 1-inch (2.5 cm) intervals. Fold alternating pastry strips back halfway. Place one pastry strip across the center of the pie at 90-degree angle to the first set of strips. Unfold the folded strips and fold back the alternating strips. Place a second pastry strip across the first set of strips, about 1 inch (2.5 cm) from the center strip. Repeat with remaining strips until the lattice covers the filling. Trim overhang of bottom crust and strips to about ¾ inch (2 cm). Fold the edge under and crimp decoratively. Right before baking, lightly brush lattice with cream, milk or soy milk and sprinkle with sugar. Bake pie according to recipe.

Shortcut lattice: This is the way that I usually do my lattice tops. It's quick, easy and looks great. Roll out dough for top crust into an 11-by 7-inch (27.5 by 17.5 cm) rectangle (or a circle that's 2 to 3 inches/5 to 7.5 cm larger than the diameter of the pan and about ⅛ inch/0.25 cm thick). With a paring knife or crimped pastry roller (also known as a fluted pastry wheel), cut lengthwise into 10 strips, each approximately ½ inch (1 cm) wide. Arrange five strips across pie, at 1-inch (2.5 cm) intervals. Arrange remaining strips diagonally across first strips. Trim overhang of bottom crust and strips to about ¾ inch (2 cm). Fold the edge under and crimp decoratively. Right before baking, lightly brush lattice with cream, milk or soy milk and sprinkle with sugar. Bake pie according to recipe.

Naked-top pie: You can bake your pies without a pastry top. I call these "naked pies." They are definitely rustic looking but beautiful in their own right. The baking time might be altered slightly, but rely on visual signs of doneness to tell when the pie is fully baked.

The fruit filling should be thick and glossy, and the pastry nicely browned around the edge. Bake the pie according to the recipe, omitting the top crust.

Steam vents: Steam vents — slits or openings cut into the top crust — allow steam to escape from double-crust pies. There are many ways to make them, from a simple hole cut in the center of the pie to slits cut through the top crust in a concentric circle around the center to small shapes cut with tiny cookie cutters. Don't brush the top crust with cream, milk or soy milk until after you make the cuts in the pastry.

Single-crust pastry shells

Unbaked pie shell: Line your lightly greased pie plate with pastry dough and flute or crimp the edge. If time permits, place in freezer until very cold. Fill the shell and bake according to recipe directions.

Partially baked shell: Preheat oven to 375°F (190°C). Prick the prepared crust in several places with a fork. Refrigerate or freeze until chilled. Line the crust with parchment paper or foil and a layer of pie weights or dried beans to weigh it down. Bake for about 25 minutes or until the shell no longer looks moist and is firm to the touch. Remove from the oven. Carefully remove the pie weights and return the shell to the oven and bake just until lightly browned, about 5 minutes. Fill pie according to recipe.

Fully prebaked shell: Preheat oven to 375°F (190°C). Prick the prepared crust in several places with a fork. Refrigerate or freeze until chilled. Line the crust with parchment paper or foil and a layer of pie weights or dried beans to weigh it down. Bake for about 25 minutes or until the shell no longer looks moist and is firm to the touch. Remove from the oven. Carefully remove the pie weights and return the shell to the oven and bake until golden brown, about 10 minutes.

Quick and easy alternatives to pastry dough

Store-bought pastry shells: Many of these recipes can be made using a store-bought pastry shell for convenience. Make sure to keep the shell frozen until you're ready to fill and bake it. You don't want to thaw the shell or let it sit out for long.

Individual phyllo shells: Preheat oven to 375°F (190°C). Using a box of thawed frozen dough, unroll and place on counter. Cover phyllo with a lightly damp towel (make sure it's not too wet or it will make the dough soggy). Carefully remove one sheet at a time. Brush with melted butter, margarine, oil or cooking spray. Top with another sheet, again brushing with melted butter, margarine, oil or cooking spray. Repeat with another two layers, but don't coat top layer. This will help prevent the dough from tearing. Using a sharp paring knife, cut the dough in half lengthwise. Cut each piece crosswise into thirds so that you have six squares. Repeat process if making more than six shells. Press each square into each cup of a lightly greased muffin pan and bake in preheated oven for about 20 minutes or until golden brown and crisp. Let shells cool, transfer to a wire rack and fill with desired filling just before serving.

Puff pastry shells: Look for boxes of frozen puff pastry shells in the freezer section of grocery stores. Bake and fill according to package directions.

Apple Pies

Apple Cranberry Spice Crumb Pie

Serves 8

- Preheat oven to 400°F (200°C)
- 9-inch (23 cm) glass pie plate, greased
- Rimmed baking sheet

Here's a great autumn pie for when you're in the mood for something a little out of the ordinary. It makes a fabulous ending to a Thanksgiving meal. Try it topped with a big scoop of ice cream.

1	recipe All-Purpose Vegan Pastry Dough or Small-Batch All-Purpose Buttery Pastry Dough, chilled (see recipes, pages 182 and 180)	1

FILLING

3	large Granny Smith apples, peeled, cored and thinly sliced	3
1 cup	fresh or frozen cranberries	250 mL
¾ cup	packed light brown sugar	175 mL
¼ cup	all-purpose flour	50 mL
1 tsp	ground cinnamon	5 mL
¼ tsp	ground nutmeg	1 mL
1	recipe Brown Sugar Streusel or Cinnamon Sugar Crumb Topping (see recipes, pages 134 and 135)	1

1. On a lightly floured surface, roll out dough into a circle large enough to fit pie plate, dusting work surface and dough as necessary to keep the dough from sticking (or roll between 2 pieces of waxed or parchment paper). Press dough into prepared pie plate, crimping edge. Place pie plate in freezer or refrigerator for 15 to 20 minutes to chill while you prepare the filling.

2. *Filling:* In a large bowl, gently combine apples, cranberries, brown sugar, flour, cinnamon and nutmeg, making sure apples are well coated. Transfer filling to prepared bottom crust, gently pressing apples into pastry with your hand. Place pie plate on baking sheet and bake in preheated oven for 30 minutes.

3. Remove from oven, reduce temperature to 350°F (180°C) and sprinkle streusel over apples. Return pie to oven and continue baking for 25 to 35 minutes more or until streusel is nicely browned, apples are tender and juices are bubbling. If pie starts to get too brown before it's finished baking, cover loosely with a piece of tented foil. Let cool on a wire rack for 1 hour before serving.

Apple Raisin Crumb Pie

Serves 8

- Preheat oven to 400°F (200°C)
- 9-inch (23 cm) glass pie plate, greased
- Rimmed baking sheet

There is a wonderful, old-fashioned flair to this pie. Maybe it's the combo of apples and raisins, maybe it's the crumb topping, but whatever the case, this is a wonderful ending for a picnic or holiday feast.

Tip
For some zing, soak the raisins in dark rum and drain before using in the recipe.

Variation
Substitute dried cranberries or cherries for the raisins.

| 1 | recipe All-Purpose Vegan Pastry Dough or Small-Batch All-Purpose Buttery Pastry Dough, chilled (see recipes, pages 182 and 180) | 1 |

FILLING

4	large Granny Smith apples, peeled, cored and thinly sliced	4
¾ cup	packed light brown sugar	175 mL
½ cup	raisins (see Tip, left)	125 mL
2 tbsp	all-purpose flour	25 mL
2 tsp	vanilla paste or extract	10 mL
1 tsp	ground cinnamon	5 mL
½ tsp	ground allspice	2 mL

| 1 | recipe Brown Sugar Streusel or Cinnamon Sugar Crumb Topping (see recipes, pages 134 and 135) | 1 |

1. On a lightly floured surface, roll out dough into a circle large enough to fit pie plate, dusting work surface and dough as necessary to keep the dough from sticking (or roll between 2 pieces of waxed or parchment paper). Press dough into prepared pie plate, crimping edge. Place pie plate in freezer or refrigerator for 15 to 20 minutes to chill while you prepare the filling.

2. *Filling:* In a large bowl, gently combine apples, brown sugar, raisins, flour, vanilla, cinnamon and allspice, making sure apples are well coated. Transfer filling to prepared bottom crust, gently pressing apples into pastry with your hand. Place pie plate on baking sheet and bake in preheated oven for 30 minutes.

3. Remove from oven, reduce temperature to 350°F (180°C) and sprinkle streusel over apples. Return pie to oven and continue baking for 25 to 35 minutes more or until streusel is nicely browned, apples are tender and juices are bubbling. If pie starts to get too brown before it's finished baking, cover loosely with a piece of tented foil. Let cool on a wire rack for 1 hour before serving.

Apple Custard Pie with Lemon and Cinnamon

Serves 8

- Preheat oven to 375°F (190°C)
- 9-inch (23 cm) glass pie plate, greased
- Rimmed baking sheet

This is one stupendous pie. The lemon, cinnamon and apples play off one another so well that it's a favorite around our house. Try baking it the next time you're asked to bring dessert somewhere. You won't be disappointed.

Tip

To easily peel, core and thinly slice apples, look for one of the many available apple peeler/slicer/corer gadgets. I love mine and have used it for years.

1	recipe Small-Batch All-Purpose Buttery Pastry Dough, chilled (see recipe, page 180)	1
FILLING		
1 cup	packed light brown sugar	250 mL
1 cup	sour cream	250 mL
1	egg	1
2 tbsp	all-purpose flour	25 mL
2 tsp	grated lemon zest	10 mL
1 tsp	ground cinnamon	5 mL
1 tsp	vanilla extract	5 mL
4	large Granny Smith apples, peeled, cored and thinly sliced	4
⅓ cup	raisins	75 mL
1	recipe Brown Sugar Streusel or Cinnamon Sugar Crumb Topping (see recipes, pages 134 and 135)	1

1. On a lightly floured surface, roll out dough into a circle large enough to fit pie plate, dusting work surface and dough as necessary to keep the dough from sticking (or roll between 2 pieces of waxed or parchment paper). Press dough into prepared pie plate, crimping edge. Place pie plate in freezer or refrigerator for 15 to 20 minutes to chill while you prepare the filling.

2. *Filling:* In a large bowl, combine brown sugar, sour cream, egg, flour, lemon zest, cinnamon and vanilla, whisking until smooth. Stir in apples and raisins, making sure that they're well coated. Transfer filling to prepared bottom crust, gently pressing apples into pastry with your hand and mounding them slightly in the center. Place pie plate on baking sheet and bake in preheated oven for 40 minutes.

3. Remove from oven and sprinkle streusel over apples. Return pie to oven and continue baking for 25 to 35 minutes more or until streusel is nicely browned, apples are tender and filling looks puffed, set and not runny. If pie starts to get too brown before it's finished baking, cover loosely with a piece of tented foil. Let cool completely on a wire rack before transferring pie to refrigerator to chill for at least 2 hours before serving. This pie is best eaten on the day that it's made.

> **Variation**
> Substitute orange zest for the lemon.

Apple Raspberry Pie

Serves 8

- Preheat oven to 375°F (190°C)
- 9-inch (23 cm) glass pie plate, greased
- Rimmed baking sheet

One afternoon, after months of pie making, my son asked me if he could help me make a pie. No problem! This is the pie that we came up with, which is easy to make, very juicy and oh-so-delicious!

Tips

The dough should be pressed into the pan right after making. It shouldn't sit around or be chilled first.

If you're in a hurry, you can substitute purchased unbaked pastry dough for the oil pastry. This is an easy pie to bake with kids.

1	recipe Sweet Oil Pastry Dough (see recipe, page 185)	1

FILLING

3	large Granny Smith apples, peeled, cored and thinly sliced	3
2 cups	frozen raspberries	500 mL
⅔ cup	granulated sugar	150 mL
3 tbsp	all-purpose flour	45 mL
1 tbsp	freshly squeezed lemon juice	15 mL
1 tbsp	raspberry-flavored liqueur	15 mL
	Cream, milk or soy milk	
	Coarse or granulated sugar	

1. Press half of the dough into prepared pie plate (see Tips, left). Divide second piece of dough into 8 individual pieces and flatten into 3-inch (7.5 cm) circles. Set pieces aside on a piece of parchment paper. Alternatively, you can press or roll the second piece of dough into one solid circle to top pie. Place pie plate in refrigerator for 10 to 15 minutes to chill while you prepare the filling.

2. *Filling:* In a large bowl, gently combine apples, raspberries, sugar, flour, lemon juice and liqueur. Transfer filling to prepared bottom crust, mounding in center.

3. Place pastry circles on top of fruit, slightly overlapping pieces to decoratively top pie. (The entire top will not be covered. You will see the fruit between circles.) Lightly lift edges of circles where they touch and brush with a dab of water to adhere together. With the point of a sharp knife, slash a few vents in top of pastry to allow steam to escape during baking. Lightly brush pastry with cream and sprinkle with sugar.

4. Place pie plate on baking sheet and bake in preheated oven for about 1 hour and 20 minutes or until top is nicely browned and juices are bubbling and look thickened. If pie starts to get too brown before it's finished baking, cover loosely with a piece of tented foil. Let cool on a wire rack for 1 hour before serving.

Brown Sugar Apple Pie with Almond Crumb Topping

Serves 8

- Preheat oven to 400°F (200°C)
- 9-inch (23 cm) glass pie plate, greased
- Rimmed baking sheet

I've always heard that if you want to sell your house, you should bake a pie so that your place smells homey. I was testing this recipe while our house was on the market and I believe it was this pie that sold it. We had several offers that day — all of them requesting the recipe with the sale of the house.

Variation

You can omit the lemon zest from the filling, or substitute orange zest and juice for the lemon.

1	recipe All-Purpose Vegan Pastry Dough or Small-Batch All-Purpose Buttery Pastry Dough, chilled (see recipes, pages 182 and 180)	1

FILLING

4	large Granny Smith apples, peeled, cored and thinly sliced	4
¾ cup	packed light brown sugar	175 mL
2 tbsp	all-purpose flour	25 mL
2 tsp	grated lemon zest	10 mL
1 tbsp	freshly squeezed lemon juice	15 mL
1 tsp	ground cinnamon	5 mL
1	recipe Almond Crumb Topping (see recipe, page 134)	1

1. On a lightly floured surface, roll out dough into a circle large enough to fit pie plate, dusting work surface and dough as necessary to keep the dough from sticking (or roll between 2 pieces of waxed or parchment paper). Press dough into prepared pie plate, crimping edge. Place pie plate in freezer or refrigerator for 15 to 20 minutes to chill while you prepare the filling.

2. *Filling:* In a large bowl, gently combine apples, brown sugar, flour, lemon zest, lemon juice and cinnamon, making sure apples are well coated. Transfer filling to prepared bottom crust, gently pressing apples into pastry with your hand. Place pie plate on baking sheet and bake in preheated oven for 30 minutes.

3. Remove from oven, reduce temperature to 350°F (180°C) and sprinkle crumb topping over apples. Return pie to oven and continue baking for 25 to 30 minutes more or until the crumb topping is nicely browned, apples are tender and juices are bubbling. If pie starts to get too brown before it's finished baking, cover loosely with a piece of tented foil. Let cool on a wire rack for 1 hour before serving.

Double-Crust Spiced Apple Pie

Serves 8

- Preheat oven to 425°F (220°C)
- 9-inch (23 cm) glass pie plate, greased
- Rimmed baking sheet

My husband, who can be quite picky about his apple pie, declared this pie perfect. The apples are soft as silk, the flavor is light, and everything is wrapped up in a rich, crisp crust. I dedicate this pie to you, Jay.

Tips

You may need slightly more sugar, depending on the tartness of the apples.

Add an additional tablespoon (15 mL) all-purpose flour if your apples are very juicy.

To easily peel, core and thinly slice apples, look for one of the many available apple peeler/slicer/corer gadgets. I love mine and have used it for years.

1	recipe Buttery Pie Pastry Dough or Large-Batch All-Purpose Vegan Pastry Dough, chilled (see recipes, pages 181 and 183)	1

FILLING

6	large Granny Smith apples, peeled, cored and thinly sliced	6
1 cup	granulated sugar (see Tips, left)	250 mL
¼ cup	all-purpose flour (see Tips, left)	50 mL
1 tbsp	sweet Marsala, optional	15 mL
1 tsp	ground cinnamon	5 mL
1 tsp	ground nutmeg	5 mL
½ tsp	ground allspice	2 mL
	Cream, milk or soy milk	
	Coarse or granulated sugar	

1. Divide pastry dough into 2 pieces, one slightly larger than the other. On a lightly floured surface, roll out larger piece of dough into a circle large enough to fit pie plate, dusting work surface and dough as necessary to keep the dough from sticking (or roll between 2 pieces of waxed or parchment paper). Press dough into prepared pie plate. Place pie plate in freezer or refrigerator for 15 to 20 minutes to chill while you prepare the filling. Roll out remaining dough for top crust and set aside at room temperature on sheet of parchment paper.

2. *Filling:* In a large bowl, gently combine apples, sugar, flour, Marsala, if using, cinnamon, nutmeg and allspice, making sure apples are well coated. Transfer filling to prepared bottom crust, gently pressing the apples into pastry with your hand and mounding them slightly in the center. Lightly brush edge of pastry with a little water. Place top crust over apples, trimming and fluting edge. Cut steam vents in top of pie. Brush top with cream and sprinkle with sugar.

3. Place pie plate on baking sheet and bake in preheated oven for 25 minutes. Reduce heat to 350°F (180°C) and continue baking for 50 to 60 minutes more or until top is nicely browned, apples are tender and juices are bubbling. Insert a knife through one of the vents in top of pie to make sure that apples are tender. If pie starts to get too brown before it's finished baking, cover loosely with a piece of tented foil. Let cool on a wire rack for 1 hour before serving.

Variation
Substitute your favorite spirit for the Marsala, such as whiskey, bourbon or rum.

Sour Cream Apple Pie

Serves 8

- Preheat oven to 375°F (190°C)
- 9-inch (23 cm) glass pie plate, greased
- Rimmed baking sheet

I have to dedicate this pie to Jill Karabell, who started me on my pie-making journey many years ago. Her fabulous sour cream apple pie has always been one of my favorites. Jill, I hope this one comes close.

Tips

To easily peel, core and thinly slice apples, look for one of the many available apple peeler/slicer/corer gadgets.

This pie is best eaten on the day that it's made.

Variation

Add 1 tsp (5 mL) ground cinnamon to the filling for a bolder flavor.

1	recipe Small-Batch All-Purpose Buttery Pastry Dough, chilled (see recipe, page 180)	1

FILLING

1 cup	sour cream	250 mL
¾ cup + 2 tbsp	granulated sugar	200 mL
1	egg	1
2 tbsp	all-purpose flour	25 mL
1 tbsp	dark rum	15 mL
1 tsp	vanilla extract	5 mL
½ tsp	ground nutmeg	2 mL
5	large Granny Smith apples, peeled, cored and thinly sliced	5
1	recipe Brown Sugar Streusel or Cinnamon Sugar Crumb Topping (see recipes, pages 134 and 135)	1

1. On a lightly floured surface, roll out dough into a circle large enough to fit pie plate, dusting work surface and dough as necessary to keep the dough from sticking (or roll between 2 pieces of waxed or parchment paper). Press dough into prepared pie plate, crimping edge. Place pie plate in freezer or refrigerator for 15 to 20 minutes to chill while you prepare the filling.

2. *Filling:* In a large bowl, combine sour cream, sugar, egg, flour, rum, vanilla and nutmeg, whisking until smooth. Stir in apples, making sure they're well coated. Transfer to bottom crust, gently pressing apples into pastry with your hand and mounding them slightly in the center. Place pie plate on baking sheet and bake in preheated oven for 40 minutes.

3. Remove from oven and sprinkle streusel over apples. Return pie to oven and continue baking for 20 to 30 minutes more or until streusel is nicely browned, apples are tender and filling looks puffed, set and not runny. If pie starts to get too brown before it's finished baking, cover loosely with a piece of tented foil. Let cool completely on a wire rack before transferring pie to refrigerator to chill for at least 2 hours before serving.

Berry Pies & Tarts

Blackberry Raspberry Crumb Pie

Serves 8

- Preheat oven to 400°F (200°C)
- 9-inch (23 cm) glass pie plate, greased
- Rimmed baking sheet

I like to use a combo of berries in pies, as the flavors really play well off each other. This is a very tasty duo, especially with freshly picked berries.

Tips

If your berries are pretty tart, you can increase the sugar in the recipe by up to ¼ cup (50 mL).

You can also use frozen (unthawed) berries for this pie, but the cold berries might need an additional 15 minutes or longer in Step 3 for the pie to bake.

If using a frozen store-bought pastry crust for this recipe, make sure to keep it frozen until you're ready to fill and bake it.

| 1 | recipe All-Purpose Vegan Pastry Dough or Small-Batch All-Purpose Buttery Pastry Dough, chilled (see recipes, pages 182 and 180) | 1 |

FILLING

2½ cups	fresh raspberries	625 mL
2 cups	fresh blackberries or Marionberries	500 mL
¾ cup	granulated sugar (see Tips, left)	175 mL
3½ tbsp	cornstarch	52 mL
1 tbsp	freshly squeezed lemon juice	15 mL
⅛ tsp	ground cinnamon	0.5 mL
1	recipe Brown Sugar Streusel, Almond Crumb Topping or Cinnamon Sugar Crumb Topping (see recipes, pages 134 and 135)	1

1. On a lightly floured surface, roll out dough into a circle large enough to fit pie plate, dusting work surface and dough as necessary to keep the dough from sticking (or roll between 2 pieces of waxed or parchment paper). Press dough into prepared pie plate, crimping edge. Place pie plate in freezer or refrigerator for 15 to 20 minutes to chill while you prepare the filling.

2. *Filling:* In a large bowl, gently combine raspberries, blackberries, sugar, cornstarch, lemon juice and cinnamon, making sure that cornstarch is not lumpy. Transfer filling to prepared bottom crust. Place pie plate on baking sheet and bake in preheated oven for 45 minutes.

3. Remove from oven, reduce temperature to 350°F (180°C) and sprinkle streusel over pie, avoiding juicy edge. Return pie to oven and continue baking for 15 minutes more or until nicely browned and juices are bubbling and thickened around edge. If pie starts to get too brown before it's finished baking, cover loosely with a piece of tented foil. Let cool on a wire rack for 1 to 2 hours before serving.

Blueberry Pie

Serves 8

- Preheat oven to 375°F (190°C)
- 9-inch (23 cm) deep-dish glass pie plate, greased
- Rimmed baking sheet

This blueberry pie recipe is an old family favorite. I spent most of my childhood in Southern California, so I didn't discover blueberry season until a stint in the Pacific Northwest. After experiencing freshly picked blueberries, my desserts were never the same.

Tips

If your blueberries are pretty tart, you can increase the sugar to 1 cup (250 mL).

Use a good-quality store-bought refrigerated pie crust in place of the homemade pastry dough if you're in a rush.

1	recipe Buttery Pie Pastry Dough or Large-Batch All-Purpose Vegan Pastry Dough, chilled (see recipes, pages 181 and 183)	1

FILLING

5 cups	fresh blueberries	1.25 L
¾ cup	granulated sugar (see Tips, left)	175 mL
⅓ cup	all-purpose flour	75 mL
½ tsp	ground nutmeg	2 mL
	Cream, milk or soy milk	
	Coarse or granulated sugar	

1. Divide pastry dough into 2 pieces, one slightly larger than the other. On a lightly floured surface, roll out larger piece of dough into a circle large enough to fit pie plate, dusting work surface and dough as necessary to keep the dough from sticking (or roll between 2 pieces of waxed or parchment paper). Press dough into prepared pie plate. Place pie plate in freezer or refrigerator for 15 to 20 minutes to chill while you prepare the filling. Roll out remaining dough for top crust and set aside at room temperature on sheet of parchment paper.

2. *Filling:* In a large bowl, gently combine blueberries, sugar, flour and nutmeg. Transfer filling to prepared bottom crust, mounding fruit slightly in the center. Lightly brush edge of pastry with a little water. Place top crust over berries, trimming and fluting edge. Cut steam vents in top of pie. Brush top with cream and sprinkle with coarse sugar.

3. Place pie plate on baking sheet and bake in preheated oven for 50 to 65 minutes or until top is nicely browned and juices are bubbling and thickened. If pie starts to get too brown before it's finished baking, cover loosely with a piece of tented foil. Let cool completely on a wire rack before serving.

Blueberry Tart

Serves 8 to 12

- Preheat oven to 375°F (190°C)
- 9- or 10-inch (23 or 25 cm) tart pan

To me, this tart conjures up images of dining al fresco in the garden, surrounded by family and friends on a warm summer afternoon. Once blueberry season hits, I'm all over the blueberry farms picking berries.

1	recipe The Best Tart Dough (see recipe, page 187)	1
1	recipe Cheesecake Mousse Filling or Vanilla Pastry Cream (see recipes, pages 200 and 206)	1
3 cups	fresh blueberries, approx.	750 mL
	Flavored whipped cream or ice cream, optional	

1. Prepare fully baked tart shell according to recipe directions. Let cool.

2. Spread filling in bottom of cooled tart shell. Evenly spread blueberries over filling, mounding them in the center, if desired.

3. Refrigerate tart until ready to serve. This tart is best eaten the day that it is prepared. Serve with a dollop of flavored whipped cream or serve with a scoop of ice cream, if desired.

Boysenberry Tart

Serves 8 to 12

- Preheat oven to 375°F (190°C)
- 9- or 10-inch (23 or 25 cm) tart pan

If you haven't made a fruit tart with pastry cream, then you should head right to the kitchen and start baking! This tart is sublime, with a wonderful crisp cookie crust, silky pastry cream and juicy, fresh berries.

1	recipe The Best Tart Dough (see recipe, page 187)	1
1	recipe Vanilla Pastry Cream (see recipe, page 206)	1
3 cups	fresh boysenberries, approx.	750 mL

1. Prepare fully baked tart shell according to recipe directions. Let cool.

2. Spread Vanilla Pastry Cream in bottom of cooled tart shell. Evenly spread boysenberries over pastry cream, either in a single layer or mounding berries slightly in the center, depending on the look you want.

3. Refrigerate tart until ready to serve. This tart is best eaten the day that it is prepared.

Apple Raspberry Pie (page 24)
Overleaf: Double-Crust Spiced Apple Pie (page 26)

Boysenberry Cherry Pie

Serves 8

- Preheat oven to 400°F (200°C)
- 9-inch (23 cm) glass pie plate, greased
- Rimmed baking sheet

I love picking fruit in the summer months. The flavor is sweet, the fruit is fragrant, and it makes for the most amazing pies. This is another recipe inspired by freshly picked summer fruit that will not disappoint.

Tip

If you like the fruit filling in your pie a little juicier rather than thicker, you can reduce the cornstarch to 3 tbsp (45 mL).

Variation

For a pretty topping, instead of using a solid top crust, cut out large shapes with cookie cutters. Arrange them decoratively, overlapping slightly, over fruit. Lightly brush with cream or milk and sprinkle with sugar before baking.

1	recipe All-Purpose Buttery Pastry Dough, Buttery Pie Pastry Dough or Large-Batch All-Purpose Vegan Pastry Dough, chilled (see recipes, pages 179, 181 and 183)	1

FILLING

2 cups	fresh boysenberries	500 mL
2 cups	fresh Bing or other sweet cherries, pitted	500 mL
1 cup	granulated sugar	250 mL
3½ tbsp	cornstarch (see Tip, left)	52 mL
	Cream, milk or soy milk	
	Coarse or granulated sugar	

1. Divide pastry dough into 2 pieces, one slightly larger than the other. On a lightly floured surface, roll out larger piece of dough into a circle large enough to fit pie plate, dusting work surface and dough as necessary to keep the dough from sticking (or roll between 2 pieces of waxed or parchment paper). Press dough into prepared pie plate. Place pie plate in freezer or refrigerator for 15 to 20 minutes to chill while you prepare the filling. Roll out remaining dough for top crust and set aside at room temperature on sheet of parchment paper.

2. *Filling:* In a large bowl, gently combine boysenberries, cherries, sugar and cornstarch, making sure that cornstarch is not lumpy. Transfer filling to prepared bottom crust, mounding fruit slightly in the center. Lightly brush edge of pastry with a little water. Place top crust over fruit, trimming and fluting edge. Cut steam vents in top of pie. Brush top with cream and sprinkle with coarse sugar.

3. Place pie plate on baking sheet and bake in preheated oven for 30 minutes. Reduce temperature to 350°F (180°C) and continue baking for 40 to 50 minutes more or until top is nicely browned and juices are bubbling and thickened. If pie starts to get too brown before it's finished baking, cover loosely with a piece of tented foil. Let cool on a wire rack for 1 hour before serving.

Lemon Pucker Pie (page 48)
Overleaf: Blackberry Raspberry Crumb Pie (page 30)

Boysenberry Peach Crumble Pie

Serves 8

- Preheat oven to 400°F (200°C)
- 9-inch (23 cm) glass pie plate, greased
- Rimmed baking sheet

I love that peaches and boysenberries are often ripe and in season around the same time in the summer. This is where you can have lots of fun with your pie making. Take this pie, for example — tangy-sweet berries combine with juicy, sweet peaches for one amazing dessert.

> **Tip**
> Depending on your oven, the pie might take longer to bake than the recipe states. Check for visual signs of doneness: the top is nicely browned and juices are bubbling and thickened around edge. When in doubt, it's better to bake the pie a little longer, rather than not long enough, so that the cornstarch is fully cooked.

> **Variation**
> Use frozen berries and/or peaches instead of fresh, increasing baking time by 20 to 30 minutes.

| 1 | recipe All-Purpose Vegan Pastry Dough or Small-Batch All-Purpose Buttery Pastry Dough, chilled (see recipes, pages 182 and 180) | 1 |

FILLING

3 cups	sliced pitted peeled ripe peaches (see Tip, page 52)	750 mL
2 cups	fresh boysenberries	500 mL
1 cup	granulated sugar	250 mL
¼ cup	cornstarch	50 mL
1	recipe Brown Sugar Streusel, Almond Crumb Topping or Cinnamon Sugar Crumb Topping (see recipes, pages 134 and 135)	1

1. On a lightly floured surface, roll out dough into a circle large enough to fit pie plate, dusting work surface and dough as necessary to keep the dough from sticking (or roll between 2 pieces of waxed or parchment paper). Press dough into prepared pie plate. Place pie plate in freezer or refrigerator for 15 to 20 minutes to chill while you prepare the filling.

2. *Filling:* In a large bowl, gently combine peaches, boysenberries, sugar and cornstarch, making sure that cornstarch is not lumpy. Transfer filling to prepared pastry. Place pie plate on baking sheet and bake in preheated oven for 45 minutes.

3. Remove from oven, reduce temperature to 350°F (180°C) and sprinkle streusel over pie, avoiding juicy edge. Return pie to oven and continue baking for 15 minutes more or until nicely browned and juices are bubbling and thickened around edge. If pie starts to get too brown before it's finished baking, cover loosely with a piece of tented foil. Let cool on a wire rack for 1 to 2 hours before serving.

Boysenberry Pie

Serves 8

- Preheat oven to 400°F (200°C)
- 9-inch (23 cm) glass pie plate, greased
- Rimmed baking sheet

Every summer, as I drag my family to pick berries at our local berry farm, my daughter complains bitterly. I think it's a reasonably fair trade: a few hours of picking berries in scorching heat for a plethora of fresh berry pies.

Tips

Depending on the sweetness of the berries, you may want to add an additional ¼ cup (50 mL) granulated sugar.

In a hurry? Use a good-quality refrigerated pastry dough instead of homemade.

Variation

Add 1 tbsp (15 mL) cassis to the berry mixture before baking.

1	recipe Buttery Pie Pastry Dough, All-Purpose Buttery Pastry Dough or Large-Batch All-Purpose Vegan Pastry Dough, chilled (see recipes, pages 181, 179 and 183)	1

FILLING

4 cups	fresh boysenberries	1 L
¾ cup	granulated sugar (see Tips, left)	175 mL
3½ tbsp	cornstarch	52 mL
Pinch	ground cinnamon	Pinch
	Cream, milk or soy milk	
	Granulated sugar	

1. Divide pastry dough into 2 pieces, one slightly larger than the other. On a lightly floured surface, roll out larger piece of dough into a circle large enough to fit pie plate, dusting work surface and dough as necessary to keep the dough from sticking (or roll between 2 pieces of waxed or parchment paper). Press dough into prepared pie plate. Place pie plate in freezer or refrigerator for 15 to 20 minutes to chill while you prepare the filling. Roll out remaining dough for top crust and set aside at room temperature on sheet of parchment paper.

2. *Filling:* In a large bowl, gently combine boysenberries, sugar, cornstarch and cinnamon, making sure that cornstarch is not lumpy. Transfer filling to prepared pastry, mounding fruit in the center. Lightly brush edge of pastry with a little water. Place top crust over berries, trimming and fluting edge. Cut steam vents in top of pie. Brush top with cream and sprinkle with sugar.

3. Place pie plate on baking sheet and bake in preheated oven for 30 minutes. Reduce temperature to 350°F (180°C) and continue baking for 40 to 50 minutes more or until top is nicely browned and juices are bubbling and thickened. If pie starts to get too brown before it's finished baking, cover loosely with a piece of tented foil. Let cool on a wire rack for 1 hour before serving.

Bumbleberry Crumb Pie

Serves 8

- Preheat oven to 400°F (200°C)
- 9-inch (23 cm) glass pie plate, greased
- Rimmed baking sheet

This is a great pie to make in the winter, when you're pining away for a berry pie and berry season is so far away. You will begin to feel like summer is right around the corner.

Tips

Look for bags of mixed frozen berries in big box stores. The ones I have found contain large berries and have great flavor.

If you like your pie a little sweeter, you can increase the sugar in the recipe by up to ¼ cup (50 mL).

Variation

Substitute 1 tbsp (15 mL) raspberry-flavored liqueur for the lemon juice.

1	recipe All-Purpose Vegan Pastry Dough, All-Purpose Buttery Pastry Dough or Small-Batch All-Purpose Buttery Pastry Dough, chilled (see recipes, pages 182, 179 and 180)	1

FILLING

4½ cups	frozen unsweetened mixed berries, such as blueberries, raspberries and blackberries, partially thawed (see Tips, left)	1.125 L
¾ cup	granulated sugar (see Tips, left)	175 mL
3½ tbsp	cornstarch	52 mL
1 tbsp	freshly squeezed lemon juice	15 mL
1	recipe Brown Sugar Streusel, Almond Crumb Topping or Cinnamon Sugar Crumb Topping (see recipes, pages 134 and 135)	1

1. On a lightly floured surface, roll out dough into a circle large enough to fit pie plate, dusting work surface and dough as necessary to keep the dough from sticking (or roll between 2 pieces of waxed or parchment paper). Press dough into prepared pie plate, crimping edge. Place pie plate in freezer or refrigerator for 15 to 20 minutes to chill while you prepare the filling.

2. *Filling:* In a large bowl, gently combine berries, sugar, cornstarch and lemon juice, making sure that cornstarch is not lumpy. Transfer filling to prepared pastry. Place pie plate on baking sheet and bake in preheated oven for 45 minutes.

3. Remove from oven, reduce temperature to 350°F (180°C) and sprinkle streusel over pie, avoiding juicy edge. Return pie to oven and continue baking for 15 to 25 minutes more or until nicely browned and juices are bubbling and thickened around edge. If pie starts to get too brown before it's finished baking, cover loosely with a piece of tented foil. Let cool on a wire rack for 1 hour before serving.

Cranberry Boysenberry Pie

Serves 8

- Preheat oven to 400°F (200°C)
- 9-inch (23 cm) glass pie plate, greased
- Rimmed baking sheet

I thought about naming this Cranbo Pie, but I was afraid it might be confused with a certain movie of a similar-sounding name, thus losing its delicate nature.

Tips

Depending on your oven, the pie might take longer to bake than the recipe states. Check for visual signs of doneness: the top is nicely browned and juices are bubbling and thickened around edge. When in doubt, it's better to bake the pie a little longer, rather than not long enough, so that the cornstarch is fully cooked. Pies made with frozen berries usually take a bit longer to bake, about an extra 15 minutes, than those made with fresh.

Variation

Substitute unsweetened frozen cherries for the boysenberries.

| 1 | recipe Buttery Pie Pastry Dough, All-Purpose Buttery Pastry Dough or Large-Batch All-Purpose Vegan Pastry Dough, chilled (see recipes, pages 181, 179 and 183) | 1 |

FILLING

3 cups	fresh boysenberries	750 mL
1 cup	frozen cranberries	250 mL
1 cup	granulated sugar, or to taste	250 mL
3 tbsp	cornstarch	45 mL
	Cream, milk or soy milk	
	Coarse or granulated sugar	

1. Divide pastry dough into 2 pieces, one slightly larger than the other. On a lightly floured surface, roll out larger piece of dough into a circle large enough to fit pie plate, dusting work surface and dough as necessary to keep the dough from sticking (or roll between 2 pieces of waxed or parchment paper). Press dough into prepared pie plate. Place pie plate in freezer or refrigerator for 15 to 20 minutes to chill while you prepare the filling. Roll out remaining dough for top crust and set aside at room temperature on sheet of parchment paper.

2. *Filling:* In a large bowl, gently combine boysenberries, cranberries, sugar and cornstarch, making sure that cornstarch is not lumpy. Transfer filling to prepared bottom crust, mounding fruit slightly in the center. Lightly brush edge of pastry with a little water. Place top crust over berries, trimming and fluting edge. Cut steam vents in top of pie. Brush top with cream and sprinkle with sugar.

3. Place pie plate on baking sheet and bake in preheated oven for 30 minutes. Reduce temperature to 375°F (190°C) and continue baking for 40 to 50 minutes more or until top is nicely browned and juices are bubbling and thickened. If pie starts to get too brown before it's finished baking, cover loosely with a piece of tented foil. Let cool on a wire rack for 2 hours before serving.

Deep-Dish Blueberry Pie

Serves 8

- Preheat oven to 425°F (220°C)
- 10-inch (25 cm) deep-dish glass pie plate, lightly greased
- Rimmed baking sheet

Blueberry pie is another one of my favorites, one of those desserts that I dream about all year long. When the beginning of July rolls around, I pick copious amounts of blueberries to have at the ready so that I can make lots of blueberry pies. This pie is pretty quick to make, as it only has a top crust.

> **Tip**
> Use a good-quality store-bought refrigerated pie crust in place of the homemade pastry dough if you're in a rush.

1	recipe All-Purpose Vegan Pastry Dough or Small-Batch All-Purpose Buttery Pastry Dough, chilled (see recipes, pages 182 and 180)	1

FILLING

6 cups	fresh blueberries	1.5 L
1 cup	granulated sugar	250 mL
6 tbsp	cornstarch	90 mL
2 tsp	lightly packed grated lemon zest, optional	10 mL
1 tbsp	freshly squeezed lemon juice	15 mL
1/4 tsp	ground nutmeg	1 mL
	Cream, milk or soy milk	
	Coarse or granulated sugar	

1. On a lightly floured surface, roll out dough into a circle slightly larger than the top of the pie plate for top crust. If necessary, dust work surface and dough with a little more flour as necessary to keep the dough from sticking. Set aside on sheet of parchment paper.

2. *Filling:* In a large bowl, gently combine blueberries, sugar, cornstarch, lemon zest, if using, lemon juice and nutmeg, making sure that cornstarch is not lumpy. Transfer filling to prepared pie plate. Place rolled pastry over berries to edge of pie plate, crimping edge. Cut steam vents in top of pie. Brush top with cream and sprinkle with sugar.

3. Place pie plate on baking sheet and bake in preheated oven for 20 minutes. Reduce temperature to 375°F (190°C) and continue baking for 40 to 50 minutes more or until top is nicely browned and juices are bubbling and thickened. If pie starts to get too brown before it's finished baking, cover loosely with a piece of tented foil. Let cool on a wire rack for 1 hour before serving.

Diane's Thanksgiving Cranberry Blueberry Pie

Serves 8 to 10

- Preheat oven to 400°F (200°C)
- 10-inch (25 cm) glass pie plate, greased
- Rimmed baking sheet

This delicious recipe comes to us from the talented cookbook author Diane Morgan. The recipe appears in her book *The Thanksgiving Table*. Diane said that her children would be terribly disappointed if this pie were missing from their Thanksgiving feast.

Variation

If you have access to fresh or frozen huckleberries, you can substitute them for the blueberries.

1	recipe Sour Cream Pie Pastry Dough, chilled (see recipe, page 184)	1
FILLING		
½	small orange, including peel, seeded and quartered	½
4 cups	fresh or frozen blueberries	1 L
3 cups	fresh or frozen cranberries	750 mL
1⅔ cups	granulated sugar	400 mL
3 tbsp	cornstarch	45 mL
½ tsp	salt	2 mL
	Cream, milk or soy milk	
	Coarse or granulated sugar	

1. Divide pastry dough into 2 pieces, one slightly larger than the other. On a lightly floured surface, roll out larger piece of dough into a circle large enough to fit pie plate, dusting work surface and dough as necessary to keep the dough from sticking. Press dough into prepared pie plate. Place pie plate in freezer or refrigerator for 15 to 20 minutes to chill while you prepare the filling. Roll out remaining dough for top crust and set aside at room temperature on sheet of parchment paper.

2. *Filling:* In a food processor or blender, coarsely grind orange. In a large saucepan over medium heat, stir together orange, cranberries, blueberries, sugar, cornstarch and salt. Bring to a boil. Reduce heat and simmer, stirring constantly, until mixture is thickened and sugar is dissolved, about 4 minutes. Let cool completely.

3. Transfer filling to bottom crust, mounding fruit slightly in the center. Lightly brush edge of pastry with cream. Place top crust over mixture, trimming and fluting edge. Cut steam vents in top of pie. Brush top with cream and sprinkle with sugar.

4. Place pie plate on baking sheet and bake in preheated oven for 50 minutes or until top is nicely browned and juices are bubbling and thickened. Let cool on a wire rack for 1 hour before serving.

Easy Berry Pie

Serves 8

This is a simple pie to make with fresh ripe summer fruit or berries, but it's still impressive enough to serve to company. It's so easy to prepare with a store-bought crust. Top with some billowy whipped cream and you're good to go.

Tip
Top pie with whipped cream before serving.

Variation
Substitute sliced pitted peeled peaches for some of the fresh berries.

1	9-inch (23 cm) store-bought refrigerated pastry crust	1
4 cups	mixed fresh berries	1 L
⅔ cup	granulated sugar	150 mL
3 tbsp + 1 tsp	cornstarch	45 mL + 5 mL
1 cup	frozen mixed berries	250 mL

1. Bake pastry crust according to package directions. Let cool.

2. Place fresh berries in cooled crust, mounding fruit slightly in the center. Set aside.

3. In a saucepan, whisk together sugar and cornstarch. Slowly whisk in 1 tbsp (15 mL) water until smooth. Stir in frozen berries and bring to a simmer over medium heat, stirring continuously. Cook, stirring, until mixture is thick, 4 to 5 minutes. Continue cooking for 1 minute more and remove from heat. Whisk in additional 1 tbsp (15 mL) water. Spoon as much hot topping into pie plate as will fit over fresh berries (there may be some filling left over). Let pie stand until filling is cool. Cover and refrigerate for 4 hours before serving.

Fresh Glazed Strawberry Pie

Serves 8

For me, this is one of the pies that signify the beginning of summer. There's nothing so sweet as fresh summer berries, especially local strawberries from the farmer's market.

Tips

This recipe won't work with frozen berries.

If the strawberries are on the sour side, you can increase the sugar to 1 cup (250 mL).

Variation

Substitute a graham cracker crust for the pastry crust.

1	9-inch (23 cm) store-bought refrigerated pastry crust	1
6 cups	fresh strawberries, hulled	1.5 L
3 tbsp	cornstarch	45 mL
1 cup	water, divided	250 mL
¾ cup	granulated sugar	175 mL
1 tsp	grated lemon zest	5 mL
	Red food coloring, optional	

1. Bake pastry crust according to package directions. Let cool.

2. Place strawberries in cooled crust, mounding fruit slightly in the center. Set aside.

3. In a small bowl, whisk together cornstarch and 3 tbsp (45 mL) water. In a large saucepan, combine cornstarch mixture, sugar and remaining water, whisking until smooth. Cook over medium heat, stirring, until mixture is thick and clear. Stir in lemon zest and red food coloring, if using. Let cool for 5 minutes.

4. Carefully pour mixture over strawberries. Place pie plate in refrigerator and chill until firm, about 4 hours.

Fresh Raspberry Tart

Serves 8 to 12

- Preheat oven to 375°F (190°C)
- 9- or 10-inch (23 or 25 cm) tart pan

Fresh fruit tarts are my favorite French pastry, bringing back memories of strolling past patisseries in Paris. This is my take on the classic.

1	recipe The Best Tart Dough (see recipe, page 187)	1
1	recipe Cheesecake Mousse Filling (see recipe, page 200)	1
2 to 3 cups	fresh raspberries	500 to 750 mL

1. Bake tart shell according to recipe directions. Let cool.

2. Spread mousse filling in bottom of cooled tart shell. Evenly spread raspberries over mousse, either in a single layer or mounding berries slightly in the center depending on the look you want.

3. Refrigerate tart until ready to serve.

Raspberry Lemon Crumb Pie

Serves 8

- Preheat oven to 400°F (200°C)
- 9-inch (23 cm) glass pie plate, greased
- Rimmed baking sheet

While I was testing this pie recipe, we had a workman at our house. It was early in the morning and I offered him a piece of pie. He declared, "This is the best breakfast I've ever had." I gave him the rest of the pie to take home.

Tip

You can substitute an unbaked store-bought pastry for the homemade crust in this recipe, but make sure to keep it frozen until you're ready to use it.

1	recipe All-Purpose Vegan Pastry Dough or Small-Batch All-Purpose Buttery Pastry Dough, chilled (see recipes, pages 182 and 180)	1

FILLING

4½ cups	fresh raspberries	1.125 L
¾ cup	granulated sugar	175 mL
3½ tbsp	cornstarch	52 mL
1 tbsp	freshly squeezed lemon juice	15 mL
1 tsp	packed grated lemon zest	5 mL
1	recipe Brown Sugar Streusel, Almond Crumb Topping or Cinnamon Sugar Crumb Topping (see recipes, pages 134 and 135)	1

1. On a lightly floured surface, roll out dough into a circle large enough to fit pie plate, dusting work surface and dough as necessary to keep the dough from sticking (or roll between 2 pieces of waxed or parchment paper). Press dough into prepared pie plate. Place pie plate in freezer or refrigerator for 15 to 20 minutes to chill while you prepare the filling.

2. *Filling:* In a large bowl, gently combine raspberries, sugar and cornstarch, making sure that cornstarch is not lumpy. Transfer filling to prepared bottom crust. Place pie plate on baking sheet and bake in preheated oven for 45 minutes.

3. Remove from oven, reduce temperature to 350°F (180°C) and sprinkle streusel over pie, avoiding juicy edge. Return pie to oven and continue baking for 15 minutes more or until nicely browned and juices are bubbling and thickened around edge. If pie starts to get too brown before it's finished baking, cover loosely with a piece of tented foil. Let cool on a wire rack for 1 hour before serving.

Raspberry Orange Pie

Serves 8

- Preheat oven to 425°F (220°C)
- 9-inch (23 cm) glass pie plate, greased
- Rimmed baking sheet

Citrus complements raspberries beautifully without masking the wonderful flavor of the berries. This pie is incredible topped with a scoop of homemade Orange Vanilla Ice Cream (see recipe, page 223).

Tip

You can substitute unbaked store-bought double-crust pastry for the homemade crust in this recipe, but make sure to keep it frozen until you're ready to use it.

Variation

Substitute orange-flavored liqueur for the orange juice.

1	recipe Buttery Pie Pastry Dough or Large-Batch All-Purpose Vegan Pastry Dough, chilled (see recipes, pages 181 and 183)	1

FILLING

4½ cups	fresh raspberries	1.125 L
¾ cup	granulated sugar	175 mL
3½ tbsp	cornstarch	52 mL
2 tsp	grated orange zest	10 mL
1 tbsp	freshly squeezed orange juice	15 mL
	Cream, milk or soy milk	
	Coarse sugar	

1. Divide pastry dough into 2 pieces, one slightly larger than the other. On a lightly floured surface, roll out larger piece of dough into a circle large enough to fit pie plate, dusting work surface and dough as necessary to keep the dough from sticking (or roll between 2 pieces of waxed or parchment paper). Press dough into prepared pie plate. Place pie plate in freezer or refrigerator for 15 to 20 minutes to chill while you prepare the filling. Roll out remaining dough for top crust and set aside at room temperature on sheet of parchment paper.

2. *Filling:* In a large bowl, gently combine raspberries, sugar, cornstarch and orange zest and juice, making sure that cornstarch is not lumpy. Transfer filling to prepared bottom crust, mounding fruit slightly in the center. Lightly brush edge of pastry with a little water. Place top crust over berries, trimming and fluting edge. Cut steam vents in top of pie. Brush top with cream and sprinkle with sugar.

3. Place pie plate on baking sheet and bake in preheated oven for 15 minutes. Reduce temperature to 350°F (180°C) and continue baking for 40 to 50 minutes more or until top is nicely browned and juices are bubbling and thickened. If pie starts to get too brown before it's finished baking, cover loosely with a piece of tented foil. Let cool on a wire rack for 1 hour before serving.

Razzleberry Pie

Serves 8

- Preheat oven to 400°F (200°C)
- 9-inch (23 cm) glass pie plate, greased
- Rimmed baking sheet

OK, so there aren't really berries called razzleberries (or at least not that I know of), but it seemed like a perfect name for this pie. The combo of raspberries and boysenberries is divine.

Tips

Depending on the sweetness of the berries, you can add up to another ¼ cup (50 mL) granulated sugar.

If you like your pie filling a little runny, rather than thick, you can reduce the cornstarch to 3 tbsp (45 mL).

You can use frozen berries instead of fresh in this recipe. Make sure not to thaw them. If you use frozen berries, increase the baking time at 350°F (180°C) by 15 to 30 minutes.

| 1 | recipe Buttery Pie Pastry Dough or Large-Batch All-Purpose Vegan Pastry Dough, chilled (see recipes, pages 181 and 183) | 1 |

FILLING

2 cups	fresh boysenberries	500 mL
2 cups	fresh raspberries	500 mL
¾ cup	granulated sugar (see Tips, left)	175 mL
3½ tbsp	cornstarch	52 mL
	Cream, milk or soy milk	
	Granulated sugar	

1. Divide pastry dough into 2 pieces, one slightly larger than the other. On a lightly floured surface, roll out larger piece of dough into a circle large enough to fit pie plate, dusting work surface and dough as necessary to keep the dough from sticking (or roll between 2 pieces of waxed or parchment paper). Press dough into prepared pie plate. Place pie plate in freezer or refrigerator for 15 to 20 minutes to chill while you prepare the filling. Roll out remaining dough for top crust and set aside at room temperature on sheet of parchment paper.

2. *Filling:* In a large bowl, gently combine boysenberries, raspberries, sugar and cornstarch, making sure that cornstarch is not lumpy. Transfer filling to prepared bottom crust, mounding fruit slightly in the center. Lightly brush edge of pastry with a little water. Place top crust over berries, trimming and fluting edge. Cut steam vents in top of pie. Brush top with cream and sprinkle with sugar.

3. Place pie plate on baking sheet and bake in preheated oven for 20 minutes. Reduce temperature to 350°F (180°C) and continue baking for 40 to 50 minutes more or until top is nicely browned and juices are bubbling and thickened. If pie starts to get too brown before it's finished baking, cover loosely with a piece of tented foil. Let cool on a wire rack for 2 hours before serving.

Fruit, Pumpkin & Other Pies & Tarts

Fruit Pies & Tarts

Pumpkin & Other Pies

Almond Cherry Tart

Serves 8 to 10

- Preheat oven to 350°F (180°C)
- 8- or 9-inch (20 or 23 cm) round silicone pan or metal springform pan, greased and floured

I love when I can throw together a dessert with a few items on hand and wind up with something impressive, like this Almond Cherry Tart.

¾ cup + 2 tbsp	all-purpose flour	200 mL
¼ cup	almond flour	50 mL
1¼ tsp	baking powder	6 mL
½ cup	butter, softened	125 mL
1 cup	granulated sugar	250 mL
2	eggs	2
1 tsp	almond extract	5 mL
1	package (1 lb/500 g) frozen pitted dark sweet cherries, thawed and drained (about 3 cups/750 mL)	1
	Confectioner's (icing) sugar for dusting	

1. In a bowl, combine all-purpose and almond flours and baking powder. Set aside.

2. In a large bowl of a stand mixer fitted with paddle attachment, beat together butter and sugar until light and fluffy. Add eggs, one at a time, beating well after each addition. Add almond extract, mixing until combined. Add flour mixture, mixing just until thoroughly combined. Batter should be very thick. Scrape mixture into prepared pan and, using a rubber spatula, smooth the surface. (The batter will be shallow in the pan.) Spread drained cherries evenly over batter.

3. Bake tart in preheated oven for 55 to 65 minutes or until golden brown and a tester inserted in the center comes out clean.

4. Let cool in pan on a wire rack for about 10 minutes. Dust top of cooled tart with confectioner's sugar just before serving. Serve at room temperature.

Deep-Dish Raspberry Rhubarb Pie

Serves 8

- Preheat oven to 425°F (220°C)
- 9-inch (23 cm) deep-dish glass pie plate, greased
- Rimmed baking sheet

After tasting literally hundreds of pies, my son became a bit jaded about his taste-testing duties (as I'm sure any teenage boy might). So I was a bit surprised that he attacked this pie with such gusto, loving the sweet and tart flavor. I agree with Noah: you can't beat rhubarb and raspberries.

Tip
If you're in a hurry, use unbaked store-bought pastry dough for the crusts.

Variation
Sprinkle berry mixture with a little ground cinnamon before putting on top crust.

1	recipe Large-Batch All-Purpose Vegan Pastry Dough or All-Purpose Buttery Pastry Dough, chilled (see recipes, pages 183 and 179)	1

FILLING

3 cups	fresh or frozen raspberries or 1 bag (12 oz/340 g) frozen raspberries	750 mL
3 cups	sliced fresh rhubarb (1/4-inch/0.5 cm thick slices)	750 mL
1 cup	granulated sugar	250 mL
5 tbsp	cornstarch	75 mL
	Cream, milk or soy milk	
	Coarse or granulated sugar	

1. Divide pastry dough into 2 pieces, one slightly larger than the other. On a lightly floured surface, roll out larger piece of dough into a circle large enough to fit pie plate, dusting work surface and dough as necessary to keep the dough from sticking (or roll between 2 pieces of waxed or parchment paper). Press dough into prepared pie plate. Place pie plate in freezer or refrigerator for 15 to 20 minutes to chill while you prepare the filling. Roll out remaining dough for top crust and set aside at room temperature on sheet of parchment paper.

2. *Filling:* In a large bowl, gently combine raspberries, rhubarb, sugar and cornstarch, making sure that cornstarch is not lumpy. Transfer filling to prepared bottom crust, mounding fruit slightly in the center. Lightly brush edge of pastry with a little water. Place top crust over filling, trimming and fluting edge. Cut steam vents in top of pie. Brush top with cream and sprinkle with sugar.

3. Place pie plate on baking sheet and bake in preheated oven for 20 minutes. Reduce temperature to 350°F (180°C) and continue baking for 45 to 60 minutes more or until top is nicely browned and juices are bubbling and thickened. If pie starts to get too brown before it's finished baking, cover loosely with a piece of tented foil. Let cool on a wire rack for 2 hours before serving.

Lemon Pucker Pie

Serves 8

● Preheat oven to
350°F (180°C)

One of my fondest lemon pie memories is from age 13, when I decided to bake one for my mother. It took me three attempts to get it right — I kept breaking the crusts and curdling the filling. The final pie was delicious, made from fresh lemons right off our tree. This recipe is adapted from my mother's tried-and-true recipe, which I believe was originally clipped from a *Better Homes and Gardens* magazine. It's one fantastic pie!

1	9-inch (23 cm) store-bought refrigerated pie shell or Small-Batch All-Purpose Buttery Pastry Dough (see recipe, page 180)	1
3	eggs	3
1²⁄₃ cups	granulated sugar, divided	400 mL
3 tbsp	cornstarch	45 mL
3 tbsp	all-purpose flour	45 mL
4 tsp	grated lemon zest, divided	20 mL
¹⁄₃ cup	freshly squeezed lemon juice	75 mL
¹⁄₈ tsp	pure lemon oil (see Tip, right)	0.5 mL
¹⁄₄ tsp	cream of tartar	1 mL

1. Prepare fully baked pastry crust according to package or recipe directions. Let cool.

2. Separate eggs, placing whites in metal bowl of stand mixer and yolks in a separate bowl. Whisk ¼ cup (50 mL) water into egg yolks, whisking until smooth. Set both aside.

3. In a saucepan, combine 1¹⁄₃ cups (325 mL) of the sugar, cornstarch and flour, stirring well. Gradually whisk in 1¼ cups (300 mL) water, whisking until smooth. Cook mixture over medium-high heat, whisking continuously, until thick and bubbling. Reduce temperature to medium and cook, whisking, for 2 minutes more. Remove from heat.

4. Whisk egg yolk mixture and, while whisking, gradually add half of the hot filling, making sure that yolks don't scramble. Whisk egg yolk mixture back into saucepan, whisking until smooth.

5. Return saucepan to medium-low heat and cook, whisking continuously, until mixture starts to bubble. Reduce temperature and simmer, whisking, for 2 minutes more. Remove saucepan from heat and whisk in 3 tsp (15 mL) of the lemon zest, lemon juice and lemon oil. Pour hot mixture into cooled crust.

6. Add cream of tartar to egg whites. Using an electric mixer with whisk attachment, beat on medium speed until very foamy and soft peaks just start to form. Gradually add remaining ⅓ cup (75 mL) of sugar, 1 tbsp (15 mL) at a time, and beat on high speed until stiff glossy peaks form, about 4 minutes. Stir in remaining 1 tsp (5 mL) lemon zest.

7. Spread meringue topping immediately over hot pie filling, making sure to spread to the edges of pastry crust, sealing in filling. Bake in preheated oven for 15 minutes or until lightly browned around edge and egg whites are set. Let cool on a wire rack for 45 minutes. Place in refrigerator to chill for 3 hours before serving. This pie is best served on the day that it is made.

Tip

Look for pure lemon oil in well-stocked grocery or health food stores. Do not substitute lemon extract for the oil, as it will not taste the same. Lemon oil tastes like fresh lemons, and it is worth the trouble to seek this product out. You can also order it directly from Boyajian (see Sources, page 246).

Mango Raspberry Pie

Serves 8

- Preheat oven to 375°F (190°C)
- 9-inch (23 cm) deep-dish glass pie plate, greased
- Rimmed baking sheet

This is one delicious pie. Even if you're not a huge mango fan, you might be pleasantly surprised by the unusual flavor combination of the mangoes and fresh raspberries, which is almost peach-like.

Tip

When slicing mangoes, slice off the sides of the fruit (called "cheeks"), avoiding the large pit in the center. I like to use one of those great mango-cutting gadgets for this very purpose. Gently score the cheeks, being careful not to cut all the way through the skin. Invert the cheeks and cut the mango into cubes.

Variations

Substitute lemon juice for the lime juice.

This pie would also work well with a lattice top (see instructions, page 17).

1	recipe Buttery Pie Pastry Dough or Large-Batch All-Purpose Vegan Pastry Dough, chilled (see recipes, pages 181 and 183)	1

FILLING

3 cups	chopped pitted peeled mangoes (about 4) (see Tip, left)	750 mL
2½ cups	fresh raspberries	625 mL
⅔ cup	granulated sugar	150 mL
3 tbsp	cornstarch	45 mL
2 tbsp	freshly squeezed lime juice	25 mL
	Cream, milk or soy milk	
	Coarse or granulated sugar	

1. Divide pastry dough into 2 pieces, one slightly larger than the other. On a lightly floured surface, roll out larger piece of dough into a circle large enough to fit pie plate, dusting work surface and dough as necessary to keep the dough from sticking (or roll between 2 pieces of waxed or parchment paper). Press dough into prepared pie plate. Place pie plate in freezer or refrigerator for 15 to 20 minutes to chill while you prepare the filling. Roll out remaining dough for top crust and set aside at room temperature on sheet of parchment paper.

2. *Filling:* In a large bowl, gently combine mangoes, raspberries, sugar, cornstarch and lime juice, making sure that cornstarch is not lumpy. Transfer filling to prepared bottom crust. Lightly brush edge of pastry with a little water. Place top crust over fruit mixture, trimming and fluting edge. Cut steam vents in top of pie. Brush top with cream and sprinkle with sugar.

3. Place pie plate on baking sheet and bake in preheated oven for 60 to 70 minutes or until top is nicely browned and juices are bubbling and thickened. If pie starts to get too brown before it's finished baking, cover loosely with a piece of tented foil. Let cool on a wire rack for 1 hour before serving.

Peach Raspberry Pie

Serves 8

- Preheat oven to 400°F (200°C)
- 9-inch (23 cm) glass pie plate, greased
- Rimmed baking sheet

I absolutely love this pie. Of course, berry pie and peach pie are two of my all-time favorites, so a combo can only be better. The color of this pie is so pretty, too, as the raspberries turn the peaches a soft pink blush color.

Tips
You will need 1¾ lbs (875 g) peaches to yield 4 cups (1 L) sliced peaches.

Depending on the sweetness of the fruit, add up to ¼ cup (50 mL) more sugar.

Variation
This pie would also work well with a lattice top (see instructions, page 17).

1	recipe Buttery Pie Pastry Dough or Large-Batch All-Purpose Vegan Pastry Dough, chilled (see recipes, pages 181 and 183)	1

FILLING

4 cups	sliced pitted peeled ripe peaches (see Tip, page 52)	1 L
1 cup	fresh raspberries	250 mL
¾ cup	granulated sugar (see Tips, left)	175 mL
¼ cup	cornstarch	50 mL
	Cream, milk or soy milk	
	Coarse or granulated sugar	

1. Divide pastry dough into 2 pieces, one slightly larger than the other. On a lightly floured surface, roll out larger piece of dough into a circle large enough to fit pie plate, dusting work surface and dough as necessary to keep the dough from sticking (or roll between 2 pieces of waxed or parchment paper). Press dough into prepared pie plate. Place pie plate in freezer or refrigerator for 15 to 20 minutes to chill while you prepare the filling. Roll out remaining dough for top crust and set aside at room temperature on sheet of parchment paper.

2. *Filling:* In a large bowl, gently combine peaches, raspberries, sugar and cornstarch, making sure that cornstarch is not lumpy. Transfer filling to prepared bottom crust. Lightly brush edge of pastry with a little water. Place top crust over fruit, trimming and fluting edge. Cut steam vents in top of pie. Brush top with cream and sprinkle with sugar.

3. Place pie plate on baking sheet and bake in preheated oven for 20 minutes. Reduce temperature to 350°F (180°C) and continue baking for 40 minutes more or until nicely browned and juices are bubbling and thickened. If pie starts to get too brown before it's finished baking, cover loosely with a piece of tented foil. Let cool on a wire rack for 2 hours before serving.

Peach Pie

Serves 8

- Preheat oven to 400°F (200°C)
- 9-inch (23 cm) glass pie plate, greased
- Rimmed baking sheet

I still remember the first peach pie I baked. We had a peach tree in our backyard that was literally falling over from too much fruit. I thought it would be a perfect moment to try my hand at peach pie. The pie gods must have been with me that day because it was one of the best pies I'd ever had.

Tip

To easily peel peaches: With a sharp paring knife, make a shallow X on the bottom of each peach. Carefully place 3 or 4 peaches in a pot of boiling water. Boil for 30 to 40 seconds. Remove with a slotted spoon and submerge in a bowl of cold water. Repeat with remaining peaches. Drain when cool. The peels should come right off. To prevent the peaches from turning brown, you can sprinkle them with a little lemon juice.

1	recipe Buttery Pie Pastry Dough or Large-Batch All-Purpose Vegan Pastry Dough, chilled (see recipes, pages 181 and 183)	1

FILLING

5 cups	sliced pitted peeled ripe peaches (see Tip, left)	1.25 L
¾ cup	granulated sugar (see Tips, right)	175 mL
¼ cup	cornstarch	50 mL
½ tsp	ground cinnamon	2 mL
¼ tsp	ground nutmeg	1 mL

CINNAMON SUGAR TOPPING

1 tbsp	granulated sugar	15 mL
¼ tsp	ground cinnamon	1 mL
	Cream, milk or soy milk	

1. Divide pastry dough into 2 pieces, one slightly larger than the other. On a lightly floured surface, roll out larger piece of dough into a circle large enough to fit pie plate, dusting work surface and dough as necessary to keep the dough from sticking (or roll between 2 pieces of waxed or parchment paper). Press dough into prepared pie plate. Place pie plate in freezer or refrigerator for 15 to 20 minutes to chill while you prepare the filling. Roll out remaining dough for top crust and set aside at room temperature on sheet of parchment paper.

2. *Filling:* In a large bowl, gently combine peaches, sugar, cornstarch, cinnamon and nutmeg, making sure that cornstarch is not lumpy. Transfer filling to prepared bottom crust. Lightly brush edge of pastry with a little water. Place top crust over peaches, trimming and fluting edge. Cut steam vents in top of pie.

3. *Cinnamon Sugar Topping:* In a small bowl, mix together sugar and cinnamon. Brush top of pie with cream and sprinkle with cinnamon sugar topping.

4. Place pie plate on baking sheet and bake in preheated oven for 30 minutes. Reduce temperature to 375°F (190°C) and continue baking for 35 minutes more or until top is nicely browned and juices are bubbling and thickened. If pie starts to get too brown before it's finished baking, cover loosely with a piece of tented foil. Let cool on a wire rack for 1 hour before serving.

Tips

You will need 2¼ lbs (1.125 kg) peaches to yield 5 cups (1.25 L) sliced peaches.

Depending on the sweetness of the fruit, add up to ⅓ cup (75 mL) more sugar.

Top with Brown Sugar Cinnamon Ice Cream, Vanilla Bean Ice Cream or Whipped Rum Topping (see recipes, pages 213, 229 and 245).

Variations

Omit spices and add 1 tbsp (15 mL) brandy or ½ tsp (2 mL) almond extract to peaches before baking.

This pie would also work well with a lattice top (see instructions, page 17).

Sour Cherry Boysenberry Pie

Serves 8

- Preheat oven to 375°F (190°C)
- 9-inch (23 cm) glass pie plate, greased
- Rimmed baking sheet

Cherries and boysenberries are a perfect match, making a truly glorious pie. With the boundless varieties of summer fruit, I can't help but combine them in different ways.

Tips

Depending on the sweetness of the fruit, you can add up to ¼ cup (50 mL) more sugar.

If using frozen berries, the baking time may increase by 15 to 30 minutes.

| 1 | recipe Buttery Pie Pastry Dough or Large-Batch All-Purpose Vegan Pastry Dough, chilled (see recipes, pages 181 and 183) | 1 |

FILLING

3 cups	fresh or frozen boysenberries	750 mL
2 cups	pitted fresh or frozen sour cherries	500 mL
¾ cup	granulated sugar	175 mL
3 tbsp	cornstarch	45 mL
¼ tsp	almond extract	1 mL
	Cream, milk or soy milk	
	Coarse or granulated sugar	

1. Divide pastry dough into 2 pieces, one slightly larger than the other. On a lightly floured surface, roll out larger piece of dough into a circle large enough to fit pie plate, dusting work surface and dough as necessary to keep the dough from sticking (or roll between 2 pieces of waxed or parchment paper). Press dough into prepared pie plate. Place pie plate in freezer or refrigerator for 15 to 20 minutes to chill while you prepare the filling. Roll out remaining dough for top crust and set aside at room temperature on sheet of parchment paper.

2. *Filling:* In a large bowl, gently combine boysenberries, cherries, sugar, cornstarch and almond extract, making sure that cornstarch is not lumpy. Transfer filling to prepared bottom crust. Lightly brush edge of pastry with a little water. Place top crust over fruit, trimming and fluting edge. Cut steam vents in top of pie. Brush top with cream and sprinkle with sugar.

3. Place pie plate on baking sheet and bake in preheated oven for 55 to 65 minutes or until top is nicely browned and juices are bubbling and thickened. If pie starts to get too brown before it's finished baking, cover loosely with a piece of tented foil. Let cool on a wire rack for 1 hour before serving.

Sour Cherry Pie

Serves 8

- Preheat oven to 375°F (190°C)
- 9-inch (23 cm) glass pie plate, greased
- Rimmed baking sheet

Summer cherry picking became a family tradition about 18 years ago, shortly after my husband and I got married. He really had no idea the fun that was in store for him. Now, like clockwork, I drag the family out to local farms to pick fresh cherries right off the trees. There's nothing like it.

Tip

If you can't find fresh sour cherries, you can substitute drained canned (not cherry pie filling) or frozen sour cherries (do not thaw if using frozen). Just remember that when using frozen fruit, baking time may increase by 15 to 30 minutes.

1	recipe Buttery Pie Pastry Dough or Large-Batch All-Purpose Vegan Pastry Dough, chilled (see recipes, pages 181 and 183)	1

FILLING

5 cups	pitted fresh sour cherries (see Tip, left)	1.25 L
1 cup	granulated sugar	250 mL
3 tbsp + 1 tsp	cornstarch	50 mL
¼ tsp	almond extract	1 mL
	Cream, milk or soy milk	
	Coarse or granulated sugar	

1. Divide pastry dough into 2 pieces, one slightly larger than the other. On a lightly floured surface, roll out larger piece of dough into a circle large enough to fit pie plate, dusting work surface and dough as necessary to keep the dough from sticking (or roll between 2 pieces of waxed or parchment paper). Press dough into prepared pie plate. Place pie plate in freezer or refrigerator for 15 to 20 minutes to chill while you prepare the filling. Roll out remaining dough for top crust and set aside at room temperature on sheet of parchment paper.

2. *Filling:* In a large bowl, gently combine cherries, sugar, cornstarch and almond extract, making sure that cornstarch is not lumpy. Transfer filling to prepared bottom crust. Lightly brush edge of pastry with a little water. Place top crust over cherries, trimming and fluting edge. Cut steam vents in top of pie. Brush top with cream and sprinkle with sugar.

3. Place pie plate on baking sheet and bake in preheated oven for 60 to 65 minutes or until top is nicely browned and juices are bubbling and thickened. If pie starts to get too brown before it's finished baking, cover loosely with a piece of tented foil. Let cool on a wire rack for 1 hour before serving.

Strawberry Rhubarb Pie

Serves 8

- Preheat oven to 425°F (220°C)
- 9-inch (23 cm) glass pie plate, greased
- Rimmed baking sheet

Melanie Miller graciously shared this recipe with me when we worked together on a sugar advertising campaign (fun job, huh?). She was right when she said that this pie is utterly delicious, and it's one that I have made over and over again.

Tip

Do not substitute frozen strawberries in this recipe.

Variation

This pie would also work well with a lattice top (see instructions, page 17).

1	recipe Buttery Pie Pastry Dough or Large-Batch All-Purpose Vegan Pastry Dough, chilled (see recipes, pages 181 and 183)	1

FILLING

3 cups	sliced fresh rhubarb (½-inch/1 cm pieces)	750 mL
3 cups	fresh strawberries, cut in half (or quartered if large)	750 mL
¾ cup	granulated sugar	175 mL
⅓ cup	all-purpose flour	75 mL
	Cream, milk or soy milk	
	Coarse or granulated sugar	

1. Divide pastry dough into 2 pieces, one slightly larger than the other. On a lightly floured surface, roll out larger piece of dough into a circle large enough to fit pie plate, dusting work surface and dough as necessary to keep the dough from sticking (or roll between 2 pieces of waxed or parchment paper). Press dough into prepared pie plate. Place pie plate in freezer or refrigerator for 15 to 20 minutes to chill while you prepare the filling. Roll out remaining dough for top crust and set aside at room temperature on sheet of parchment paper.

2. *Filling:* In a large bowl, gently combine rhubarb, strawberries, sugar and flour. Transfer filling to prepared bottom crust. Lightly brush edge of pastry with a little water. Place top crust over fruit, trimming and fluting edge. Cut steam vents in top of pie. Brush top with cream and sprinkle with sugar.

3. Place pie plate on baking sheet and bake in preheated oven for 45 minutes. Reduce temperature to 375°F (190°C) and continue baking for 15 minutes more or until top is nicely browned and juices are bubbling and thickened. Let cool on a wire rack for 1 hour before serving.

Sweet Cherry Apple Crumb Pie

Serves 8

- Preheat oven to 425°F (220°C)
- 9-inch (23 cm) glass pie plate, greased
- Rimmed baking sheet

I love the combination of subtle flavors in this pie. I also love that you can make it in the middle of winter, thanks to the great variety of frozen fruit available.

Tips

Look for crisp green Granny Smith apples for this pie. Use about 3 large apples or 4 medium.

You can use a store-bought pastry crust for this pie. Just leave it in the freezer until you're ready to fill it.

Variation

Add 2 tsp (10 mL) grated lemon zest to the filling.

1	recipe All-Purpose Vegan Pastry Dough or Small-Batch All-Purpose Buttery Pastry Dough, chilled (see recipes, pages 182 and 180)	1

FILLING

3 or 4	Granny Smith apples, peeled, cored and thinly sliced (see Tips, left)	3 or 4
2 cups	pitted fresh or frozen sweet cherries	500 mL
2/3 cup	granulated sugar	150 mL
3½ tbsp	cornstarch	52 mL
1 tbsp	red wine or cherry-flavored liqueur	15 mL
1 tsp	vanilla paste or extract	5 mL
½ tsp	ground cinnamon	2 mL
1	recipe Brown Sugar Streusel, Almond Crumb Topping or Cinnamon Sugar Crumb Topping (see recipes, pages 134 and 135)	1
	Ground cinnamon	

1. On a lightly floured surface, roll out dough into a circle large enough to fit pie plate, dusting work surface and dough as necessary to keep the dough from sticking (or roll between 2 pieces of waxed or parchment paper). Press dough into prepared pie plate, crimping edge. Place pie plate in freezer or refrigerator for 15 to 20 minutes to chill while you prepare the filling.

2. *Filling:* In a large bowl, gently combine apples, cherries, sugar, cornstarch, wine, vanilla paste and cinnamon, making sure the apples are well coated. Transfer filling to prepared bottom crust, gently pressing apples into pastry and mounding fruit slightly in the center.

3. Place pie plate on baking sheet and bake in preheated oven for 30 minutes. Remove from oven, reduce temperature to 350°F (180°C) and sprinkle streusel over pie, avoiding juicy edge. Return pie to oven and continue baking for 30 to 40 minutes more or until streusel is nicely browned and juices are bubbling and thickened around edge. If pie starts to get too brown before it's finished baking, cover loosely with a piece of tented foil. Let cool on a wire rack for 1 hour before serving.

White Chocolate Key Lime Pie

Serves 8

Close your eyes and imagine yourself in the tropics. Now imagine taking a bite of a dreamy, luscious pie filled with the flavor of fresh lime juice and creamy white chocolate. Well, look no further than this recipe, made right in your own kitchen.

Tips

To melt white chocolate: Place chocolate in a microwave-safe bowl. Microwave on High for 40 to 60 seconds or just until melted. Let cool slightly.

To make chocolate curls: Use a vegetable peeler and peel curls of white chocolate directly off chocolate bar.

1	package (8 oz/250 g) cream cheese, slightly softened	1
1	can (14 oz or 300 mL) sweetened condensed milk	1
3 oz	white chocolate, melted (see Tips, left)	90 g
1 tsp	packed grated lime zest	5 mL
¾ cup	freshly squeezed lime juice	175 mL
1	8-inch (20 cm) store-bought graham cracker pie shell or Graham Cracker Crust (see recipe, page 195)	1
1 cup	whipping (35%) cream	250 mL
2 tbsp	confectioner's (icing) sugar	25 mL
	White chocolate curls (see Tips, left)	

1. In a food processor fitted with metal blade, combine cream cheese and sweetened condensed milk. Pulse until puréed and smooth. Add melted white chocolate, pulsing until smooth. Add lime juice and pulse again until smooth and creamy. Stir in lime zest.

2. Transfer filling to prepared crust, smoothing top. Refrigerate pie for several hours or until firm.

3. In a bowl, using an electric mixer, combine cream and confectioner's sugar. Whip until soft peaks form. Swirl whipped cream over top of pie. Sprinkle white chocolate curls over top of whipped cream. Serve pie at once or refrigerate until ready to serve. This pie is best eaten the day that it is made.

Bryanna's Dairy-Free Pumpkin Pie

Serves 8 to 12

- Preheat oven to 350°F (180°C)
- 9-inch (23 cm) glass pie plate, greased

The first time I had this pie, it blew me away. No one would ever suspect that it's not full of dairy, as it has a rich, spicy flavor. This wonderful pie, created by the talented cookbook author Bryanna Clark Grogan, is now a regular part of my Thanksgiving dessert buffet.

Tip

You can use a store-bought frozen deep-dish 9-inch (23 cm) pie crust for this recipe. Just make sure to keep it frozen until you're ready to fill it.

1	recipe All-Purpose Vegan Pastry Dough, chilled (see recipe, page 182)	1

FILLING

2 cups	pumpkin purée (not pie filling)	500 mL
1 cup	soy milk or almond milk (not low-fat)	250 mL
¾ cup	packed brown sugar	175 mL
4 tbsp	cornstarch	60 mL
1 tbsp	molasses	15 mL
1 tsp	ground cinnamon	5 mL
1 tsp	vanilla extract	5 mL
½ tsp	ground ginger	2 mL
½ tsp	ground nutmeg	2 mL
½ tsp	salt	2 mL
¼ tsp	ground allspice	1 mL

1. On a lightly floured surface, roll out dough into a circle large enough to fit pie plate, dusting work surface and dough as necessary to keep the dough from sticking (or roll between 2 pieces of waxed or parchment paper). Press dough into prepared pie plate, crimping edge. Place pie plate in freezer or refrigerator for 15 to 20 minutes to chill while you prepare the filling.

2. *Filling:* In a food processor fitted with metal blade, combine pumpkin and soy milk, pulsing until smooth. Add brown sugar, cornstarch, molasses, cinnamon, vanilla, ginger, nutmeg, salt and allspice, pulsing until mixture is smooth. Pour into prepared bottom crust.

3. Bake in preheated oven for 60 minutes or until the filling cracks around the edge and the center is set, covering edge with foil if it begins to brown too quickly. Let cool completely on a wire rack. Refrigerate pie overnight before serving.

Easy Sweet Potato Pie

Serves 8

● Preheat oven to
350°F (180°C)

This is an unusual but very
delicious pie. It's a fun
change from pumpkin pie
and a surprise to the taste
buds. It can be made
quickly, thanks to the use
of store-bought pie crust
and canned sweet
potatoes.

Tips
If using store-bought pie
crust, all of the filling
may not fit. Use
it to fill tarts or bake in
custard cups.

Sweet potatoes may be
labeled as yams. Be sure
to use the dark orange
type rather than a true
yam, which is quite a
different vegetable.

Variations
For a slightly spicier
pie, add a few pinches
ground nutmeg to
the filling.

Substitute 1½ cups
(375 mL) well-drained
canned sweet potatoes
for the fresh. If they
are packed in syrup,
decrease sugar to
¾ cup (175 mL).

| 1 | 9-inch (23 cm) store-bought frozen deep-dish pie shell or Small-Batch All-Purpose Buttery Pastry Dough or All-Purpose Vegan Pastry Dough, chilled (see recipes, pages 180 and 182) | 1 |

FILLING

1¼ cups	mashed cooked sweet potatoes	300 mL
3	eggs	3
1 cup	packed dark brown sugar	250 mL
1 cup	evaporated milk	250 mL
1 tsp	ground cinnamon, approx.	5 mL
1 tsp	vanilla extract	5 mL

TOPPING

1 cup	whipping (35%) cream	250 mL
3 tbsp	confectioner's (icing) sugar	45 mL
1 tbsp	bourbon	15 mL

1. Bake pastry according to package or recipe directions. Let cool.

2. *Filling:* In a food processor fitted with a metal blade, purée sweet potatoes. Add eggs, one at a time, pulsing briefly after each addition. Add brown sugar, evaporated milk, 1 tsp (5 mL) cinnamon and vanilla, pulsing until smooth. Ingredients can also be whisked together in a bowl instead. Pour into pie shell. Sprinkle top of pie with pinch ground cinnamon.

3. Bake in preheated oven for 45 minutes or until filling is set in the center and pie is slightly puffed (do not overbake). Let cool completely on a wire rack. Refrigerate pie until cold.

4. *Topping:* In a bowl, using an electric mixer, combine cream, confectioner's sugar and bourbon. Whip until soft peaks form. Swirl whipped cream over top of pie. Serve pie at once or refrigerate until ready to serve.

Libby's Pumpkin Pie

Makes 2 pies

Each pie serves 8

● Preheat oven to
425°F (220°C)

This recipe is the first
pumpkin pie I ever made.
Although I would love to
take credit for creating
the recipe (especially
since I was only 13 at the
time), it's truthfully from
Libby's canned pumpkin.
Although I don't usually
include back-of-the-can
recipes in my cookbooks,
this one is a definite
keeper. The recipe is
easy to make and
nicely spiced — a great
all-around pumpkin pie.

Tip

Cans of pumpkin purée
vary in size, often
containing between
14 and 19 oz (398 and
540 mL). This recipe
is flexible and works
with these slightly
different amounts.

2	9-inch (23 cm) store-bought frozen deep-dish pie shells or Buttery Pie Pastry Dough or All-Purpose Buttery Pastry Dough, chilled (see recipes, pages 181 and 179)	2
FILLING		
1½ cups	granulated sugar	375 mL
2 tsp	ground cinnamon	10 mL
1 tsp	ground ginger	5 mL
1 tsp	salt	5 mL
½ tsp	ground cloves	2 mL
4	eggs	4
1	can (29 oz or 796 mL) pumpkin purée (not pie filling) (see Tip, left)	1
2	cans (each 12 oz/355 mL) evaporated milk	2

1. Bake pastry according to package or recipe directions. Let cool.

2. *Filling:* In a small bowl, mix together sugar, cinnamon, ginger, salt and cloves.

3. In a large bowl, beat eggs until well mixed. Add pumpkin and sugar-and-spice mixture, beating until smooth. Gradually stir in evaporated milk. Pour into prepared pie shells.

4. Bake in preheated oven for 15 minutes. Reduce temperature to 350°F (180°C) and continue baking for 40 to 50 minutes more or until a knife inserted in the center comes out clean. Let cool completely on a wire rack. Refrigerate pie until ready to serve.

Perfect Pumpkin Pie

Serves 8

● Preheat oven to
350°F (180°C)

● 9-inch (23 cm)
deep-dish glass pie
plate, greased

This is adapted from a
wonderful recipe by Dede
Wilson, which originally
appeared in *Bon Appétit*
magazine. If you like your
pumpkin pies rich and
silky (and who doesn't?),
it will make a wonderful
addition to your
Thanksgiving feast.

Tip

If the crust bubbles
while baking, gently
press crust with the back
of a fork or a scrunched
up paper towel.

1	recipe Small-Batch All-Purpose Buttery Pastry Dough, chilled (see recipe, page 180)	1
FILLING		
2 cups	pumpkin purée (not pie filling) (see Tip, page 61)	500 mL
¾ cup	packed light brown sugar	175 mL
1 tsp	ground cinnamon	5 mL
1 tsp	ground ginger	5 mL
½ tsp	ground allspice	2 mL
½ tsp	ground nutmeg	2 mL
3	eggs	3
¾ cup	whipping (35%) cream	175 mL
2 tbsp	pure maple syrup	25 mL

1. On a lightly floured surface, roll out dough into a circle
large enough to fit pie plate, dusting work surface and
dough as necessary to keep the dough from sticking
(or roll between 2 pieces of waxed or parchment paper).
Press dough into prepared pie plate, crimping edge to
form a high border. Line crust with a double layer of foil
and bake in preheated oven for 15 minutes. Remove
foil and continue baking just until edge is light golden.
Let cool for 10 minutes.

2. *Filling:* In a food processor fitted with metal blade,
purée pumpkin, brown sugar, cinnamon, ginger,
allspice and nutmeg until smooth. Add eggs, one at a
time, pulsing briefly after each addition. Add cream
and maple syrup, pulsing just until smooth.

3. Pour filling into warm crust and bake for 60 to
65 minutes or until puffed around edge and firm
in the center. Let cool completely on a wire rack.
Refrigerate pie until ready to serve.

Cream Pies

Banana Fanna Pie

Serves 8

- Preheat oven to 375°F (190°C)
- 9-inch (23 cm) glass pie plate, greased

My friend Erika and I used to make banana cream pies together all the time. I've added chocolate chips to our original recipe, taking it from fabulous to amazing.

Tip

Keep this pie refrigerated until ready to serve. It's best served the day that it is made.

| 1 | recipe All-Purpose Vegan Pastry Dough or Small-Batch All-Purpose Buttery Pastry Dough, chilled (see recipes, pages 182 and 180) | 1 |

FILLING

½ cup	semisweet chocolate chips	125 mL
2 tbsp	whipping (35%) cream	25 mL
3	egg yolks	3
¾ cup	granulated sugar	175 mL
¼ cup	all-purpose flour	50 mL
¼ cup	cornstarch	50 mL
⅛ tsp	salt	0.5 mL
3 cups	half-and-half (10%) cream, divided	750 mL
2 tbsp	butter	25 mL

TOPPING

1 cup	whipping (35%) cream	250 mL
1 tbsp	confectioner's (icing) sugar	15 mL
¼ tsp	vanilla extract	1 mL
2	bananas, sliced	2
	Chocolate chips	

1. On a lightly floured surface, roll out dough into a circle large enough to fit pie plate, dusting work surface and dough as necessary to keep the dough from sticking (or roll between 2 pieces of waxed or parchment paper). Press dough into prepared pie plate, crimping edge. Lightly prick bottom and side of crust with a fork (be careful not to make large holes). Place pie plate in freezer for 15 to 20 minutes to chill.

2. Line the chilled crust with parchment paper or foil and a layer of dried beans or pie weights to weigh it down. Bake for 20 to 25 minutes or until the shell is golden brown and the bottom is no longer moist. If you use a glass pie plate, you can look at the bottom to check that all of the moisture has baked out of the crust. Remove paper and weights. Return crust to oven and bake for 5 minutes more or just until lightly browned.

3. *Filling:* In a microwave-safe bowl, combine chocolate chips and cream. Microwave on High for 40 seconds, stirring partway through, or until chocolate chips are softened. Stir chocolate mixture until smooth. Spread over bottom of cooled crust. Refrigerate crust until chocolate is firm.

4. In a small bowl, whisk together egg yolks, sugar, flour, cornstarch and salt. Whisk in ½ cup (125 mL) of the half-and-half cream, whisking until smooth. In a large saucepan, bring remaining half-and-half cream to a boil over medium-high heat. Remove saucepan from heat and slowly whisk into egg yolk mixture. Return mixture to saucepan and whisk continuously over medium-low heat for 3 to 4 minutes or until thick and smooth. Whisk in butter. Pour custard into a clean bowl and press a sheet of plastic wrap directly onto the surface to prevent a skin from forming. Let cool completely.

5. *Topping:* In a bowl, using an electric mixer, combine cream, confectioner's sugar and vanilla and whip until soft peaks form. Layer banana slices over chocolate in crust. Spoon cooled custard over bananas. Top pie with whipped cream topping and sprinkle with chocolate chips. Chill for several hours before serving.

Variation

Whisk ¾ cup (175 mL) semisweet chocolate chips into hot custard mixture for a double chocolate banana pie.

Better than Robert Redford Pie

Serves 8 to 12

OK, I know you're wondering what this name is all about. For years my mom has made a dessert called Sex in a Pan (also known as Better than Robert Redford in some circles), which I believe she originally clipped from the *Vancouver Sun* newspaper. I decided that the dessert needed to go in a pie shell and, well, the rest is history. Thanks, Mom, for sharing the recipe.

Tip

This pie can be prepared a day ahead.

Variation

Substitute a graham cracker crust for the chocolate crumb crust.

1	package (8 oz/250 g) cream cheese, softened	1
½ cup	confectioner's (icing) sugar	125 mL
1 tbsp	dark rum	15 mL
2	tubs (each 8 oz or 500 mL) whipped topping, thawed, divided	2
1	9-inch (23 cm) store-bought or homemade Cookie Crumb Crust (see recipe, page 195)	1
1¾ cups	milk	425 mL
1	package (4-serving size) instant chocolate pudding	1
	Chocolate shavings or broken chocolate sandwich cookies	

1. In bowl of stand mixer fitted with whisk attachment, combine cream cheese, confectioner's sugar and rum. Beat until smooth. Gently stir in half of the whipped topping. Spread mixture in prepared crust.

2. In a large bowl, combine milk and pudding, whisking until smooth and thickened. Spread pudding over cream cheese mixture.

3. Spread remaining whipped topping over pudding. Garnish with chocolate shavings or broken cookies. Refrigerate pie for several hours before serving.

Buttermilk Pie

Serves 8

- Preheat oven to 325°F (160°C)
- 9-inch (23 cm) glass pie plate, greased

I was searching high and low for a buttermilk pie recipe when I stumbled across an article by Natalie Y. Moore on that very topic. Buttermilk pie is a delightful southern specialty, which I adore. In the article, Moore says that this is the recipe her mother uses, which is originally from *Country Cooking* by the editors of *Southern Living* magazine (Galahad Books, 1974).

Tips

You can use a frozen store-bought crust for this recipe. Just remember to leave it in the freezer until you're ready to fill it.

Don't remove the pie from the oven too soon. The pie should be firm with a boldly golden top, and the crust should be a little brown. If the pie is removed from the oven prematurely, the dessert looks like pudding spilling from a crust.

1	recipe All-Purpose Vegan Pastry Dough or Small-Batch All-Purpose Buttery Pastry Dough, chilled (see recipes, pages 182 and 180)	1

FILLING

1 cup	granulated sugar	250 mL
2 tbsp	all-purpose flour, plus a little for dusting	25 mL
1 tbsp	grated lemon zest	15 mL
3	eggs	3
1 cup	buttermilk	250 mL
½ cup	butter, melted and cooled slightly	125 mL
1 tsp	vanilla extract	5 mL

1. On a lightly floured surface, roll out dough into a circle large enough to fit pie plate, dusting work surface and dough as necessary to keep the dough from sticking (or roll between 2 pieces of waxed or parchment paper). Press dough into prepared pie plate, crimping edge. Place pie plate in freezer for 15 to 20 minutes to chill while you prepare the filling.

2. *Filling:* In a large bowl, combine sugar, flour and lemon zest. Whisk in eggs, one at a time. Add buttermilk, melted butter and vanilla, stirring well.

3. Dust prepared pastry with a little bit of flour. Pour filling into crust and sprinkle a little more flour over top.

4. Bake pie in preheated oven for 1 hour or until custard is set. Let cool on a wire rack before serving.

Butterscotch Cream Pie

Serves 8 to 12

If butterscotch pie conjures up images of sitting at a diner with an old-fashioned slice-o-pie, then you will want to give this recipe a spin. This pie is wonderfully rich, with a deep butterscotch flavor. I could eat the whole pie with a spoon.

¾ cup	packed light brown sugar	175 mL
6 tbsp	cornstarch	90 mL
¼ tsp	salt	1 mL
4	egg yolks	4
1 cup	milk (not low-fat or nonfat), divided	250 mL
2 cups	half-and-half (10%) cream	500 mL
2 tbsp	butter	25 mL
1 tbsp	Scotch	15 mL
1 tsp	vanilla extract	5 mL
1	9-inch (23 cm) store-bought or homemade Cookie Crumb Crust (see recipe, page 195)	1

TOPPING

1 cup	whipping (35%) cream	250 mL
2 tbsp	confectioner's (icing) sugar	25 mL

1. In a small bowl, whisk together brown sugar, cornstarch, salt, egg yolks and ¼ cup (50 mL) milk until smooth. In a large saucepan, bring remaining milk and half-and-half cream to a boil over medium-high heat. Remove saucepan from heat and slowly whisk into egg yolk mixture. Return mixture to saucepan and whisk continuously over medium-low heat for 3 to 4 minutes or until thick and smooth. Reduce temperature and continue whisking for 1 minute more or until filling is very thick. Remove from heat and whisk in butter, Scotch and vanilla. Strain the filling through a fine-mesh sieve into a bowl and press a piece of plastic wrap directly onto the surface to prevent a skin from forming. Let cool completely.

2. Spread filling in crust and chill, loosely covered, for 4 to 6 hours or until filling is thick enough to slice.

3. *Topping:* Just prior to serving pie, in a bowl, using an electric mixer or whisk, whip whipping cream and confectioner's sugar until soft peaks form. Swirl whipped cream on top of pie. Refrigerate pie until ready to serve. This pie is best served the day that it is made.

Cheesecake Tart with Coconut Crust

Serves 8

- 9½-inch (24 cm) tart pan with removable bottom, greased

This is similar to a cheesecake but even better. It goes together quickly and looks impressive. It's always a huge hit when I bring this to local gatherings. It looks like I spent hours in the kitchen.

Tip

Superfine sugar, also known as baker's sugar, is an ultra-fine granulated sugar that dissolves very quickly in liquid. If you cannot find it in your local grocery store, you can make your own. Process granulated sugar in a food processor until very finely ground.

10	whole graham crackers (about ¾ cup/175 mL)	10
⅓ cup	sweetened flaked coconut	75 mL
5 tbsp	butter, melted	75 mL
FILLING		
12 oz	cream cheese, softened	375 g
½ cup	superfine sugar (see Tip, left)	125 mL
1¾ cups	whipping (35%) cream	425 mL
2½ tbsp	rum	32 mL

1. In a food processor fitted with metal blade, pulse graham crackers until fine crumbs. Place crumbs in a bowl and stir in coconut and butter. Press mixture onto side and bottom of prepared tart pan. Place tart pan in freezer to chill while you prepare the filling.

2. *Filling:* In bowl of stand mixer fitted with whisk attachment, combine cream cheese and sugar. Whip until creamy, scraping down side of bowl as necessary. Add cream and rum, whipping until mixture looks like whipped cream and soft peaks form.

3. Remove crust from freezer. Spread whipped cream mixture in crust, using back of spoon to decoratively swirl mixture. Refrigerate for several hours before serving.

Chocolate Bottom Vanilla Cream Pie

Serves 8 to 12

This cream pie is to live for! The super-creamy filling is speckled with vanilla flecks and cradled in a chocolate-covered crust. Wow! I could definitely eat this entire pie with a spoon.

Tip
This pie is best served the day that it is made.

¾ cup	granulated sugar	175 mL
⅓ cup	cornstarch	75 mL
¼ cup	all-purpose flour	50 mL
¼ tsp	salt	1 mL
3	egg yolks	3
3 cups	half-and-half (10%) cream, divided	750 mL
2 tbsp	butter	25 mL
2 tsp	vanilla paste or extract	10 mL
2 oz	semisweet or bittersweet chocolate, melted	60 g
1	9-inch (23 cm) store-bought or homemade Cookie Crumb Crust (see recipe, page 195)	1

TOPPING

1¼ cups	whipping (35%) cream	300 mL
2 tbsp	confectioner's (icing) sugar	25 mL
1 tsp	vanilla paste or extract	5 mL

1. In a small bowl, whisk together sugar, cornstarch, flour, salt and egg yolks. Whisk in ½ cup (125 mL) of the half-and-half cream, whisking until smooth. In a large saucepan, bring remaining half-and-half cream to boil over medium-high heat. Remove saucepan from heat and slowly whisk into egg yolk mixture. Return mixture to saucepan and whisk continuously over medium-low heat for 3 to 4 minutes or until thick and smooth. Reduce temperature to low and continue whisking for 1 minute more or until filling is very thick. Remove saucepan from heat and whisk in butter and vanilla paste. Strain filling through a fine-mesh sieve into a bowl and press a piece of plastic wrap directly onto the surface to prevent a skin from forming. Let cool completely.

2. In a microwave-safe bowl, heat chocolate for 20 seconds on High or just until chocolate is shiny and almost melted. Remove from microwave, stirring until smooth. If chocolate isn't completely melted, heat an additional 10 to 20 seconds. Spoon melted chocolate into bottom of prepared crust, spreading evenly. Refrigerate crust for 15 minutes or until chocolate is firm.

3. Stir filling and spread in crust. Chill, loosely covered, for 4 to 6 hours or until filling is thick enough to slice.

4. *Topping:* Just prior to serving pie, in a bowl, using an electric mixer or whisk, whip together cream, confectioner's sugar and vanilla just until stiff peaks form. Swirl whipped cream on top of pie. Refrigerate pie until ready to serve.

Chocolate Coffee Cream Pie

Serves 8

Coffee and chocolate are truly a match made in heaven. That is why this pie cannot be beat, especially if you're a big fan of a nice custard pie in a chocolate crumb crust. Holy moly, this is good!

Tip
Keep this pie refrigerated until ready to serve. This pie is best served the day that it is made.

Variation
Garnish the top with chocolate shavings for an extra-special touch.

¾ cup	granulated sugar	175 mL
¼ cup	cornstarch	50 mL
¼ tsp	salt	1 mL
4	egg yolks	4
1 cup	milk (not low-fat or nonfat), divided	250 mL
1½ cups	half-and-half (10%) cream	375 mL
½ cup	strong brewed coffee, cooled	125 mL
4 tsp	instant coffee granules	20 mL
¾ cup	semisweet chocolate chips	175 mL
1 oz	unsweetened chocolate, chopped	30 g
1 tsp	vanilla extract	5 mL
1	9-inch (23 cm) store-bought or homemade Cookie Crumb Crust (see recipe, page 195)	1

TOPPING

1 cup	whipping (35%) cream	250 mL
2 tbsp	confectioner's (icing) sugar	25 mL
2 tsp	instant coffee granules	10 mL

1. In a small bowl, whisk together sugar, cornstarch, salt and egg yolks. Whisk in ½ cup (125 mL) of the milk until smooth. In a large saucepan, bring remaining milk, cream and brewed and instant coffees to a boil over medium heat. Remove saucepan from heat and slowly whisk into egg yolk mixture. Return mixture to saucepan and whisk continuously over medium-low heat for 3 to 4 minutes or until mixture is very thick and smooth. Remove from heat and whisk in chocolate chips, unsweetened chocolate and vanilla. Strain filling through a fine-mesh sieve into a bowl and press a piece of plastic wrap directly onto the surface to prevent a skin from forming. Let cool completely.

2. Stir filling and spread in crust. Chill, loosely covered, for 4 to 6 hours or until filling is thick enough to slice.

3. *Topping:* Just prior to serving pie, in a bowl, using an electric mixer or whisk, whip together whipping cream, confectioner's sugar and instant coffee until soft peaks form. Swirl whipped cream over top of pie.

Chocolate Cream Pie

Serves 8 to 12

This pie is definitely an oldie but a goodie. When I eat it, I'm reminded of diners and drive-ins. You will fall in love with its creamy dark chocolate filling and whipped cream top.

Tips
Bittersweet, also known as dark, chocolate must have at least 35% chocolate liquor, but many brands now go beyond that up to 90%. When I use dark chocolate in my baking, I often reach for a 70% bar. If you like a sweeter chocolate, use semisweet, which has a less-intense chocolate flavor than bittersweet. For a darker, more intense chocolate flavor, reach for one of the darker higher percentage bars.

Keep this pie refrigerated until ready to serve. This pie is best served the day that it is made.

¾ cup	granulated sugar	175 mL
¼ cup	cornstarch	50 mL
¼ tsp	salt	1 mL
4	egg yolks	4
2 cups	whole milk, divided	500 mL
1 cup	whipping (35%) cream	250 mL
6 oz	bittersweet or semisweet chocolate, chopped (see Tips, left)	175 g
1 oz	unsweetened chocolate, chopped	30 g
1 tsp	vanilla extract	5 mL
1	9-inch (23 cm) store-bought or homemade Cookie Crumb Crust (see recipe, page 195)	1

TOPPING

1¼ cups	whipping (35%) cream	300 mL
1 tbsp	confectioner's (icing) sugar	15 mL
1 tsp	vanilla extract	5 mL
	Chocolate shavings, optional	

1. In a heavy saucepan, whisk together sugar, cornstarch, salt and egg yolks until well combined. Add ½ cup (125 mL) of the milk, whisking well. Whisk in remaining milk and cream. Bring to a simmer over medium heat, whisking. Reduce temperature and simmer, whisking, for 1 minute or until filling is very thick. Remove from heat and whisk in bittersweet and unsweetened chocolates and vanilla. Strain filling through a fine-mesh sieve into a bowl and press a piece of plastic wrap directly onto the surface to prevent a skin from forming. Let cool completely.

2. Stir filling and spread in crust. Chill, loosely covered, for at least 6 hours.

3. *Topping:* Just prior to serving pie, in a bowl, using an electric mixer or whisk, whip together cream, confectioner's sugar and vanilla until soft peaks form. Swirl whipped cream over top of pie and garnish with chocolate shavings, if desired.

Chocolate Peanut Butter Mousse Pie

Serves 8

This is a recipe that I developed for a chocolate demo that I did in Seattle. I wanted to show not just how versatile tofu can be but also how utterly delicious it is when whipped with peanut butter and melted chocolate. No one will guess the secret ingredient, but they will fall in love with the silky flavors of this pie.

Tips

This pie can be made up to 1 day ahead. The texture becomes more truffle-like the longer it's refrigerated.

If you are vegan, be sure to use both vegan chocolate sandwich cookies and vegan chocolate for the shavings.

1½ cups	semisweet chocolate chips	375 mL
½ cup	chocolate-flavored soy milk	125 mL
1	package (12.3 oz/400 g) firm silken tofu	1
1 cup	creamy natural peanut butter	250 mL
½ cup	confectioner's (icing) sugar	125 mL
1	9-inch (23 cm) store-bought vegan chocolate cookie crumb crust or Cookie Crumb Crust (see recipe, page 195)	1
	Chocolate shavings or broken chocolate sandwich cookies (see Tips, left)	

1. In a microwave-safe bowl, combine chocolate chips and soy milk. Microwave on High for 30 seconds. Stir chocolate and heat for 20 seconds more or just until soy milk is warm. Remove from microwave and stir until chocolate is melted and mixture is smooth. If necessary, heat chocolate mixture for 10 seconds more or as needed. Do not overheat or chocolate will burn.

2. In a blender, blend tofu until very smooth. Add chocolate mixture and peanut butter, blending until smooth. Add sugar, blending until smooth.

3. Spread chocolate mixture in crust and top with chocolate shavings or broken chocolate sandwich cookies. Refrigerate for several hours or until pie is firm enough to slice.

Coconut Cream Pie

Serves 8 to 12

Since we can't take romantic vacations in Hawaii as often as we'd like, I present you with this luscious tropical pie. One whiff of the coconut will send your senses reeling. Not only does the pie taste great, it will save you thousands in travel expenses.

Tip

This pie is wonderful served with chocolate sauce or Hot Fudge Sauce (see recipe, page 235) on the side.

Variation

Substitute the Toasted Coconut Crust (see recipe, page 196) for the Graham Cracker Crust.

1 cup	granulated sugar	250 mL
1/4 cup	cornstarch	50 mL
Pinch	salt	Pinch
1 cup	unsweetened coconut milk	250 mL
4	egg yolks	4
2 cups	whole milk	500 mL
1 cup	packed sweetened flaked coconut	250 mL
1 tbsp	butter	15 mL
1	9-inch (23 cm) store-bought or homemade Graham Cracker Crust (see recipe, page 195)	1

TOPPING

1 1/4 cups	whipping (35%) cream	300 mL
2 tbsp	confectioner's (icing) sugar	25 mL
1/4 cup	sweetened flaked coconut, toasted	50 mL

1. In a large saucepan, whisk together sugar, cornstarch and salt. Whisk in coconut milk until smooth. Whisk in egg yolks until smooth. Whisk in milk. Cook mixture over medium heat, whisking continuously, until thick and bubbly. Reduce temperature to low and continue to cook, whisking, for 2 minutes more or until mixture is very thick.

2. Remove saucepan from heat and strain filling through a fine-mesh sieve into a bowl. Stir in coconut and butter until butter is melted. Pour into prepared pie crust, pressing a piece of plastic wrap directly onto the surface to prevent a skin from forming. Let cool completely. Refrigerate pie for 4 to 6 hours or until filling is firm enough to slice.

3. *Topping:* Just prior to serving pie, in a bowl, using an electric mixer or whisk, whip together cream and confectioner's sugar until soft peaks form. Swirl whipped cream over top of pie and garnish with toasted coconut.

Custard Pie

Serves 8

- Preheat oven to 375°F (190°C)
- 9-inch (23 cm) glass pie plate, greased

I love this old-fashioned pie. In fact, I wasn't the only one. When I was testing this recipe, I couldn't keep my kids away from it. They were literally requesting it for breakfast, lunch and dinner.

Tip

Try to make sure that both the filling and the pastry are hot when the pie is assembled. This helps to set the custard. Also be careful not to overbake the pie.

| 1 | recipe All-Purpose Vegan Pastry Dough or Small-Batch All-Purpose Buttery Pastry Dough, chilled (see recipes, pages 182 and 180) | 1 |

FILLING

4	eggs	4
½ cup	granulated sugar	125 mL
½ cup	whipping (35%) cream	125 mL
1½ cups	milk (not low-fat or nonfat), heated until steaming	375 mL
	Ground nutmeg	

1. On a lightly floured surface, roll out dough into a circle large enough to fit pie plate, dusting work surface and dough as necessary to keep the dough from sticking (or roll between 2 pieces of waxed or parchment paper). Press dough into prepared pie plate, crimping edge. Lightly prick bottom and side of crust with a fork (be careful not to make large holes). Place pie plate in freezer for 15 to 20 minutes to chill while you prepare the filling.

2. Line pastry with a piece of parchment paper filled with pie weights or a double thickness of foil. Bake in preheated oven for 10 minutes or until edge start to look dry and very lightly browned. Remove pastry from oven and carefully remove parchment and pie weights, being careful not to rip the crust. Return pastry to oven and bake for 5 to 10 minutes more or until pastry is set and no longer looks wet. Remove from oven and reduce temperature to 325°F (160°C).

3. *Filling:* Meanwhile, in a large bowl, whisk together eggs, sugar and cream. Slowly whisk hot milk into egg mixture, whisking continuously so that eggs do not curdle.

4. Pour warm filling into hot pastry crust. Sprinkle with nutmeg. Bake in preheated oven for 35 to 45 minutes or until custard is set but seems slightly quivery in the center. A knife inserted near the center of the pie should come out clean. Let cool on a wire rack to room temperature. Refrigerate until ready to serve.

Easy Lemon Pie

Serves 8 to 12

Here's an easy pie that's guaranteed to delight. It's creamy, delicious and, best of all, super-easy to make. This pie is similar to a Key lime one but is infused with fresh lemon flavor in place of lime. I love that it's a no-bake pie.

Tips

This pie is best served the day that it is made.

This is a great pie to make in the heat of the summer if you use a ready-made graham cracker crust.

Variation

For a pink lemonade version, lightly tint the filling with a drop or so of red food coloring (just enough to tint it light pink).

1	can (14 oz or 300 mL) sweetened condensed milk	1
1	package (8 oz/250 g) cream cheese, softened	1
2 tsp	packed grated lemon zest	10 mL
¾ cup	freshly squeezed lemon juice	175 mL
¼ tsp	lemon oil	1 mL
1	9-inch (23 cm) store-bought or homemade Graham Cracker Crust or Toasted Coconut Crust (see recipes, pages 195 and 196)	1

TOPPING

1 cup	whipping (35%) cream	250 mL
2 tbsp	confectioner's (icing) sugar	25 mL

1. In a food processor fitted with metal blade, combine sweetened condensed milk and cream cheese. Pulse until smooth and creamy. Add lemon juice and lemon oil, pulsing until smooth. Stir in lemon zest.

2. Spread lemon mixture in prepared pie crust, smoothing top. Refrigerate for several hours or until firm.

3. *Topping:* In a bowl, using an electric mixer or whisk, whip cream and confectioner's sugar until soft peaks form. Swirl whipped cream over top of pie. Refrigerate pie for 3 to 4 hours or until firm. Keep refrigerated until ready to serve.

Old-Fashioned Chocolate Orange Pie

Serves 8

Don't let the name fool you. This dessert is a favorite with all ages. The chocolate-orange flavor lends an air of sophistication to an old-fashioned pie.

Tips

This pie is best served the day that it is made.

Small-Batch All-Purpose Buttery Pastry Dough (see recipe, page 180) would also work well here.

1	9-inch (23 cm) store-bought frozen pastry crust	1
FILLING		
¼ cup	granulated sugar	50 mL
2 tbsp	all-purpose flour	25 mL
2 tbsp	cornstarch	25 mL
⅛ tsp	salt	0.5 mL
1½ cups	milk, divided (not low-fat or nonfat)	375 mL
2	egg yolks	2
1 tsp	finely grated orange zest	5 mL
½ cup	orange juice	125 mL
1 cup	semisweet chocolate chips	250 mL
1 tbsp	butter	15 mL
½ tsp	vanilla extract	2 mL
TOPPING		
1 cup	whipping (35%) cream	250 mL
1 tbsp	confectioner's (icing) sugar	15 mL
½ tsp	vanilla extract	2 mL
	Chocolate chips, optional	

1. Bake pastry crust according to package directions. Let cool.

2. *Filling:* In a bowl, whisk together sugar, flour, cornstarch and salt. Whisk in ½ cup (125 mL) of the milk and egg yolks. Set aside.

3. In a large saucepan over medium-high heat, bring remaining milk and orange zest and juice to a simmer, whisking often (don't worry if it looks a bit curdled at this point). Remove saucepan from heat and whisk into egg yolk mixture. Return mixture to saucepan, reduce temperature to medium-low and cook, whisking continuously, until thickened. Remove from heat and whisk in chocolate chips, butter and vanilla until smooth. Transfer to a bowl, cover with plastic wrap and press a sheet of plastic wrap directly onto the surface to prevent a skin from forming. Let cool just until warm. Spread filling in prepared crust.

4. *Topping:* Just prior to serving pie, in a bowl, using an electric mixer or whisk, whip together cream, confectioner's sugar and vanilla until soft peaks form. Swirl whipped cream over top of pie and sprinkle with chocolate chips, if desired. Chill for several hours before serving.

Lemon Cream Pie

Serves 8 to 12

I'm not sure that you can ever have enough recipes for lemon pie, especially if each one is a little different and unique. This is a light and fluffy lemon cream pie, with not a stitch of baking or cooking involved. Easy-peasy pie.

Tips

This pie is best served the day that it is made.

If desired, you can serve the pie with a drizzle of raspberry sauce.

1	can (14 oz or 300 mL) sweetened condensed milk	1
2 tsp	grated lemon zest	10 mL
⅓ cup + 2 tbsp	freshly squeezed lemon juice	100 mL
¼ tsp	lemon oil	1 mL
2 cups	whipping (35%) cream	500 mL
2 tbsp	confectioner's (icing) sugar	25 mL
1	9-inch (23 cm) store-bought or homemade Graham Cracker Crust (see recipe, page 195), cooled	1

1. In a large bowl, whisk together sweetened condensed milk and lemon zest, juice and oil. Set aside.
2. In bowl of stand mixer fitted with whisk attachment or in a large bowl with a hand mixer, combine cream and confectioner's sugar. Beat until soft peaks form. Fold whipped cream into milk mixture, blending well. Spread in crust and refrigerate for at least 2 hours. Serve pie chilled.

Hand Pies

Brown Sugar Hand Pies

Makes 4 hand pies

- Preheat oven to 425°F (220°C)
- Baking sheet, lined with parchment paper

My husband has always had a deep love for cinnamon toaster pastries — you know, the kind that you buy in the supermarket and pop in a toaster oven, with a brown sugar filling and a sweet white glaze. So Jay set out to make a homemade version, knowing that there would be no comparison in flavor between home-baked and store-bought. He was right — these are some of the tastiest pies around.

> **Tip**
> In a hurry? You can make these hand pies with store-bought refrigerated pastry.
>
> **Variation**
> Add 1 to 2 tsp (5 to 10 mL) grated orange zest to the filling.

½ cup	packed brown sugar	125 mL
¼ cup	granulated sugar	50 mL
2 tbsp	butter or margarine, at room temperature	25 mL
1 tsp	ground cinnamon	5 mL
1	recipe All-Purpose Vegan Pastry Dough or Small-Batch All-Purpose Buttery Pastry Dough, chilled (see recipes, pages 182 and 180)	1
	Cream, milk or soy milk	
1	recipe Vanilla Bean Glaze or Cinnamon Glaze (see recipes, pages 242 and 240) or coarse sugar	1

1. In a bowl, using an electric mixer, beat together brown sugar, granulated sugar, butter and cinnamon until smooth.

2. On a lightly floured surface, roll out dough into a 12-inch (30 cm) circle, dusting work surface and dough as necessary to keep the dough from sticking (or roll between 2 pieces of waxed or parchment paper). Cut dough into quarters. Spoon sugar mixture evenly in a strip down the center of each quarter. Lightly brush edges with a little water. Fold dough in half to make a triangle, making sure to lightly press top of pastry to distribute the filling evenly. Seal edges together with tines of a fork, dipping the fork into flour as necessary (see Tips, page 85).

3. Place pies on prepared baking sheet. Brush tops with cream and top with glaze or sugar.

4. Bake pies in preheated oven for 15 to 20 minutes or until golden brown. Let cool on baking sheet for 10 minutes. Serve warm or transfer to a wire rack and let cool completely.

Cherry Jam Half-Moon Pies

Makes 14 pastries

- Preheat oven to 375°F (190°C)
- 2 baking sheets, lined with parchment paper
- 4-inch (10 cm) round cookie or biscuit cutter

This is a great recipe to make at the spur of the moment, because you can throw it together quickly with just a few ingredients on hand. With some cherry preserves and a good-quality refrigerated pastry dough, you can put these together in no time.

Variation

Instead of sprinkling the pies with sugar before baking, glaze the baked and cooled pies with Vanilla Bean Glaze or Almond Glaze (see recipes, pages 242 and 240).

1	recipe Buttery Pie Pastry Dough or Large-Batch All-Purpose Vegan Pastry Dough (see recipes, pages 181 and 183) or store-bought refrigerated pastry dough, chilled	1
½ cup	cherry jam or preserves, approx.	125 mL
	Cream, milk or soy milk	
	Coarse or granulated sugar, optional	

1. On a lightly floured surface, roll out dough slightly thinner than ⅛ inch (0.25 cm) thick, dusting work surface and dough as necessary to keep the dough from sticking (or roll between 2 pieces of waxed or parchment paper). Cut dough into 14 circles with a 4-inch (10 cm) round cookie or biscuit cutter.

2. Spoon 1 to 2 tsp (5 to 10 mL) of the jam in the center of each circle. Lightly brush edges with a little water. Fold each circle in half, making sure to lightly press top of pastry to distribute the filling evenly. Seal edges together with tines of a fork, dipping the fork into flour as necessary. Pierce tops with tines of a fork. Place on prepared baking sheets. Refrigerate for 15 minutes.

3. Brush tops of pies with cream. If desired, sprinkle sugar over cream.

4. Bake pies in preheated oven for 25 to 35 minutes or until golden brown. Let cool on pans for 10 minutes. Transfer to a wire rack and let cool completely.

Cherry Turnovers

Makes 8 turnovers

- Preheat oven to 400°F (200°C)
- Baking sheet, lined with parchment paper

This turnover recipe is one of my daughter's favorites. The cherry filling is completely irresistible, especially with the crisp puff pastry. I love to throw these turnovers together for a quick company dessert, as they can bake while everyone's enjoying dinner.

Tips

If you have a smaller package of puff pastry, the pastry may be thinner but will still work.

These pastries are best eaten within a few hours of baking.

1	box (18 oz/540 g) frozen puff pastry, thawed (see Tips, left)	1
½	recipe Cherry Pie Filling or Cherry Berry Filling (see recipes, page 201)	½
	Cream, milk or soy milk	
	Granulated sugar	
	Confectioner's (icing) sugar, optional	

1. On a lightly floured surface, unroll one puff pastry sheet. If necessary, roll out into a 9¾- by 9½-inch (24 by 23.75 cm) rectangle. Cut rectangle into 4 pieces. Place one-eighth of the cherry filling in the center of each square. Lightly brush two adjacent edges with a little water. Fold over dough into a triangle and crimp edges with a fork. Repeat with remaining pastry and filling.

2. Place pastries on prepared baking sheet. Lightly brush with cream and sprinkle with sugar. Bake in preheated oven for 20 to 25 minutes or until puffed and lightly browned. Let cool on pan for 10 minutes. Transfer to a wire rack to finish cooling completely.

3. If desired, dust turnovers with confectioner's sugar before serving.

Chocolate Babka Hand Pies

Makes 4 hand pies

- Preheat oven to 425°F (220°C)
- Baking sheet, lined with parchment paper

The stuffing for this hand pie recipe was inspired by Marcy Goldman's chocolate babka in her cookbook *Jewish Holiday Baking*. It makes a fabulous filling for these toaster pies.

Tips

You can make these hand pies with store-bought refrigerated and rolled pastry. Bring to room temperature before rolling out.

I have found that it's not always necessary to seal your pastry edge with water. It really depends on the dough. I have included that step in this recipe, but if your dough is soft and doesn't seem to need it, don't worry.

Variation

Brush tops of unbaked pies with cream, milk or soy milk and sprinkle with granulated sugar and bake as directed.

FILLING

¼ cup	semisweet chocolate chips	50 mL
1½ tbsp	light brown sugar	22 mL
1 tbsp	butter or margarine	15 mL
1½ tsp	unsweetened Dutch-process cocoa powder	7 mL
¼ tsp	ground cinnamon	1 mL
1	recipe All-Purpose Vegan Pastry Dough or Small-Batch All-Purpose Buttery Pastry Dough, chilled (see recipes, pages 182 and 180) Confectioner's (icing) sugar	1

1. *Filling:* In a food processor fitted with metal blade, pulse together chocolate chips, brown sugar, butter, cocoa powder and cinnamon until mixture is blended.

2. On a lightly floured surface, roll out dough into a 12-inch (30 cm) circle, dusting work surface and dough as necessary to keep the dough from sticking (or roll between 2 pieces of waxed or parchment paper). Cut dough into quarters. Spoon chocolate mixture into center of each quarter. Lightly brush edges with a little water (see Tips, left). Fold dough in half to make a triangle, making sure to lightly press top of pastry to distribute the filling evenly. Seal edges together with tines of a fork, dipping the fork into flour as necessary. Place pies on prepared baking sheet.

3. Bake pies in preheated oven for 15 to 20 minutes or until golden brown. Let cool on pan for 10 minutes. Serve warm or transfer to a wire rack and let cool completely. Before serving, lightly dust tops of pies with confectioner's sugar.

Chocolate Hand Pies

Makes 4 hand pies

- Preheat oven to 425°F (220°C)
- Baking sheet, lined with parchment paper

My inspiration for these lovely pies came while watching my son tear into a chocolate bar. I thought that a nice big piece of dark chocolate sandwiched between pastry would make a fantastic pie!

Tips

You can make these hand pies with store-bought refrigerated and rolled pastry. Be sure to bring to room temperature before rolling out.

I have found that it's not always necessary to seal your pastry edge with water. It really depends on the dough. I have included that step in this recipe, but if your dough is soft you can omit it.

Variations

Substitute white chocolate for the dark.

Instead of topping the pies with Almond Glaze, top with Cinnamon Glaze (see recipe, page 240).

1	recipe All-Purpose Vegan Pastry Dough or Small-Batch All-Purpose Buttery Pastry Dough, chilled (see recipes, pages 182 and 180)	1
3 oz	bittersweet chocolate bar, broken into small pieces, or semisweet chocolate chips	90 g
1	recipe Almond Glaze (see recipe, page 240)	1

1. On a lightly floured surface, roll out dough into a 12-inch (30 cm) circle, dusting work surface and dough as necessary to keep the dough from sticking (or roll between 2 pieces of waxed or parchment paper). Cut dough into quarters. Place chocolate in center of each quarter. Lightly brush edges with a little water (see Tips, left). Fold dough in half to make a triangle. Seal edges together with tines of a fork, dipping the fork into flour as necessary. Place pies on prepared baking sheet.

2. Bake pies in preheated oven for 15 to 20 minutes or until golden brown. Let cool on pan for 10 minutes. Serve warm or transfer to a wire rack and let cool completely.

3. Place wire rack on a baking sheet. Spread glaze over tops of pies. Let stand until glaze is firm.

Chocolate Raspberry Moon Pies

Makes 8 pastries

- Preheat oven to 375°F (190°C)
- Baking sheet, lined with parchment paper
- 4-inch (10 cm) round cookie or biscuit cutter

Although these pies make a great dessert, I love eating them even more for breakfast. Who says that jam pies can't be a breakfast of champions?

Tip

Bittersweet, also known as dark, chocolate must have at least 35% chocolate liquor, but many brands now go beyond that up to 90%. When I use dark chocolate in my baking, I often reach for a 70% bar. If you like a sweeter chocolate, use semisweet, which has a less-intense chocolate flavor than bittersweet. For a darker, more intense chocolate flavor, reach for one of the darker, higher percentage bars.

Variation

Substitute apricot jam or preserves for the raspberry.

1	recipe Large-Batch All-Purpose Vegan Pastry Dough or All-Purpose Buttery Pastry Dough, chilled (see recipes, pages 183 and 179)	1
½ cup	raspberry jam or preserves	125 mL
3 oz	bittersweet or semisweet chocolate, approx., coarsely chopped (see Tip, left)	90 g
	Cream, milk or soy milk	
	Granulated sugar	

1. On a lightly floured surface, roll out both pieces of dough slightly thinner than ⅛ inch (0.25 cm) thick, dusting work surface and dough as necessary to keep the dough from sticking (or roll between 2 pieces of waxed or parchment paper). Cut dough into 16 circles with a 4-inch (10 cm) round cookie or biscuit cutter, rerolling scraps.

2. Spoon about 1 tbsp (15 mL) of the jam into the center of each of 8 of the circles. Gently press a piece of chocolate on top of jam. Lightly brush edges with a little cream or water (see Tips, page 86). Place a second circle of pastry on top of chocolate, making sure to lightly press top of pastry to distribute the filling evenly. Seal edges together with tines of a fork, dipping the fork into flour as necessary. Place pies on prepared baking sheet. Refrigerate for 20 to 30 minutes.

3. Brush tops of pies with cream and sprinkle with sugar.

4. Bake pies in preheated oven for 25 to 35 minutes or until golden brown. Let cool on pan for 10 minutes. Transfer to a wire rack and let cool completely.

Double Almond Hand Pies

Makes 8 hand pies

- Preheat oven to 425°F (220°C)
- 2 baking sheets, lined with parchment paper

I'm reminded of Paris when I bite into these flaky pies. The flavor is similar to that of an almond croissant, with a lovely American pastry twist.

Tips

Almond paste is also available in 7-oz (210 g) tubes in some areas and is suitable for this recipe.

You can make these hand pies with store-bought refrigerated pastry.

I have found that it's not always necessary to seal your pastry edge with water. It really depends on the dough. I have included that step in this recipe, but if your dough is soft and doesn't seem to need it, don't worry.

Variation

Top pies with a drizzle of melted chocolate instead of the Almond Glaze.

1	recipe Buttery Pie Pastry Dough or Large-Batch All-Purpose Vegan Pastry Dough, chilled (see recipes, pages 181 and 183)	1
1	can or package (8 oz/250 g) almond paste (see Tips, left)	1
1	recipe Almond Glaze (see recipe, page 240)	1
	Sliced almonds	

1. Divide dough into 2 pieces. On a lightly floured surface, roll out one piece of the dough into a 12-inch (30 cm) circle, dusting work surface and dough as necessary to keep the dough from sticking (or roll between 2 pieces of waxed or parchment paper). (While rolling out the first piece of dough to make the first 4 hand pies, keep the remaining piece covered and refrigerated until you're ready to roll it.)

2. Cut dough into quarters. Spoon about one-eighth of the almond paste into your hand and lightly press into a long triangle. Place one piece in center of each quarter. Lightly brush edges with a little water (see Tips, left). Fold dough in half to make a triangle. Seal edges together with tines of a fork, dipping the fork into flour as necessary. Place pies on one of the prepared baking sheets. Repeat with remaining dough and filling.

3. Bake pies in preheated oven for 15 to 20 minutes or until golden brown. Let cool on pan for 10 minutes. Transfer to a wire rack and let cool completely.

4. Place wire rack on a baking sheet. Spread glaze over tops of pies. Sprinkle a few sliced almonds on top of glaze. Let stand until glaze is firm.

Plum Hand Pies

Makes 8 hand pies

- Preheat oven to 425°F (220°C)
- 2 baking sheets, lined with parchment paper

Now that prunes have had a makeover and are officially called "dried plums," I think it's safe to call these delicious gems "plum pies." The pies taste like bakery pastries and are lightly sweet with a nice bit of tanginess. They make a perfect breakfast pie.

Tips

Prune filling, also known as lekvar, is available in the international food section in large grocery stores or can be ordered online (see Sources, page 246).

You can make these hand pies with store-bought refrigerated pastry.

Variation

Substitute Lemon Glaze (see recipe, page 241) for the Vanilla Bean Glaze.

1	recipe Buttery Pie Pastry Dough or Large-Batch All-Purpose Vegan Pastry Dough, chilled (see recipes, pages 181 and 183)	1
1	can (12 oz/340 g) prune pie filling, about 1¼ cups (300 mL) (see Tips, left)	1
1	recipe Vanilla Bean Glaze (see recipe, page 242)	1

1. Divide dough into 2 pieces. On a lightly floured surface, roll out one piece of the dough into a 12-inch (30 cm) circle, dusting work surface and dough as necessary to keep the dough from sticking (or roll between 2 pieces of waxed or parchment paper). (While rolling out the first piece of dough to make the first 4 hand pies, keep the remaining piece covered and refrigerated until you're ready to roll it.)

2. Cut dough into quarters. Spoon one-eighth of the prune filling in a strip down center of each quarter, leaving a border. Lightly brush edges with a little water. Fold dough in half to make a triangle, making sure to lightly press top of pastry to distribute the filling evenly. Seal edges together with tines of a fork, dipping the fork into flour as necessary. Place pies on one of the prepared baking sheets. Repeat with remaining dough and filling.

3. Bake pies in preheated oven for 15 to 20 minutes or until golden brown. Let cool on pan for 10 minutes. Transfer to a wire rack and let cool completely.

4. Place wire rack on a baking sheet. Spread glaze over tops of pies. Let stand until glaze is firm.

Poppy Seed Hand Pies

Makes 8 hand pies

- Preheat oven to 425°F (220°C)
- 2 baking sheets, lined with parchment paper

These sweet pies remind me of pastries from the neighborhood deli, but without the hours of effort involved in making a traditional Danish.

Tips

Poppy seed filling is often available in the international food section in large grocery or specialty stores or can be ordered online (see Sources, page 246).

You can make these hand pies with store-bought refrigerated pastry.

1	recipe Buttery Pie Pastry Dough or Large-Batch All-Purpose Vegan Pastry Dough, chilled (see recipes, pages 181 and 183)	1
1	can (11 oz/312 g) poppy seed filling, about 1 ⅛ cups (275 mL) (see Tips, left)	1
1	recipe Vanilla Bean Glaze or Almond Glaze (see recipes, pages 242 and 240)	1

1. Divide dough into 2 pieces. On a lightly floured surface, roll out one piece of the dough into a 12-inch (30 cm) circle, dusting work surface and dough as necessary to keep the dough from sticking (or roll between 2 pieces of waxed or parchment paper). (While rolling out the first piece of dough to make the first 4 hand pies, keep the remaining piece covered and refrigerated until you're ready to roll it.)

2. Cut dough into quarters. Spoon one-eighth of the poppy seed filling in a strip down the center of each quarter, leaving a border. Lightly brush edges with a little water. Fold dough in half to make a triangle, making sure to lightly press top of pastry to distribute the filling evenly. Seal edges together with tines of a fork, dipping the fork into flour as necessary. Place pies on one of the prepared baking sheets. Repeat with remaining dough and filling.

3. Bake pies in preheated oven for 15 to 20 minutes or until golden brown. Let cool on pan for 10 minutes. Transfer to a wire rack and let cool completely.

4. Place wire rack on a baking sheet. Spread glaze over tops of pies. Let stand until glaze is firm.

Quick and Easy Blueberry Turnovers

Makes 8 turnovers

- Preheat oven to 400°F (200°C)
- Baking sheet, lined with parchment paper

I have to give credit for this recipe to my friend Vicki Hodge, as I was so inspired after seeing her recipe for cherry turnovers. These are not only delicious but also extremely quick to prepare. You've got to love easy recipes.

Tips

If you have a smaller package of puff pastry, the pastry may be thinner but will still work.

These pastries are best eaten within a few hours of baking.

1	box (18 oz/540 g) frozen puff pastry, thawed (see Tips, left)	1
1	recipe Blueberry Pie Filling (see recipe, page 199)	1
	Freshly grated nutmeg	
	Granulated sugar	
	Confectioner's (icing) sugar, optional	

1. On a lightly floured surface, unroll one puff pastry sheet. If necessary, roll out into a 9¾- by 9½-inch (24 by 23.75 cm) rectangle. Cut rectangle into 4 pieces. Place one-eighth of the blueberry filling in the center of each square. Lightly brush two adjacent edges with a little water. Fold dough into a triangle and crimp edges with a fork. Repeat with remaining pastry and filling.

2. Place pastries on prepared baking sheet and sprinkle with nutmeg and granulated sugar. Bake in preheated oven for 20 to 25 minutes or until puffed and lightly browned. Let cool on pan for 10 minutes. Transfer to a wire rack and let cool completely.

3. If desired, dust turnovers with confectioner's sugar before serving.

Strawberry Hand Pies

Makes 4 hand pies

- Preheat oven to 425°F (220°C)
- Baking sheet, lined with parchment paper

My daughter, Sydney, loved making these jam hand pies when she was a little girl. Now that she's older, she's less into making them and more into eating them, especially for breakfast. I think Sydney's onto something here.

Tips

You can make these hand pies with store-bought refrigerated pastry.

These hand pies can be made a day ahead.

Variations

Top pies with a sprinkle of ground cinnamon before baking.

Omit the sugar topping and drizzle cooled pies with melted chocolate.

1	recipe All-Purpose Vegan Pastry Dough or Small-Batch All-Purpose Buttery Pastry Dough, chilled (see recipes, pages 182 and 180)	1
6 tbsp	strawberry jam or preserves, approx.	90 mL
	Cream, milk or soy milk	
	Granulated sugar	

1. On a lightly floured surface, roll out dough into a 12-inch (30 cm) circle, dusting work surface and dough as necessary to keep the dough from sticking (or roll between 2 pieces of waxed or parchment paper). Cut dough into quarters. Spoon one-quarter of the jam in a strip down the center of each quarter, leaving borders. Lightly brush edges with a little water. Fold dough in half to make a triangle, making sure to lightly press top of pastry to distribute the filling evenly. Seal edges together with tines of a fork, dipping the fork into flour as necessary. Place pies on prepared baking sheet. Brush tops with a little cream and sprinkle with sugar.

2. Bake pies in preheated oven for 15 to 20 minutes or until golden brown. Let cool on pan for 10 minutes. Transfer to a wire rack and let cool completely.

Little Pies & Tarts

Almond Peach Galettes

Makes 8 pastries

- Preheat oven to 400°F (200°C)
- 2 baking sheets, lined with parchment paper

A galette is really just a rustic French tart with a fancy name, and it sounds like you slaved all day in a hot kitchen. This is a very easy dessert, relying on store-bought puff pastry, a simple almond filling and canned peaches.

1	box (18 oz/540 g) frozen puff pastry, thawed (see Tips, page 91)	1
1	recipe Almond Cream Filling (see recipe, page 198)	1
8	drained canned peach halves	8
	Coarse or granulated sugar	

1. On a lightly floured surface, unroll pastry sheets or roll each out to a 9¾- by 9½-inch (24 by 23.75 cm) rectangle. Cut each pastry sheet into 4 squares. Spread 1 to 2 tbsp (15 to 25 mL) almond cream filling in the center of each piece. Top each with a peach half, cut side down. Fold corners up to peach half.

2. Arrange pastries on prepared baking sheets and sprinkle with sugar. Bake in preheated oven for 20 to 30 minutes or until pastry is puffed and golden brown. Let cool on baking sheet for 10 minutes.

VEGAN FRIENDLY

Chocolate Mousse Tartlets

Makes 22 tartlets

- Preheat oven to 375°F (190°C)
- Twenty-two 2½-inch (6 cm) tartlet molds, greased

My son, Noah, is crazy for these tarts. The delicate flaky pastry crust combined with the smooth chocolate filling and fresh strawberries is irresistible.

1	recipe Small-Batch Mini Tart Dough (see recipe, page 192)	1
1	recipe Dairy-Free Chocolate Mousse Tart Filling or Dark Chocolate Mousse (see recipes, pages 202 and 203)	1
24	fresh strawberries	24

1. Bake tart dough according to recipe and let cool completely. Remove from tins.

2. Working with one cooled tart shell at a time, place a scoop of chocolate mousse inside each. Cut each strawberry into 3 or 4 slices and arrange on top of tart. Repeat with remaining tart shells, mousse and strawberries.

Chocolate Fruit Tarts

Makes 6 tarts

- Preheat oven to 350°F (180°C)
- Baking sheet, lined with parchment paper

Here's a quick and easy dessert that looks like it took hours to prepare. Simply top some cookie dough, which has been baked into tart-shaped cookies, with a chocolate ganache and fresh fruit. The fruit can be varied depending on the season, making this a spectacular dessert any time of the year.

Tip

If using bananas, melt ⅓ cup (75 mL) apricot jelly or jam in microwave until warm and soft. Using a pastry brush, paint a thin coating of melted jelly over fruit. This will help prevent the bananas from turning brown.

Variation

Substitute store-bought refrigerated sugar cookie or chocolate chip cookie dough for the crust.

CRUST

1½ cups	all-purpose flour	375 mL
½ cup	packed light brown sugar	125 mL
1 tsp	baking powder	5 mL
½ cup	salted butter, cut into small pieces	125 mL
1	egg yolk	1
2 tsp	vanilla extract	10 mL

FILLING

½ cup	whipping (35%) cream	125 mL
5 oz	semisweet chocolate, chopped	150 g

TOPPING

Fresh or dried fruit of choice, such as sliced bananas (see Tip, left), fresh strawberries, fresh raspberries or a combination of fruit

1. *Crust:* In a food processor fitted with metal blade, pulse together flour, brown sugar and baking powder until mixed. Add butter, egg yolk and vanilla, pulsing until dough is smooth and begins to form a ball.

2. Scoop ¼-cup (50 mL) measures of dough onto prepared baking sheet. Flatten dough into 4-inch (10 cm) circles, crimping edges so they are slightly raised. Bake in preheated oven for 18 to 20 minutes or until golden brown and just firm to the touch. Let cool.

3. *Filling:* In a microwave-safe bowl or measuring cup, combine cream and chocolate. Microwave on High for 30 to 60 seconds or until cream is hot and chocolate is soft and almost melted. Stir until chocolate is melted and mixture is thick and smooth. If chocolate is not completely melted, return to microwave for 10 to 20 seconds more or until chocolate is soft and melted. Stir well. Spread filling over crusts, leaving a small border uncovered.

4. *Topping:* Top chocolate with fruit, arranging decoratively. Arrange on a clean baking sheet lined with parchment paper. Refrigerate until chocolate is firm. Keep refrigerated until ready to serve. For best results, serve within several hours.

Chocolate Macaroon Tarts

Makes 12 tarts

- Preheat oven to 350°F (180°C)
- 12-cup mini muffin pan, greased

These miniature tarts are decadent. They taste like a chocolate macaroon but look more elegant. They are at their best the day that they are made, and look beautiful as part of a dessert buffet.

Tips

These tarts look very pretty lightly dusted with confectioner's (icing) sugar.

If you're not serving them right away, refrigerate the tarts until almost ready to serve.

These tarts are best served the day that they are made.

1½ cups	packed sweetened flaked coconut	375 mL
2 tbsp	granulated sugar	25 mL
2 tbsp	all-purpose flour	25 mL
2	egg whites	2
½ tsp	almond extract	2 mL
½ cup	whipping (35%) cream	125 mL
5 oz	semisweet or bittersweet chocolate, chopped (see Tips, page 73)	150 g

1. In a bowl, mix together coconut, sugar and flour. Add egg whites and almond extract, mixing well.

2. Scoop balls of dough and press into bottom and up sides of muffin cups. Bake in preheated oven for 15 to 20 minutes or until golden brown. Let cool in pan on a wire rack.

3. When cool, carefully remove each tart shell from pan. If shells are too fragile, leave them in the pan to fill or let them cool longer.

4. In a microwave-safe bowl, combine cream and chocolate. Microwave on High for 40 to 60 seconds or until cream is hot and chocolate is soft and almost melted. Stir until chocolate is smooth. If chocolate is not quite melted, heat for 20 to 40 seconds more or until chocolate is almost melted.

5. Spoon chocolate mixture into cooled coconut crusts and refrigerate until chocolate is firm.

Peach Raspberry Pie (page 51)
Overleaf: Perfect Pumpkin Pie (page 62)

Coconut Lemon Tarts

Makes 12 tarts

- Preheat oven to 350°F (180°C)
- 12-cup mini muffin pan, greased

Should you find yourself throwing a tea party or a baby or bridal shower, this is one of the desserts to serve. These tarts are at their best the day that they are made.

> **Tips**
> You can use store-bought lemon curd in this recipe.

1½ cups	packed sweetened flaked coconut	375 mL
2 tbsp	granulated sugar	25 mL
2 tbsp	all-purpose flour	25 mL
2	egg whites	2
½ tsp	almond extract, optional	2 mL
1	recipe Lemon Curd (see recipe, page 203)	1

1. In a bowl, mix together coconut, sugar and flour. Add egg whites and almond extract, if using, mixing well.
2. Scoop balls of dough and press into bottom and up sides of muffin cups. Bake in preheated oven for 15 to 20 minutes or until golden brown. Let cool in pan on a wire rack.
3. When cool, carefully remove each tart shell from pan. If shells are too fragile, leave them in the pan to fill or let them cool longer.
4. Spoon lemon curd into cooled coconut crusts and serve immediately.

Little Lemon Tarts

Makes 22 tarts

- 24-cup mini muffin pan, greased

I love serving little tarts for dessert, because sometimes they are just the thing after a large dinner. Guests love these decadent nibbles, which hit the spot with their rich, tangy-sweet filling.

1	recipe Small-Batch Mini Tart Dough (see recipe, page 192)	1
1½ cups	lemon curd, approx.	375 mL
22	fresh mint leaves, optional	22
	Whipped cream, optional	

1. Bake tart dough according to recipe and let cool completely. Remove from tins.
2. Spoon a dollop of lemon curd into each cooled tart shell.
3. Garnish each tart with a mint leaf, if desired. Top with a dollop of plain or flavored whipped cream, if desired. The tarts are best served at room temperature.

Cherry Jam Half-Moon Pies (page 83)
Overleaf: Coconut Cream Pie (page 75)

Cookie Tarts

Makes 18 tarts

- Preheat oven to 350°F (180°C)
- 24-cup muffin pan, greased

Although this seems like a complicated recipe, it is really easy to make. The tart shells can be made a day ahead. The recipe can be simplified even further by using prepared sugar cookie dough for the tart shells and prepared chocolate pudding or pudding mix for the filling.

CRUST

1⅓ cups	all-purpose flour	325 mL
⅓ cup	unsweetened Dutch-process cocoa powder, sifted	75 mL
3 tbsp	granulated sugar	45 mL
¼ tsp	salt	1 mL
⅔ cup	cold butter, cut into pieces	150 mL
3 tbsp	whipping (35%) cream	45 mL

FILLING

½ cup	chocolate milk, divided	125 mL
2 tsp	granulated sugar	10 mL
1 tbsp	cornstarch	15 mL
Pinch	salt	Pinch
2 oz	milk chocolate, chopped	60 g

TOPPING

½ cup	whipping (35%) cream	125 mL
1 tbsp	confectioner's (icing) sugar	15 mL
1 oz	milk chocolate, finely chopped	30 g

1. *Crust:* In a food processor fitted with metal blade, pulse together flour, cocoa powder, sugar and salt until combined. Add butter and pulse until mixture is crumbly and resembles coarse meal. Add cream and pulse just until mixture starts to come together and form a ball.

2. Scoop balls of dough and press into bottom and up sides of prepared muffin cups. Place pan in freezer to chill while you prepare the filling.

3. *Filling:* In a saucepan over medium heat, heat ⅓ cup (75 mL) of the chocolate milk and sugar until just warm to the touch. In a small bowl, whisk together remaining chocolate milk, cornstarch and salt. Whisk cornstarch mixture into hot milk, whisking continuously until thick. Remove saucepan from heat and whisk in milk chocolate until smooth. Pour filling into a bowl and press a sheet of plastic wrap directly onto the surface to prevent a skin from forming. Let cool for 20 minutes.

4. Bake tart shells in preheated oven for 15 to 20 minutes or until shells are starting to pull away from sides of pan. Let cool in pan for 15 minutes. Transfer to a wire rack to finish cooling completely.

5. Spoon filling into cooled tart shells.

6. *Topping:* In a bowl, using an electric mixer, whip cream and confectioner's sugar until soft peaks form. Spoon dollops of whipped cream over filling in tart shells. Sprinkle chopped chocolate over whipped cream.

Tip
The tarts will keep for up to 2 days in the refrigerator, though the tart shells will soften slightly. If making ahead of time, add the whipped cream topping right before serving.

Variation
Garnish tops with semisweet or white chocolate chips instead of the chopped chocolate.

Individual Peach and Berry Pies

Makes six 5-inch (12.5 cm) pies

- Preheat oven to 400°F (200°C)
- Six 5-inch (12.5 cm) metal or foil pie plates, greased
- Rimmed baking sheet

Little pies are so much fun to make and are even more fun to eat. I'm a big fan of individual desserts.

Tips

I would suggest raspberries, blueberries or blackberries for this recipe.

If fruit is very sweet, you can reduce the sugar to ¾ cup (175 mL).

Variation

For a peach-only version, omit berries and add additional 1 cup (250 mL) peaches.

1	recipe Buttery Pie Pastry Dough or Large-Batch All-Purpose Vegan Pastry Dough, chilled (see recipes, pages 181 and 183)	1

FILLING

4 cups	sliced pitted peeled ripe peaches	1 L
1 cup	fresh berries (see Tips, left)	250 mL
1 cup	granulated sugar (see Tips, left)	250 mL
¼ cup	cornstarch	50 mL
	Cream, milk or soy milk	
	Coarse or granulated sugar	

1. Divide pastry dough into 2 pieces. On a lightly floured surface, roll out one piece of the dough to about ⅛ inch (3 mm) thickness, dusting work surface and dough as necessary to keep the dough from sticking (or roll between 2 pieces of waxed or parchment paper). Cut dough into 6-inch (15 cm) circles, re-rolling scraps as necessary to make 6 circles. Press dough into prepared pie plates. Roll out remaining dough and cut into 6 more 6-inch (15 cm) circles, re-rolling scraps as necessary, for top crusts. Set aside at room temperature on sheet of parchment paper.

2. *Filling:* In a large bowl, gently combine peaches, berries, sugar and cornstarch, making sure that cornstarch is not lumpy. Divide peach mixture equally among prepared bottom crusts. Brushing edges of pastry with a little water.

3. Place top crusts over fruit, trimming and fluting edges. Cut steam vents in tops of pies. Brush tops of pies with cream and sprinkle with coarse sugar.

4. Place pie plates on baking sheet and bake in preheated oven for 15 minutes. Reduce temperature to 350°F (180°C) and continue baking for 50 minutes more or until tops are nicely browned and juices are bubbling and thickened. If pies start to get too brown before they're finished baking, cover loosely with a piece of tented foil. Let cool in pie plates on a wire rack for 1 hour before serving.

Individual Peach Lattice Pies

Makes six 5-inch (12.5 cm) pies

- Preheat oven to 400°F (200°C)
- Six 5-inch (12.5 cm) metal or foil pie plates, greased
- Rimmed baking sheet

My son can be a bit picky from time to time, so I'm always happy when he gets excited over a new recipe. Well, this is one of those recipes. Noah absolutely loved them, with the light spiced flavor of the peaches and the individual size of the pies. What kid (or adult) wouldn't want to have their own pie?

Tip

If peaches are super-sweet, you can reduce the amount of sugar by as much as ¼ cup (50 mL). If the peaches aren't very sweet, you can add an additional 1 to 2 tbsp (15 to 25 mL) sugar.

| 1 | recipe Buttery Pie Pastry Dough or Large-Batch All-Purpose Vegan Pastry Dough, chilled (see recipes, pages 181 and 183) | 1 |

FILLING

5½ cups	sliced pitted peeled ripe peaches	1.375 L
1 cup	granulated sugar	250 mL
¼ cup	cornstarch	50 mL
1 tsp	vanilla paste or extract	5 mL
¼ tsp	ground cinnamon	1 mL
	Cream, milk or soy milk	
	Coarse or granulated sugar	

1. Divide pastry dough into 2 pieces, one slightly larger than the other. On a lightly floured surface, roll out larger piece of dough to about ⅛-inch (3 mm) thickness, dusting work surface and dough as necessary to keep the dough from sticking (or roll between 2 pieces of waxed or parchment paper). Cut dough into six 6-inch (15 cm) circles, re-rolling scraps as necessary. Press dough into pie plates. Roll out remaining dough to roughly a 19- by 7-inch (47.5 by 17.5 cm) rectangle. Trim edges to straighten and cut into thirty-six 6- by ½-inch (15 by 1 cm) strips for lattice tops and set aside at room temperature on sheet of parchment paper.

2. *Filling:* In a large bowl, toss together peaches, sugar, cornstarch, vanilla and cinnamon, making sure that cornstarch is not lumpy. Divide peach mixture equally among prepared bottom crusts.

3. Lightly brush edges of bottom pastry with a little water. Place 6 strips of pastry on top of each pie, weaving a lattice design (see page 17). Brush tops lightly with cream and sprinkle with sugar.

4. Place pie plates on baking sheet and bake for 15 minutes. Reduce temperature to 350°F (180°C) and continue baking for 40 to 50 minutes more or until top is nicely browned and juices are bubbling and thickened. If pies start to get too brown, cover loosely with a piece of tented foil. Let cool in pie plates on a wire rack for 1 hour.

Little Chocolate Hazelnut Tarts

Makes 22 small tarts

● 24-cup mini muffin
  pan, greased

My children came up with
this recipe. I had some
extra tart shells sitting
around and they were in
the mood for something
sweet. So they got creative
and filled them with
chocolate hazelnut spread.
The consensus was that
these tarts were not only
easy, but delicious, too.

1	recipe Small-Batch Mini Tart Dough (see recipe, page 192)	1
1 cup	chocolate hazelnut spread, approx.	250 mL
22	toasted hazelnuts	22

1. Bake tart dough according to recipe and let cool completely. Remove from tins.

2. Spoon a dollop of chocolate hazelnut spread into each cooled tart shell.

3. Garnish each tart with a toasted hazelnut. The tarts are best served at room temperature.

Mini Caramel Tarts

Makes 22 small tarts

● 24-cup mini muffin
  pan, greased
● Rimmed baking sheet

There is something so
irresistible about caramel,
and these tarts are no
exception. I couldn't get
my son to stop eating
these sweet little tarts. In
fact, word spread around
the neighborhood so fast
that I suddenly had a
houseful of kids asking
for them.

1	recipe Small-Batch Mini Tart Dough (see recipe, page 192) or store-bought refrigerated pastry	1
1	recipe Brown Sugar Caramel Tart Filling (see recipe, page 200)	1
4 oz	semisweet or bittersweet chocolate, chopped (see Tips, page 73)	125 g

1. Bake the tart shells according to recipe or package directions. Let cool.

2. Place tart shells on baking sheet. Spoon caramel filling into tart shells. Let filling cool to room temperature.

3. In a microwave-safe bowl, microwave chocolate on Medium for 1 minute, stirring every 30 seconds, or until chocolate is soft and almost melted. Stir until chocolate is completely melted and smooth. Drizzle melted chocolate decoratively over tarts.

4. Refrigerate tarts until chocolate is firm. Keep refrigerated until ready to serve.

Little Raspberry Pies

Makes 12 pies

- Preheat oven to 375°F (190°C)
- 12-cup muffin pan, greased and floured
- Rimmed baking sheet

These little pies are baked in a regular-size muffin pan, which makes for a fun presentation.

Tip

Silicone muffin pans are great for making these little pies. Because the silicone is so flexible, it makes removal a snap. Silicone liners in a regular metal muffin pan work well, too.

| 1 | recipe Buttery Pie Pastry Dough or Large-Batch All-Purpose Vegan Pastry Dough, chilled (see recipes, pages 181 and 183) | 1 |

FILLING

4 cups	frozen unsweetened raspberries (do not thaw)	1 L
¾ cup	granulated sugar	175 mL
3 tbsp	cornstarch	45 mL
	Cream, milk or soy milk	
	Coarse or granulated sugar	

1. Divide pastry dough into 2 pieces, one slightly larger than the other. On a lightly floured surface, roll out larger piece of dough to slightly less than ⅛-inch (3 mm) thickness, dusting work surface and dough as necessary to keep the dough from sticking (or roll between 2 pieces of waxed or parchment paper). Cut out twelve 4½-inch (11 cm) circles or the size large enough to fit into muffin cups, re-rolling scraps as necessary. Press dough into muffin cups pressing dough to about ¼ inch (0.5 cm) above edge of pan. Place pan in freezer or refrigerator for 15 to 20 minutes to chill while you prepare the filling. Roll out remaining dough and cut into twelve 3¼-inch (8 cm) circles or the size large enough to cover cups for top crusts, re-rolling scraps, and set aside at room temperature on a sheet of parchment paper.

2. *Filling:* In a large bowl, toss together raspberries, sugar and cornstarch, making sure cornstarch is not lumpy. Divide berries equally among prepared bottom crusts. Lightly brush edges of pastry with a little water.

3. Place top crusts over raspberries, pinching and fluting edges. Cut a few steam vents in tops of pies. Brush tops with cream and sprinkle with sugar.

4. Place muffin pan on baking sheet and bake in preheated oven for 40 to 55 minutes or until tops are nicely browned and juices are bubbling and thickened.

5. Let pies cool for 10 minutes before carefully removing them from muffin tin.

Miniature Cheesecakes

Makes 12 miniature cheesecakes

- Preheat oven to 350°F (180°C)
- 12-cup muffin pan, lined with foil liners

Cheesecakes are often a bit temperamental and labor-intensive to make, so here I offer you a delicious alternative. These miniature cheesecakes taste every bit as rich and creamy as the original, but they go together in a snap and always receive rave reviews.

Tip
Do not use paper liners for cheesecakes. Use only foil liners or silicone muffin pans for making these little pies. Because the silicone is so flexible, it makes removal very easy.

Variations
Add ½ cup (125 mL) semisweet chocolate chips or chopped white chocolate to the batter for a chocolate version.

Spoon a dollop of Cherry Pie Filling or Blueberry Pie Filling (see recipes, pages 201 and 199) over tops of cheesecakes.

CRUST
7	whole graham crackers, ground (¾ cup/175 mL crumbs)	7
3 tbsp	butter, melted	45 mL
1 tbsp	packed light brown sugar	15 mL

FILLING
12 oz	cream cheese, softened	375 g
½ cup	granulated sugar	125 mL
¼ cup	sour cream	50 mL
2	eggs	2

TOPPING
¾ cup	sour cream	175 mL
3 tbsp	granulated sugar	45 mL

1. *Crust:* In a small bowl, mix together graham cracker crumbs, butter and brown sugar. Press crumb mixture into bottoms of prepared muffin cups.

2. *Filling:* In a food processor fitted with metal blade, blend cream cheese until smooth. Add sugar, pulsing until smooth. Add sour cream and process until smooth. Add eggs, pulsing until smooth (don't overprocess the mixture — just process until smooth; see Tip, page 107). Spoon evenly over graham crusts in muffin pan.

3. Bake cheesecakes in preheated oven for 18 to 22 minutes or until the centers are set. Remove from oven and place pan on a wire rack. Let cheesecakes stand for 5 minutes, leaving oven on.

4. *Topping:* In a small bowl, stir together sour cream and sugar. Gently spoon and swirl mixture with the back of a spoon over tops of cheesecakes, covering tops. Return pan to oven and bake for 4 minutes more. Let cool in pan on a wire rack to room temperature. Refrigerate for several hours or overnight to chill completely.

Miniature Lemon Cheesecakes

Makes 12 miniature cheesecakes

- Preheat oven to 350°F (180°C)
- 12-cup muffin pan, lined with foil liners

Not only are these precious little cheesecakes beautiful, they are also absolutely delicious! Lemon curd adds a big hit of fresh lemon flavor and is a perfect complement to the creamy cheesecake center.

Tip

Once baked and cooled, these cheesecakes freeze very well for up to 1 month without the lemon curd topping. Once you have defrosted the cheesecakes, top with the lemon curd.

Variation

Place a small dollop of whipped cream over the lemon curd before serving.

CRUST

7	whole graham crackers, ground (¾ cup/175 mL crumbs)	7
3 tbsp	butter, melted	45 mL
1 tbsp	packed light brown sugar	15 mL

FILLING

12 oz	cream cheese, softened	375 g
½ cup	granulated sugar	125 mL
¼ cup	sour cream	50 mL
2	eggs	2
1 tsp	grated lemon zest	5 mL
¾ cup	store-bought or homemade Lemon Curd (see recipe, page 203)	175 mL

1. *Crust:* In a small bowl, mix together graham cracker crumbs, butter and brown sugar. Press crumb mixture into bottoms of prepared muffin cups.

2. *Filling:* In a food processor fitted with metal blade, blend cream cheese until smooth. Add sugar, pulsing until smooth. Add sour cream and process until smooth. Add eggs and lemon zest, pulsing until smooth (don't overprocess the mixture — just process until smooth; see Tip, page 107). Spoon evenly over graham crusts in muffin pan.

3. Bake cheesecakes in preheated oven for 18 to 22 minutes or until the centers are set. Let cool in pan on a wire rack to room temperature. Refrigerate for several hours or overnight to chill completely. Before serving, place a dollop of lemon curd over tops of cheesecakes, swirling lightly with the back of a spoon.

Miniature Chocolate Cheesecakes

Makes 12 miniature cheesecakes

- Preheat oven to 350°F (180°C)
- 12-cup muffin pan, lined with foil liners

Cheesecake cannot get any easier than this. Instead of a traditional crust, simply place a whole chocolate sandwich cookie in the bottom of each muffin cup. Then top with a blend of cream cheese and melted chocolate. This is definitely a to-die-for dessert.

Tips

If you have a sweet tooth, add up to 1 tbsp (15 mL) more granulated sugar.

These cheesecakes freeze very well for up to 1 month. I like to package my cheesecakes for freezing in heavy-duty or resealable freezer bags. Arrange them in a single layer, being careful not to overstuff the bag to keep them from smashing, and place on a flat shelf or surface in the freezer.

12	chocolate sandwich cookies	12
3 oz	bittersweet or semisweet chocolate, chopped (see Tips, page 73)	90 g
1 oz	unsweetened chocolate, chopped	30 g
12 oz	cream cheese, softened	375 g
½ cup	granulated sugar (see Tips, left)	125 mL
¼ cup	sour cream	50 mL
2 tbsp	chocolate cream liqueur	25 mL
2	eggs	2

TOPPING

¾ cup	sour cream	175 mL
3 tbsp	granulated sugar	45 mL
1 tbsp	chocolate cream liqueur	15 mL
	Unsweetened Dutch-process cocoa powder, sifted	

1. Place one chocolate sandwich cookie in bottom of each prepared muffin cup and set aside.

2. In a microwave-safe bowl, combine bittersweet and unsweetened chocolates. Microwave on High for 45 to 50 seconds or until chocolate is soft and almost melted. Stir until completely melted and smooth. Set aside and let cool slightly.

3. In a food processor fitted with metal blade, blend cream cheese until smooth. Add sugar, pulsing until smooth. Add melted chocolate and process until smooth. Add sour cream and liqueur, blending well. Add eggs, pulsing until smooth (don't overprocess the mixture — just process until smooth; see Tip, right). Spoon evenly over cookies in muffin pan.

4. Bake cheesecakes in preheated oven for 18 to 22 minutes or until the centers are set. Remove from oven and place pan on a wire rack. Let cheesecakes stand for 5 minutes, leaving oven on.

5. *Topping:* In a small bowl, stir together sour cream, sugar and liqueur. Gently spoon and swirl mixture with the back of a spoon over tops of cheesecakes, covering tops. Return pan to oven and bake for 4 minutes more. Let cool in pan on a wire rack to room temperature. Refrigerate for several hours or overnight to chill completely. Just before serving, sprinkle tops of cheesecakes with cocoa powder.

Tip

Make sure not to overprocess the cheesecake filling or there will be lots of bubbles in the batter. At the same time, make sure that you blend the cream cheese and sugar together enough so that it is smooth and lump-free.

Variations

Omit sour cream topping. Just before serving, whip together ¾ cup (175 mL) whipping (35%) cream, 2 tbsp (25 mL) confectioner's (icing) sugar and ½ tsp (2 mL) vanilla extract. Spread or dollop whipped cream over tops of cheesecakes. Sprinkle grated chocolate over whipped cream and serve.

You can use crème de cacao in place of chocolate cream liqueur.

Mini Milk Chocolate Caramel Tarts with Sea Salt

Makes 22 tarts

- 24-cup mini muffin pan, greased
- Rimmed baking sheet

While salt and caramel may seem like a strange combination, it's not. I first tasted the combo when I was in Seattle at Fran's Chocolates. After one taste, I was hooked forever.

Tip

Don't let caramel cool for longer than 5 minutes or it will be difficult to get it into the shells.

1	recipe Small-Batch Mini Tart Dough (see recipe, page 192) or store-bought refrigerated pastry	1
1	recipe Brown Sugar Caramel Tart Filling (see recipe, page 200)	1
4 oz	milk chocolate, chopped	125 g
	Fleur de sel or coarse sea salt	

1. Bake the tart shells according to recipe or package directions. Let cool.

2. Place cooled tart shells on a baking sheet. Spoon caramel filling into tart shells. Let filling cool to room temperature.

3. In a microwave-safe bowl, microwave chocolate on Medium for 1 minute, stirring every 30 seconds, or until chocolate is soft and almost melted. Stir until chocolate is completely melted and smooth. Drizzle melted chocolate over top of cooled tarts with the tines of a fork.

4. Refrigerate tarts until chocolate is firm. Sprinkle or grind a pinch of salt over tarts and serve.

Chocolate & Nut Pies & Tarts

Almond, Coconut and Chocolate Chip Tart

Serves 12

- Preheat oven to 350°F (180°C)
- 11-inch (27.5 cm) metal tart pan with removable bottom, greased

This tart is both elegant and delicious. It is an adaptation of a recipe that I developed for *Bon Appétit* Magazine.

Tips

If light (white) corn syrup is unavailable, you can substitute golden.

To toast almonds: Preheat oven to 350°F (180°C). Spread nuts on a baking sheet lined with foil or parchment paper. Bake almonds for 5 to 10 minutes or until light brown and fragrant.

Garnish the tart with a light dusting of confectioner's (icing) sugar, if desired.

CRUST

1½ cups	all-purpose flour	375 mL
¼ cup	granulated sugar	50 mL
½ cup	cold butter, cut into pieces	125 mL
2 tbsp	whipping (35%) cream, approx.	25 mL
1½ tsp	vanilla extract	7 mL

FILLING

¾ cup	light (white) corn syrup (see Tips, left)	175 mL
¼ cup	packed light brown sugar	50 mL
¼ cup	butter, melted and cooled	50 mL
3	eggs	3
1 tsp	vanilla extract	5 mL
2 cups	whole almonds, toasted and coarsely chopped (see Tips, left)	500 mL
1 cup	semisweet chocolate chips	250 mL
½ cup	lightly packed sweetened flaked coconut	125 mL

1. *Crust:* In a food processor fitted with metal blade, pulse flour and sugar to combine. Add butter and pulse just until mixture resembles coarse meal. Add cream and vanilla, pulsing just until moist clumps form. If necessary, add additional cream, 1 tbsp (15 mL) at a time or as needed, to make a smooth dough (dough should not be wet). Pulse again just until dough starts to form a ball. Press dough into prepared pan.

2. *Filling:* In a large bowl, whisk together corn syrup, brown sugar and butter. Whisk in eggs and vanilla. Mix in almonds, chocolate chips and coconut. Transfer filling to prepared bottom crust.

3. Bake tart in preheated oven for 50 minutes or until firmly set in center and top is golden brown. Let cool in pan on a wire rack. Push up bottom of pan to release tart. Serve warm or at room temperature.

Brownie Tart

- Preheat oven to 350°F (180°C)
- 10-inch (25 cm) deep-dish glass pie plate, greased

This pie is a year-round favorite of my kids. It's easy enough for children to make it (with the guidance of an adult), and not only does it make a fabulous dessert, but it is also a fun alternative to standard birthday cakes.

Tips

Serve tart with a scoop of Vanilla Bean Ice Cream (see recipe, page 229).

Instead of refrigerating tart until firm, it can be served warm. If it's not refrigerated, this tart is soft, chewy and slightly gooey in the center.

Variation

Substitute chopped chocolate sandwich cookies or another candy of your choice for the chocolate-covered mints.

¾ cup	all-purpose flour	175 mL
¾ cup	unsweetened Dutch-process cocoa powder, sifted	175 mL
1¼ tsp	baking powder	6 mL
1 cup	butter, melted	250 mL
1 cup	granulated sugar	250 mL
¾ cup	packed light brown sugar	175 mL
2 tsp	vanilla extract	10 mL
2	eggs	2
1 cup	coarsely chopped chocolate-covered mints (peppermint patties)	250 mL
¼ cup	semisweet chocolate chips	50 mL

1. In a small bowl, mix together flour, cocoa powder and baking powder. Set aside.

2. In a large bowl, using an electric mixer, beat together butter and granulated and brown sugars. Add vanilla, beating well. Add eggs, one at a time, beating well after each addition. Add flour mixture, beating just until smooth.

3. Spread batter in prepared pie plate, smoothing top. Sprinkle chopped chocolate-covered mints and chocolate chips on top. Lightly press chocolates into batter, but not too much.

4. Bake in preheated oven for 35 to 40 minutes or until tart is somewhat firm but not hard to the touch. Let cool on a wire rack. Refrigerate tart until firm.

Chocolate Chip Brownie Tart

Serves 8

- Preheat oven to 325°F (160°C)
- 10- or 11-inch (25 or 27.5 cm) scalloped glass tart dish or quiche dish, greased

This tart will keep, refrigerated, for several days. For such a humble dessert, this delicious tart has a fancy look to it.

Tip

Serve the brownie tart with a scoop of homemade ice cream, such as Brown Sugar Cinnamon Ice Cream (see recipe, page 213), or your favorite store-bought variety.

Variation

For a mint chocolate version, substitute 1 tsp (5 mL) mint extract for the vanilla.

⅓ cup	all-purpose flour	75 mL
⅛ tsp	salt	0.5 mL
4 oz	unsweetened chocolate, chopped	125 g
½ cup	butter	125 mL
1¼ cups	packed light brown sugar	300 mL
2	eggs	2
1 tsp	vanilla extract	5 mL
½ cup	semisweet chocolate chips	125 mL

1. In a small bowl, mix together flour and salt. Set aside.

2. In a large microwave-safe bowl, combine unsweetened chocolate and butter. Microwave on High for 1 to 2 minutes, stopping and stirring every 20 seconds or until butter is melted and chocolate is soft and almost melted. Whisk together until chocolate is melted and mixture is smooth. If mixture is hot, let cool to lukewarm. Whisk in sugar, eggs and vanilla. Stir in flour mixture just until blended.

3. Spread mixture in prepared dish and sprinkle with chocolate chips. Bake in preheated oven for 30 to 35 minutes or until a toothpick inserted into the center comes out clean. Let cool in dish on a wire rack. Refrigerate for several hours or overnight.

Chocolate Chip Cheese Tart

Serves 8

- 9½-inch (24 cm) metal tart pan with removable bottom, greased

This is similar to a cheesecake, only better. It goes together quickly and looks impressive, and you don't even have to turn your oven on!

Tip

Superfine sugar, also known as baker's sugar, is an ultra-fine granulated sugar that dissolves very quickly in liquid. If you cannot find it in your local grocery store, you can make your own. Process granulated sugar in a food processor until very finely ground.

Variation

Substitute light rum for the coconut rum.

CRUST

10	whole graham crackers (or 1½ cups/375 mL crumbs)	10
⅓ cup	sweetened flaked coconut	75 mL
5 tbsp	butter, melted	75 mL

FILLING

12 oz	cream cheese, softened	375 g
½ cup	superfine sugar (see Tip, left)	125 mL
1¾ cups	whipping (35%) cream	425 mL
2½ tbsp	coconut rum	32 mL
½ cup	semisweet chocolate chips	125 mL
1½ tsp	shortening	7 mL
⅓ cup	miniature semisweet chocolate chips	75 mL

1. *Crust:* In a food processor fitted with metal blade, pulse graham crackers until in fine crumbs. Transfer crumbs to a mixing bowl and stir in coconut and butter. Press into bottom and up side of prepared tart pan. Place pan in freezer to chill while you prepare the filling.

2. *Filling:* In a stand mixer fitted with whisk attachment, combine cream cheese and sugar. Whip until creamy, scraping down side of bowl as necessary. Add cream and rum, whipping until soft peaks form.

3. Remove crust from freezer. Spread whipped cream mixture in crust, using back of spoon to decoratively swirl. In a microwave-safe dish, combine ½ cup (125 mL) chocolate chips and shortening. Microwave for 20 seconds or until chocolate is soft and almost melted. Stir until melted, smooth and shiny. If necessary, microwave chocolate for 10 to 20 seconds more or until almost melted. Drizzle over top of cheese mixture. Sprinkle with miniature chocolate chips and refrigerate for several hours before serving. This tart is best served the day that it is made.

Chocolate Chip Coconut Pie

Serves 8

● Preheat oven to
350°F (180°C)

This dessert tastes like a warm chocolate chip cookie in a crisp pie shell. It's a fun dessert to serve to kids, as it has familiar flavors.

Tip
Serve the pie with a scoop of homemade Vanilla Bean Ice Cream, White Chocolate Cheesecake Ice Cream or Coconut Sorbet (see recipes, pages 229, 230 and 213).

Variations
For variety, vary the flavor of the pie by substituting peanut butter or butterscotch chips for the chocolate chips.

Substitute finely chopped pecans for the coconut.

1 cup	granulated sugar	250 mL
1 cup	semisweet chocolate chips	250 mL
½ cup	all-purpose flour	125 mL
½ cup	sweetened flaked coconut	125 mL
⅛ tsp	salt	0.5 mL
½ cup	unsalted butter, melted and cooled slightly	125 mL
2	eggs	2
1 tsp	vanilla extract	5 mL
1	9-inch (23 cm) store-bought frozen deep-dish pie crust, unbaked, or All-Purpose Vegan Pastry Dough or Small-Batch All-Purpose Buttery Pastry Dough (see recipes, pages 182 and 180)	1
	Confectioner's (icing) sugar	

1. In a large bowl, mix together sugar, chocolate chips, flour, coconut and salt. Add butter, eggs and vanilla, stirring well. Transfer to prepared bottom crust.

2. Bake in preheated oven for 45 minutes or until a knife inserted into the center comes out almost clean. Let cool completely in pan on a wire rack.

3. Lightly dust top of cooled pie with confectioner's sugar.

Chocolate Chip Pecan Pie

Serves 8

- Preheat oven to 375°F (190°C)
- 9-inch (23 cm) glass pie plate, greased

For Thanksgiving, I was busy baking chocolate chip pecan pies but could not get them to set. Our friend Rick, who is from New Orleans, suggested that I follow the recipe he uses for pecan pie. This is my version of Rick's favorite recipe.

Tips

If light (white) corn syrup is unavailable, you can substitute golden.

To toast pecans: Preheat oven to 350°F (180°C). Spread pecans on a baking sheet lined with parchment paper and bake for 8 to 10 minutes or until lightly browned.

For longer storage, keep your pecans in the freezer. Pecan pie can be made a day ahead. This really saves time, especially if you're preparing a Thanksgiving feast and need to make some dishes ahead of time.

Variation

Substitute walnuts for the pecans.

1	recipe Small-Batch All-Purpose Buttery Pastry Dough, chilled (see recipe, page 180)	1

FILLING

3	eggs	3
¾ cup	light (white) corn syrup (see Tips, left)	175 mL
⅔ cup	dark brown sugar, not packed	150 mL
2 tbsp	unsalted butter, melted and cooled slightly	25 mL
1 tbsp	all-purpose flour	15 mL
1 tsp	vanilla extract	5 mL
⅛ tsp	salt	0.5 mL
⅓ cup	semisweet chocolate chips	75 mL
1⅓ cups	pecan halves, toasted (see Tips, left)	325 mL

1. On a lightly floured surface, roll out dough into a circle large enough to fit pie plate, dusting work surface and dough as necessary to keep the dough from sticking (or roll between 2 pieces of waxed or parchment paper). Press dough into prepared pie plate, crimping edge. Place pie plate in freezer or refrigerator for 15 to 20 minutes to chill while you prepare the filling.

2. *Filling:* In a large bowl, whisk eggs. Add corn syrup, brown sugar, butter, flour, vanilla and salt, whisking well. Stir in chocolate chips.

3. Place pecans in prepared bottom crust. Pour filling over pecans. Bake in preheated oven for 50 to 55 minutes or until filling is puffed around edge and fairly set in the center. If pie starts to get too brown before it's finished baking, cover loosely with a piece of tented foil. Let pie cool completely on a wire rack before serving. Once cool, refrigerate to firm up completely.

Chocolate Orange Pecan Pie

Serves 8

- Preheat oven to 375°F (190°C)

When I was pregnant and in the throes of my food cravings, I sent my husband out very late one night to hunt down a berry pie. He was gone quite some time and entered triumphantly with a pecan pie. I replied, "But I don't like pecan pie!" Oh how my tastes, not to mention my state of mind, have changed.

Tips

If using a frozen crust, leave in freezer until ready to fill.

I like to bake my pecan pies the day before I plan to serve them. That way, it gives the pie a chance to firm up.

Variation

Omit the chocolate chips and replace the liqueur with dark rum for a chocolate-free version.

⅔ cup	granulated sugar	150 mL
3 tbsp	butter, melted and cooled slightly	45 mL
1 tbsp	all-purpose flour	15 mL
¾ cup	dark (golden) corn syrup	175 mL
2 tbsp	chocolate-flavored liqueur	25 mL
1 tsp	vanilla extract	5 mL
¼ tsp	orange oil or 2 tsp (10 mL) grated orange zest	1 mL
3	eggs	3
1¼ cups	toasted pecan halves (see Tips, page 115)	300 mL
½ cup	semisweet chocolate chips	125 mL
1	9-inch (23 cm) store-bought frozen pie crust, unbaked, or All-Purpose Vegan Pastry Dough or Small-Batch All-Purpose Buttery Pastry Dough (see recipes, pages 182 and 180)	1

1. In a large bowl, whisk together sugar, butter and flour until smooth. Whisk in corn syrup, liqueur, vanilla and orange oil. Add eggs, one at a time, whisking until smooth. Stir in pecans and chocolate chips.

2. Transfer filling to prepared bottom crust. Bake in preheated oven for 45 to 55 minutes or until filling is puffed around edge and set in the center. If pie starts to get too brown before it's finished baking, cover loosely with a piece of tented foil.

3. Let cool on a wire rack. Once cool, refrigerate pie to firm up completely.

Chocolate Truffle Tart

Serves 12

- Preheat oven to 375°F (190°C)
- 10-inch (25 cm) metal tart pan with removable bottom, greased

Back in my bakery days, this chocolate tart was a huge seller. The tart filling is adapted from an old recipe that I found in *Food & Wine* magazine. This dark chocolate tart is sure to please.

1	recipe The Best Tart Dough (see recipe, page 187)	1
¾ cup	whipping (35%) cream	175 mL
⅓ cup	milk (not low-fat or nonfat)	75 mL
7 oz	bittersweet chocolate, chopped (see Tips, page 73)	210 g
2 tbsp	granulated sugar	25 mL
1	egg, lightly beaten	1
1 tbsp	dark rum	15 mL
	Unsweetened Dutch-process cocoa powder, sifted	

1. Prepare fully baked tart shell in a 10-inch (25 cm) pan according to recipe directions. Let cool in pan on a wire rack.

2. In a saucepan over medium heat, combine cream and milk and bring to a simmer. Remove saucepan from heat and add chocolate and sugar, stirring until melted. Strain chocolate cream into a bowl and let cool. Whisk in egg and rum until blended.

3. Pour chocolate mixture into cooled tart shell. Bake tart in preheated oven for 15 to 20 minutes or until filling is almost firm but still trembling slightly in the center. Let tart cool completely in pan on a wire rack. Push up bottom of pan to release tart. Dust with cocoa powder before serving.

Tips

There may be some extra mixture left after filling the tart crust, because tart pans can be slightly different sizes. Pour this extra filling into a ramekin or two (or ovenproof espresso or small coffee mug) and bake alongside the tart for the same amount of time.

This recipe can be halved for a smaller tart pan.

Rum Pecan Pie

Serves 8

● Preheat oven to
375°F (190°C)

My husband is totally
crazy for pecan pie. As I
was testing the recipes for
this book and serving him
slice after slice of berry
pie, he kept asking me the
same question: "When are
you making pecan pie?"
So, Jay, here's a delicious
pecan pie just for you. For
an extra-rich treat, serve
with a scoop of homemade
ice cream.

Tips

If light (white) corn
syrup is unavailable, you
can substitute golden.

Pecan pie can be made
a day ahead. This really
saves time, especially
if you're preparing a
holiday feast and need
to make some dishes
ahead of time.

¾ cup	packed light brown sugar	175 mL
3 tbsp	butter, melted and cooled slightly	45 mL
1 tbsp	all-purpose flour	15 mL
¾ cup	light (white) corn syrup (see Tips, left)	175 mL
2 tbsp	dark rum	25 mL
1 tsp	vanilla extract	5 mL
3	eggs	3
1¼ cups	toasted pecan halves (see Tips, page 115)	300 mL
1	9-inch (23 cm) store-bought deep-dish pie crust, unbaked, or Small-Batch All-Purpose Buttery Pastry Dough, chilled (see recipe, page 180)	1

1. In a large bowl, whisk together brown sugar, butter and flour until smooth. Whisk in corn syrup, rum and vanilla. Add eggs, whisking until smooth. Stir in pecans.

2. Transfer filling to prepared bottom crust. Bake in preheated oven for 50 to 55 minutes or until filling is puffed around edge and fairly set in the center. If pie starts to get too brown before it's finished baking, cover loosely with a piece of tented foil.

3. Let cool completely on a wire rack. Once cool, refrigerate to firm up completely.

Crisps, Crumbles, Cobblers & Toppings

Apple Berry Crisp

Serves 6 to 8

● Preheat oven to 350°F (180°C)

● 8-inch (2 L) square glass baking dish, greased

Here's a fabulous example of a crisp that you can make year-round. I keep a stash of frozen berries so that I can make this crisp any time of the year. This dessert is one of my daughter's favorites.

> **Tip**
> If you prefer a less-sweet crisp, reduce the sugar to ⅔ cup (150 mL).

4	large Granny Smith apples, peeled, cored and thinly sliced	4
3 cups	fresh or frozen (not thawed) unsweetened mixed berries	750 mL
¾ cup	granulated sugar (see Tip, left)	175 mL
3 tbsp	all-purpose flour	45 mL
1	recipe Brown Sugar Streusel, Almond Crumb Topping or Cinnamon Sugar Crumb Topping (see recipes, pages 134 and 135)	1

1. In a large bowl, gently combine apples, berries, sugar and flour, making sure apples are well coated. Spread fruit in prepared baking dish. Bake in preheated oven for 20 minutes.

2. Sprinkle streusel over apple mixture and bake for 30 to 40 minutes more or until topping is browned and apple-berry mixture is bubbling.

3. Let cool for at least 30 minutes before serving to allow the juices to thicken.

Apricot Raspberry Cobbler

Serves 6 to 8

- Preheat oven to 375°F (190°C)
- 8-inch (2 L) square glass baking dish, greased

There are several different versions of cobbler, some with a biscuit dough baked on top of fruit, and others, like this, with a cake-type batter that actually bakes up and over the fruit. I love how easily this dessert goes together.

2 cups	fresh raspberries	500 mL
5	large fresh apricots, pitted and cut into ½-inch (1 cm) slices (about 2 cups/500 mL)	5
1 cup	granulated sugar, divided	250 mL
1 tsp	packed grated lemon zest	5 mL
1 cup	all-purpose flour	250 mL
2 tsp	baking powder	10 mL
¾ cup	cold milk or soy milk	175 mL
½ cup	butter or margarine, melted	125 mL

1. In a bowl, toss together raspberries, apricots, ¼ cup (50 mL) of the sugar and lemon zest. Set aside.

2. In another bowl, whisk together flour, baking powder and remaining sugar. Add milk and butter, whisking just until combined. Transfer batter to prepared baking dish. Place fruit mixture over top (don't stir, as batter will rise to the top as it bakes).

3. Bake in preheated oven for 50 minutes to 1 hour or until crust is golden brown and the center is just firm to the touch. Let cool on a wire rack for 20 minutes before serving.

> **Tip**
> Plan on serving this dessert within 1 to 2 hours of baking.

Blackberry Cobbler

Serves 8

- Preheat oven to 375°F (190°C)
- 10-inch (25 cm) deep-dish glass pie plate or 8-inch (2 L) square glass baking dish, greased

I first prepared this dessert for a segment that I did on a TV morning show. I had a bounty of freshly picked berries and thought this dessert would be a perfect way to showcase them. This cobbler now has many fans.

5 cups	fresh or frozen (not thawed) unsweetened blackberries	1.25 L
1 cup	granulated sugar, divided	250 mL
1 cup	all-purpose flour	250 mL
2 tsp	baking powder	10 mL
¾ cup	cold milk or soy milk	175 mL
½ cup	butter or margarine, melted	125 mL

1. In a bowl, toss blackberries with ¼ cup (50 mL) of the sugar. Set aside.

2. In another bowl, whisk together flour, baking powder and remaining sugar. Add milk and butter, whisking just until combined. Transfer batter to prepared pie plate. Place blackberries over top (don't stir, as batter will rise to the top as it bakes).

3. Bake in preheated oven for 50 minutes to 1 hour or until crust is golden brown and the center is just firm to the touch. Let cool on a wire rack for 20 minutes before serving. This cobbler is best served within 1 to 2 hours of baking.

Blackberry Skillet Crumble

Serves 6

- Preheat oven to 400°F (200°C)
- 10-inch (25 cm) cast-iron or ovenproof skillet, greased

A skillet pie is a fun dessert to serve to company. It has an old-fashioned flair and looks great served right in the skillet.

1	recipe Blackberry Filling (see recipe, page 198)	1
1	recipe Brown Sugar Streusel or Oat Crumble (see recipes, pages 134 and 136)	1

1. Prepare blackberry filling according to the recipe (without letting it cool) and transfer to prepared skillet.

2. Sprinkle streusel over filling and bake in preheated oven for 20 to 25 minutes or until topping is nicely browned. Serve warm or at room temperature. This crumble is best served the day that it's made.

Blackberry Grunt

Serves 6

- 12-inch (30 cm) deep cast-iron (or enameled iron) skillet with lid, greased (see Tip, below)

When I was in high school, I came across a grunt recipe and was enthralled with the idea of cooked berries and dumplings. I loved it and made it quite often, because it was so easy to prepare with frozen fruit. The name sounds funny, but it sure tastes great!

Tip

A cast-iron or enameled skillet works best for this recipe, but another heavy, deep skillet will also work.

DUMPLINGS

1½ cups	all-purpose flour	375 mL
2 tbsp	granulated sugar	25 mL
2 tsp	baking powder	10 mL
¼ tsp	salt	1 mL
3 tbsp	cold butter or margarine, cut into small pieces	45 mL
¾ cup	cold milk or soy milk	175 mL
1 tsp	vanilla extract	5 mL
½ tsp	pure almond extract	2 mL

FILLING

4 cups	frozen unsweetened blackberries, partially thawed with juices	1 L
½ cup	granulated sugar	125 mL
1 tbsp	cornstarch	15 mL
1 tbsp	freshly squeezed lemon juice	15 mL
1 tbsp	cassis or raspberry-flavored liqueur	15 mL

1. *Dumplings:* In a large bowl or bowl of food processor, mix together flour, sugar, baking powder and salt. Using a pastry blender or a food processor fitted with metal blade, cut butter into flour mixture until it resembles coarse crumbs. Add milk and vanilla and almond extracts, stirring or pulsing just until mixture forms a soft dough. Do not overmix. Set aside.

2. *Filling:* In prepared skillet, mix together blackberries and sugar. In a bowl or measuring cup, whisk together ¾ cup (175 mL) water and cornstarch until cornstarch is dissolved. Add to blackberry mixture and stir. Stir in lemon juice and cassis.

3. Place skillet over medium heat. Cook, stirring frequently, for 5 minutes or until mixture comes to a boil. Reduce heat to low and drop dumpling batter by tablespoonfuls (15 mL) over the simmering blackberries. Cover and simmer for 20 to 30 minutes or until a tester inserted in the center of the dumplings comes out clean. Serve warm.

Blueberry Grunt

Serves 6

- 12-inch (30 cm) deep cast-iron (or enameled iron) skillet with lid or large lidded saucepan, greased (see Tips, below)

I love to serve desserts in big cast-iron skillets. The guests love the presentation. As an added bonus, you can make this dessert year-round with frozen blueberries.

Tips

A cast-iron or enameled skillet works best for this recipe, but another heavy, deep skillet will also work.

Plan on making this right before serving it, as it's best served warm.

DUMPLINGS

1½ cups	all-purpose flour	375 mL
3 tbsp	granulated sugar	45 mL
2 tsp	baking powder	10 mL
¼ tsp	salt	1 mL
3 tbsp	cold butter or margarine, cut into small pieces	45 mL
¾ cup	cold milk or soy milk	175 mL

FILLING

4 cups	frozen unsweetened blueberries, partially thawed (about 1 lb/500 g)	1 L
½ cup	granulated sugar	125 mL
1 tbsp	cornstarch	15 mL
1 tbsp	orange-flavored liqueur	15 mL
1 tsp	grated orange zest	5 mL
½ tsp	ground nutmeg	2 mL

1. *Dumplings:* In a large bowl or bowl of food processor, mix together flour, sugar, baking powder and salt. Using a pastry blender or food processor fitted with metal blade, cut butter into flour mixture until it resembles coarse crumbs. Add milk and stir or pulse just until mixture forms a soft dough. Do not overmix. Set aside.

2. *Filling:* In prepared skillet or large saucepan, mix together blueberries and sugar. In a bowl or measuring cup, whisk together ¾ cup (175 mL) water and cornstarch until cornstarch is dissolved. Add to blueberries and stir. Stir in liqueur, orange zest and nutmeg.

3. Place skillet over medium heat. Cook, stirring frequently, for 5 minutes or until mixture comes to a boil. Reduce heat to low and drop dumpling batter by tablespoonfuls (15 mL) over the simmering blueberries. Cover and simmer for 20 to 30 minutes or until a tester inserted in the center of the dumplings comes out clean. Serve warm.

Boysenberry Skillet Crumble

Serves 6

- Preheat oven to 400°F (200°C)
- 10-inch (25 cm) cast-iron or ovenproof skillet, greased

I love making a big crumble in a skillet, not only because it becomes a one-pan dessert but also because it's so much fun to serve dessert in a skillet. If you've had a chance to let the crumble cool a bit before serving, you can scoop some ice cream right on top before serving it.

Tip

This dessert is best served the day that it's made.

4 cups	fresh or frozen (not thawed) unsweetened boysenberries	1 L
1 cup	granulated sugar	250 mL
¼ cup	cornstarch	50 mL
1	recipe Brown Sugar Streusel (see recipe, page 134)	1

1. In prepared skillet, combine boysenberries, sugar and ¼ cup (50 mL) water. Bring mixture to a simmer over medium heat. (Try not to stir to avoid mashing berries.)

2. In a small bowl, whisk together cornstarch and 3 tbsp (45 mL) water until smooth. Stir cornstarch mixture into hot boysenberries and simmer, stirring carefully, for 3 to 4 minutes or until thick and mixture is glossy.

3. Sprinkle streusel over boysenberries and bake in preheated oven for 20 to 25 minutes or until topping is nicely browned. Serve warm or cool.

Bryanna's Cranberry Apple Crumble

Serves 6 to 8

- Preheat oven to 375°F (190°C)
- 9-inch (2.5 L) square glass baking dish, greased

This recipe is from my good friend and fellow cookbook author Bryanna Clark Grogan. It appears in her *The Fiber for Life Cookbook* and is a real family favorite. As well as being delicious, it's healthy, too.

3	tart apples, such as Granny Smith, peeled, cored and cut into ¼-inch (1 cm) slices (see Tips, left)	3
3 cups	fresh or frozen cranberries	750 mL
½ cup	granulated sugar	125 mL
1 tbsp	all-purpose flour	15 mL
1	recipe Bryanna's Whole Wheat Crumble Topping (see recipe, page 135)	1

1. In a bowl, gently combine apples, cranberries, sugar and flour. Spread mixture in prepared baking dish.

2. Sprinkle topping over fruit. Bake in preheated oven for 40 minutes or until apples are soft and juices are thickened.

3. Let cool on a wire rack for 20 minutes before serving to allow juices to thicken.

Bumbleberry Cobbler

Serves 6 to 8

- Preheat oven to 375°F (190°C)
- 8-inch (2 L) square glass baking dish, greased

There really isn't a bumbleberry; it's actually a combination of mixed berries. This scrumptious dessert, with its jumble of berries, is one of my regular go-to dishes.

Tips

A combination of frozen mixed berries would work here as well.

This dessert is best served within 1 to 2 hours of baking.

1½ cups	fresh or frozen (not thawed) raspberries (see Tips, left)	375 mL
1½ cups	fresh or frozen (not thawed) blueberries	375 mL
1 cup	fresh blackberries	250 mL
1 cup	granulated sugar, divided	250 mL
¼ tsp	ground cinnamon	1 mL
1 cup	all-purpose flour	250 mL
2 tsp	baking powder	10 mL
¾ cup	cold milk or soy milk	175 mL
½ cup	butter or margarine, melted	125 mL
1 tsp	vanilla extract	5 mL

1. In a bowl, toss together raspberries, blueberries, blackberries, ¼ cup (50 mL) of the sugar and cinnamon. Set aside.

2. In another bowl, whisk together flour, baking powder and remaining sugar. Add milk, butter and vanilla, whisking just until combined. Transfer batter to prepared baking dish. Scoop berries over top (don't stir, as batter will rise to the top as it bakes).

3. Bake in preheated oven for 50 minutes to 1 hour or until crust is golden brown and the center is just firm to the touch. Let cool on a wire rack for 20 minutes before serving.

Cherry Crisp

Serves 9

● Preheat oven to
400°F (200°C)

● 8-inch (2 L) square glass
baking dish, greased

It's not always easy to
find sour cherries, which
is why I love making this
crisp with homemade
Cherry Pie Filling. This
way, you can enjoy it
year-round, hassle-free.

Variation		
Cherry Raspberry Crisp: Stir 1 cup (250 mL) fresh raspberries into cherry mixture.		

1	recipe Cherry Berry Filling (see Variation, page 201)	1
1 tbsp	cassis or cherry-flavored liqueur	15 mL
1	recipe Almond Crumb Topping or Cinnamon Sugar Crumb Topping (see recipes, pages 134 and 135)	1

1. In prepared baking dish, combine cherry filling and liqueur, mixing well.

2. Sprinkle crumb topping over cherry mixture and bake in preheated oven for 20 to 25 minutes or until topping is nicely browned. (As the filling is already cooked and thickened, you're just baking this long enough to nicely brown the top and heat the filling.) You can serve this crisp warm or at room temperature.

Lemon Blueberry Cobbler

Serves 6 to 8

- Preheat oven to 375°F (190°C)
- 10-inch (25 cm) deep-dish glass pie plate or 8-inch (2 L) square glass baking dish, greased

When I need a quick and easy dessert, this cobbler is one of my standbys. It's delicious, simple to make and fabulous when topped with a scoop of homemade ice cream, especially Brown Sugar Cinnamon Ice Cream (see recipe, page 213).

Tip

Plan on serving this dessert within 1 to 2 hours of baking.

---

5 cups	fresh or frozen (not thawed) blueberries	1.25 L
1 cup	granulated sugar, divided	250 mL
1 tsp	grated lemon zest	5 mL
1 tbsp	freshly squeezed lemon juice	15 mL
1 cup	all-purpose flour	250 mL
2 tsp	baking powder	10 mL
¾ cup	cold milk or soy milk	175 mL
½ cup	butter or margarine, melted	125 mL
	Ground nutmeg	

1. In a bowl, toss blueberries with ¼ cup (50 mL) of the sugar and lemon zest and juice. Set aside.

2. In another bowl, whisk together flour, baking powder and remaining sugar. Add milk and butter, whisking just until combined. Transfer batter to prepared pie plate. Sprinkle with nutmeg. Place blueberries over top (don't stir, as batter will rise to the top as it bakes).

3. Bake in preheated oven for 50 minutes to 1 hour or until crust is golden brown and the center is just firm to the touch. Let cool on a wire rack for 20 minutes before serving.

Peach Cherry Cobbler

Serves 8 to 10

- Preheat oven to 375°F (190°C)
- 10-inch (25 cm) deep-dish glass pie plate or 8-inch (2 L) square glass baking dish, greased

I brought this cobbler to the beach one glorious weekend when my family was graciously invited by our friend Eliot. The almond, peach and cherry flavors go together beautifully.

Tip
If fruit is a bit tart, add 1 to 2 tbsp (15 to 25 mL) more sugar.

4	ripe peaches, peeled, pitted and sliced (see Tip, page 52)	4
1 cup	fresh cherries, pitted	250 mL
1 cup	granulated sugar, divided	250 mL
¾ cup	all-purpose flour	175 mL
⅓ cup	almond meal (flour)	75 mL
2 tsp	baking powder	10 mL
¾ cup	cold milk or soy milk	175 mL
6 tbsp	butter or margarine, melted	90 mL
1½ tsp	almond extract	7 mL

1. In a bowl, toss together peaches, cherries and ¼ cup (50 mL) of the sugar. Set aside.

2. In a bowl, mix together remaining sugar, all-purpose flour, almond meal and baking powder. Add milk, butter and almond extract, stirring just until combined and almost smooth. Spread batter in prepared pie plate.

3. Scoop fruit mixture over batter, discarding any accumulated liquid in bowl (don't stir, as batter will rise to the top as it bakes). Bake for 50 minutes to 1 hour or until crust is set in center and edges are brown. Let cool on a wire rack for 20 minutes before serving.

Raspberry Orange Grunt

Serves 6

- 12-inch (30 cm) deep cast-iron (or enameled iron) skillet with lid, or large lidded saucepan greased (see Tip, below)

Frozen raspberries have a wonderful way of bringing a little summer sunshine into a winter kitchen. This dessert is old-fashioned and delicious, especially with the combination of raspberries and orange.

> **Tip**
> A cast-iron or enameled skillet works best for this recipe, but another heavy, deep skillet will also work.

DUMPLINGS

1½ cups	all-purpose flour	375 mL
2 tbsp	granulated sugar	25 mL
2 tsp	baking powder	10 mL
¼ tsp	salt	1 mL
3 tbsp	cold butter or margarine, cut into small pieces	45 mL
¾ cup	cold milk or soy milk	175 mL

FILLING

4 cups	frozen unsweetened raspberries, partially thawed (about 1 lb/500 g)	1 L
½ cup	granulated sugar	125 mL
1 tbsp	cornstarch	15 mL
1 tsp	lightly packed grated orange zest	5 mL

1. *Dumplings:* In a large bowl or bowl of food processor, mix together flour, sugar, baking powder and salt. Using a pastry blender or food processor fitted with metal blade, cut butter into flour mixture until it resembles coarse crumbs. Add milk, stirring or pulsing just until mixture forms a soft dough. Do not overmix. Set aside.

2. *Filling:* In prepared skillet or saucepan, combine raspberries and sugar. In a bowl or measuring cup, whisk together ¾ cup (175 mL) water and cornstarch until cornstarch is dissolved. Add to raspberry mixture and stir. Stir in zest.

3. Place skillet over medium heat. Cook, stirring frequently, for 5 minutes or until mixture comes to a boil. Reduce heat to low and drop batter by tablespoonfuls (15 mL) over the simmering raspberries. Cover and simmer for 20 to 30 minutes or until a tester inserted in the center of the dumplings comes out clean. Serve warm.

Rhubarb Boysenberry Cobbler

Serves 6 to 8

- Preheat oven to 375°F (190°C)
- 8-inch (2 L) square glass baking dish, greased

Rhubarb is one of those incredibly delicious ingredients that signifies the beginning of summer. Once I start seeing it in grocery stores or at the farmer's market, I buy what I can and run home to bake. This is a flavorful cobbler and a great way to use fresh rhubarb.

Tip
Plan on serving this dessert within 1 to 2 hours of baking.

5 tbsp	freshly squeezed orange juice	75 mL
3 cups	sliced fresh rhubarb	750 mL
2 cups	fresh boysenberries or other berries	500 mL
1 cup	granulated sugar, divided	250 mL
1 cup	all-purpose flour	250 mL
2 tsp	baking powder	10 mL
¾ cup	cold milk or soy milk	175 mL
½ cup	butter or margarine, melted	125 mL
1 tsp	vanilla extract	5 mL
	Ground cinnamon	

1. In a large nonstick skillet, heat orange juice over medium-high heat. Reduce heat to medium and add rhubarb. Cook rhubarb, gently stirring occasionally, for 5 minutes or just until rhubarb starts to soften. Remove skillet from heat and gently fold in boysenberries and ¼ cup (50 mL) of the sugar, being careful not to mash the fruit. Set aside.

2. In a bowl, whisk together flour, baking powder and remaining sugar. Add milk, butter and vanilla, whisking just until combined. Transfer batter to prepared baking dish. Sprinkle with cinnamon. Scoop fruit mixture over top (don't stir, as batter will rise to the top as it bakes).

3. Bake in preheated oven for 50 minutes to 1 hour or until crust is golden brown and the center is just firm to the touch. Let cool on a wire rack for 20 minutes before serving.

Strawberry Rhubarb Crisp

Serves 6 to 8

• Preheat oven to
400°F (200°C)

• 8-inch (2 L) square glass
baking dish, greased

When I see strawberries
and rhubarb at the
market, I know that
summer's just around the
corner. The wonderfully
tart flavor of rhubarb and
juicy, sweet strawberries
in this dessert is one of
the ways that I like to
welcome the new season.

Tip
If you like your desserts
sweeter, you can add an
additional 1 to 2 tbsp
(15 to 25 mL) sugar.

Variation
Use lemon juice and zest
instead of the orange
juice and zest.

3½ cups	strawberries, hulled and halved or quartered, depending on size	875 mL
3 cups	sliced fresh rhubarb	750 mL
¾ cup	granulated sugar	175 mL
3 tbsp	cornstarch	45 mL
1 tsp	lightly packed grated orange zest	5 mL
1 tbsp	orange juice	15 mL
1	recipe Oat Crumble or Cinnamon Sugar Crumb Topping (see recipes, pages 136 and 135)	1

1. In a large bowl, gently combine strawberries, rhubarb, sugar, cornstarch and orange zest and juice. Spread mixture in prepared baking dish.

2. Bake in preheated oven, carefully stirring every 10 minutes or so, for 35 to 40 minutes or until fruit mixture is thickened and the juices are becoming glossy.

3. Remove baking dish from oven and gently stir liquid mixture in bottom of baking dish with fruit. Sprinkle topping over fruit mixture. Reduce heat to 350°F (180°C), return crisp to oven and continue baking for 15 to 20 minutes more or until top is lightly browned and juices are bubbling and thickened. Let cool on a wire rack for at least 20 minutes to allow juices to thicken.

Almond Crumb Topping

**Makes 2 cups
(500 mL)**
**(enough for one 8-inch/
20 cm crisp or crumble,
or one 9-inch/23 cm pie)**

In my humble opinion,
you can never have too
many variations of crumb
toppings. This one I
developed originally for
an apple pie, but the
wonderful almond scent
works well with many
different pies.

¾ cup	all-purpose flour	175 mL
⅔ cup	granulated sugar	150 mL
¼ cup	butter or margarine, melted	50 mL
1 tsp	pure almond extract	5 mL
⅓ cup	sliced almonds	75 mL

1. In a small bowl, combine flour and sugar. Add butter
   and almond extract, stirring until incorporated. Using
   your fingertips, finish working butter into flour
   mixture, squeezing until a nice crumbly mixture forms.

2. Stir in almonds. Sprinkle topping over prepared pie,
   crisp or crumble according to recipe.

Brown Sugar Streusel

**Makes about
3 cups (750 mL)**
**(enough for one large
crisp or one 9-inch/
23 cm pie)**

When you want a
no-holds-barred buttery
topping, this is your
recipe. I dedicate this
recipe to my husband,
Jay, who would be very
happy if his crisp was
all buttery topping.

1½ cups	all-purpose flour	375 mL
¾ cup	packed light brown sugar	175 mL
½ cup	butter or margarine, softened	125 mL

1. In a small bowl, combine flour and brown sugar. Add
   butter and, using an electric mixer, a fork or a pastry
   blender, mix into flour until little bits of butter remain.
   Using your fingertips, finish working butter into flour
   mixture, squeezing until a nice crumbly mixture forms.

2. Sprinkle mixture over pie, crisp or crumble according
   to recipe.

Bryanna's Whole Wheat Crumble Topping

Makes about 1¾ cups (425 mL)
(enough for one 8-inch/ 20 cm crisp or crumble, or one 9-inch/23 cm pie)

This is Bryanna Clark Grogan's streusel recipe from her book *The Fiber for Life Cookbook*. The deliciously healthy topping bakes atop cranberries and apples in her Cranberry Apple Crumble (see recipe, page 126). The first time I tasted it, I was hooked.

⅔ cup	old-fashioned rolled oats	150 mL
⅓ cup	whole wheat flour	75 mL
⅓ cup	packed brown sugar	75 mL
1 tsp	ground cinnamon	5 mL
3 tbsp	vegetable oil	45 mL
½ cup	chopped nuts, such as pecans	125 mL

1. In a bowl, combine oats, flour, brown sugar and cinnamon. Add oil, stirring until incorporated. Using your fingertips, finish working the oil into the flour mixture, squeezing until a nice crumbly mixture forms. Stir in nuts.
2. Sprinkle on top of prepared pie, crisp or crumble according to recipe.

Cinnamon Sugar Crumb Topping

Makes about 2 cups (500 mL)
(enough for one 8-inch/ 20 cm crisp or crumble, or one 9-inch/23 cm pie)

This is a great crumb topping, rich with the flavors of cinnamon and brown sugar. It also happens to be lower in fat than most toppings, but don't tell anyone — they'd never know by the buttery taste.

¾ cup	all-purpose flour	175 mL
½ cup	packed light brown sugar	125 mL
½ tsp	ground cinnamon	2 mL
¼ cup	butter or margarine, melted	50 mL

1. In a small bowl, combine flour, brown sugar and cinnamon. Add butter, stirring until incorporated. Using your fingertips, finish working butter into flour mixture, squeezing until a nice crumbly mixture forms.
2. Sprinkle topping over prepared pie, crisp or crumble according to recipe.

Hazelnut Streusel

Makes about 2 cups (500 mL)
(enough for one 8-inch/ 20 cm crisp or crumble, or one 9-inch/23 cm pie)

- Preheat oven to 350°F (180°C)
- Baking sheet, lined with foil or parchment paper

This streusel is my nod to home, where hazelnut trees abound. I love it in the autumn, when you can pick hazelnuts growing wild, a perfect partner for fall blackberries.

⅔ cup	hazelnuts	150 mL
¾ cup	all-purpose flour	175 mL
½ cup	packed light brown sugar	125 mL
¼ cup	butter or margarine, melted	50 mL

1. Place hazelnuts in a single layer on prepared baking sheet. Bake in preheated oven for 10 to 15 minutes or until nuts are lightly browned and skins are blistered. Wrap nuts in a clean dry kitchen towel and let stand for 1 minute. Rub nuts to remove loose skins (it's OK if you can't remove all of them). Let nuts cool completely. In a food processor fitted with metal blade, coarsely chop hazelnuts.

2. In a small bowl, combine flour and brown sugar. Add butter, stirring until incorporated. Using your fingertips, finish working butter into flour mixture, squeezing until a nice crumbly mixture forms. Stir in hazelnuts.

3. Sprinkle topping over prepared pie, crisp or crumble according to recipe.

Oat Crumble

Makes about 2 cups (500 mL)
(enough for one 8-inch/ 20 cm crisp or crumble, or one 9-inch/23 cm pie)

The combination of oats, brown sugar, cinnamon and butter is a true favorite. Although I would often like to eat this topping on its own, it's pretty amazing over bubbling hot fruit.

¾ cup	all-purpose flour	175 mL
½ cup	old-fashioned rolled oats	125 mL
½ cup	packed light brown sugar	125 mL
1 tsp	ground cinnamon	5 mL
¼ cup	butter or margarine, melted	50 mL

1. In a small bowl, combine flour, oats, sugar and cinnamon. Add butter, stirring until incorporated. Using your fingertips, finish working butter into flour mixture, squeezing until a nice crumbly mixture forms.

2. Sprinkle topping over prepared pie, crisp or crumble according to recipe.

Orange Spice Crumble Topping

**Makes 2 cups
(500 mL)
(enough for one 8-inch/
20 cm crisp or crumble,
or one 9-inch/23 cm pie)**

This crumble is especially
tasty because of the grated
orange zest. I love to
sprinkle it over berry or
apple pies, which makes
a wonderful combination
of flavors.

¾ cup	all-purpose flour	175 mL
½ cup	packed light brown sugar	125 mL
1 tsp	ground cinnamon	5 mL
¼ cup	cold butter or margarine, cut into small pieces	50 mL
1 tsp	grated orange zest	5 mL

1. In a bowl, combine flour, sugar and cinnamon. Using a pastry blender or food processor fitted with metal blade, cut butter into flour mixture until it resembles coarse crumbs. Using your fingertips, finish working butter into flour mixture, squeezing until a nice crumbly mixture forms. Stir in orange zest.

2. Sprinkle mixture over prepared pie, crisp or crumble according to recipe.

Walnut Oat Topping

**Makes about 2 cups
(500 mL)
(enough for one 8-inch/
20 cm crisp or crumble,
or one 9-inch/23 cm pie)**

This delicious recipe,
which gets its rich flavor
from the walnuts, oats
and brown sugar,
complements apples and
pears beautifully. My
husband can never seem
to get enough of it.

¾ cup	all-purpose flour	175 mL
½ cup	old-fashioned rolled oats	125 mL
½ cup	packed light brown sugar	125 mL
½ cup	walnuts, chopped	125 mL
¼ cup	butter or margarine, melted	50 mL

1. In a small bowl, combine flour, oats, brown sugar and walnuts. Add butter, stirring until incorporated. Using your fingertips, finish working butter into flour mixture, squeezing until a nice crumbly mixture forms.

2. Sprinkle topping over prepared pie, crisp or crumble according to recipe.

Whole-Grain Crumble

**Makes 2 cups
(500 mL)**
**(enough for one 8-inch/
20 cm crisp or crumble,
or one 9-inch/23 cm pie)**

I used to be a bit picky
about putting whole-grain
flour in my desserts.
"What's the point?" I
thought. Well, this crumble
topping has changed
my mind completely.
It's wonderfully buttery
and nutty, perfect for
sprinkling over a berry pie.

¾ cup	whole wheat pastry flour	175 mL
½ cup	old-fashioned rolled oats	125 mL
½ cup	packed light brown sugar	125 mL
½ tsp	ground cinnamon, optional	2 mL
5 tbsp	butter or margarine, melted	75 mL

1. In a small bowl, combine flour, oats, brown sugar and cinnamon, if using. Add butter, stirring until incorporated. Using your fingertips, finish working butter into flour mixture, squeezing until a nice crumbly mixture forms.

2. Sprinkle over prepared pie, crisp or crumble according to recipe.

Tip
You can make the
topping ahead and
freeze it in a resealable
freezer bag for up to
1 month.

Rustic Pies & Tarts

Apple Galette with Chai Spices

Serves 8

- Preheat oven to 400°F (200°C)
- Rimmed baking sheet

This is a wonderful example of how easy a homemade tart can be. This is a free-form tart, meaning you simply roll out the dough, top it with fruit, fold over the edges and bake. How easy is that?

1	recipe All-Purpose Vegan Pastry Dough or Small-Batch All-Purpose Buttery Pastry Dough, chilled (see recipes, pages 182 and 180)	1
3	Granny Smith apples, peeled, cored and thinly sliced	3
½ cup	packed light brown sugar	125 mL
2 tbsp	all-purpose flour	25 mL
1 tsp	vanilla powder or extract	5 mL
1 tsp	vanilla extract	5 mL
½ tsp	ground cinnamon	2 mL
¼ tsp	ground allspice	1 mL
⅛ tsp	ground cardamom	0.5 mL
	Cream, milk or soy milk	
	Granulated sugar	

1. On a large piece of parchment paper lightly dusted with flour, roll out dough into a 13-inch (32.5 cm) circle, dusting parchment and dough as necessary to keep the dough from sticking. Slide parchment and dough onto baking sheet.

2. In a large bowl, combine apples, brown sugar, flour, vanilla powder, vanilla, cinnamon, allspice and cardamom. Arrange in center of pastry, leaving a 1½-inch (4 cm) border. Gently fold up edge of dough about 3 inches (7.5 cm) toward center over apples, pleating as necessary. Brush dough with cream, sealing well at pleats. Sprinkle entire galette with granulated sugar.

3. Bake in bottom third of preheated oven for 40 to 50 minutes or until crust is golden brown, apples are tender and juices are bubbling and thickened. Let cool on baking sheet on a wire rack for about 1 hour before serving.

Apple Tarte Tatin

Serves 8

- Preheat oven to 400°F (200°C)
- 10-inch (25 cm) cast-iron or ovenproof skillet or tarte Tatin pan

This tart takes me back to my French roots. It's as lovely for dessert as it is served for brunch. But, then again, how can you possibly go wrong with caramelized apples, sugar, butter and pastry?

Tip

If you have a smaller package of puff pastry, the pastry may be thinner but will still work.

Variation

Substitute a homemade pastry crust, such as All-Purpose Vegan Pastry Dough or Buttery Pie Pastry Dough (see recipes, pages 182 and 181) for the puff pastry.

½	box (18 oz/540 g) frozen puff pastry, thawed (see Tip, left)	½
6 tbsp	butter	90 mL
¾ cup	granulated sugar	175 mL
5	Golden Delicious apples, peeled, cored and sliced into quarters	5

1. On a lightly floured surface, unroll sheet of puff pastry and roll, if necessary, to make generous 11-inch (27.5 cm) square. Using a paring knife, cut pastry into an approximately 11-inch (27.5 cm) circle. (Don't roll the pastry too thin.) Pierce all over with a fork. Set pastry on a plate and refrigerate until ready to use.

2. In a skillet over medium heat, melt butter. Remove skillet from heat. Sprinkle sugar evenly over melted butter, stirring just to mix. Arrange apples, cut side down, in a circle around edge of pan, squeezing in as many apples as you can. Fill center of circle with remaining apples to cover pan. Cook over medium-high heat for 12 minutes or until juices darken. If juices and apples are darkening too fast, reduce heat to medium. Remove skillet from heat. Using a fork, turn each apple piece over, keeping neatly arranged. Return skillet to heat and cook for 5 minutes more or until lightly cooked on the other side.

3. Remove skillet from heat and carefully place pastry over apples, tucking sides into pan. Bake in preheated oven for 20 to 25 minutes or until pastry is puffed and nicely browned. Let cool in pan on a wire rack for 20 minutes. Carefully invert tart onto a serving platter and serve. Be careful when inverting the tart, as the juices and filling are very hot.

Blueberry Pavlova

Serves 8

This is a simple and scrumptious dessert. Even with the whipped cream, the Pavlova feels and tastes light and airy. It was originally named for the famed Russian ballerina Anna Pavlova.

1	recipe Meringue Tart Shell (see recipe, page 194)	1
1¾ cups	whipping (35%) cream	425 mL
⅓ cup	confectioner's (icing) sugar, sifted	75 mL
½ tsp	vanilla extract	2 mL
1½ cups	fresh blueberries	375 mL

1. Bake meringue shell according to recipe directions. Let cool.

2. In a large bowl, using an electric mixer, beat cream, confectioner's sugar and vanilla just until soft peaks form.

3. Scoop whipped cream over top of cooled meringue shell, swirling with the back of a spoon. Sprinkle blueberries over whipped cream and serve immediately.

Chocolate Chip Skillet Pie

Serves 8

● Preheat oven to 350°F (180°C)

● 10-inch (25 cm) cast-iron or ovenproof skillet, greased

You've got a real crowd pleaser with this dessert. Besides being utterly delicious, this pie practically bakes itself while you're enjoying dinner. Serve it with one of the homemade ice creams in this book (see recipes, starting on page 213) and you've got a fabulous dessert.

1½ cups	all-purpose flour	375 mL
½ tsp	baking powder	2 mL
1¼ cups	packed light brown sugar	300 mL
½ cup	salted butter, softened	125 mL
1 tsp	vanilla extract	5 mL
1	egg	1
1 cup	semisweet chocolate chips	250 mL

1. In a bowl, combine flour and baking powder.

2. In large bowl, using a stand mixer fitted with paddle attachment, cream together brown sugar and butter until light and fluffy. Add vanilla, mixing well. Add egg, beating until smooth. Add flour mixture and beat just until combined. Fold in chocolate chips.

3. Transfer dough to prepared skillet, smoothing top. Bake in preheated oven for 20 to 30 minutes or until puffed and lightly browned. Let cool in pan on a wire rack for 20 to 30 minutes before serving.

Cherry Almond Clafouti

Serves 6 to 8

- Preheat oven to 350°F (180°C)
- 10-inch (25 cm) deep-dish glass pie plate, greased

A clafouti is a French dessert that is almost a cross between a custard, a pancake and a fruit pie. It usually contains some kind of fresh fruit, which is my inspiration for baking it in a pie plate. This recipe is adapted from the *Moosewood Restaurant Book of Desserts*. It's one that I make often because it's so good! Clafouti makes a wonderful breakfast as well as dessert, so this is a versatile recipe.

Tips

If using frozen berries, you do not need to thaw them but you may need to extend the baking time by a few minutes.

This clafouti is best served warm, the same day that it is made.

1 cup	fresh or frozen (not thawed) cherries, pitted (see Tips, left)	250 mL
1 cup	milk	250 mL
¾ cup	all-purpose flour	175 mL
½ cup	packed brown sugar	125 mL
4	eggs	4
1 tsp	vanilla extract	5 mL
½ tsp	almond extract	2 mL
¼ tsp	ground cinnamon	1 mL

1. Place cherries in bottom of prepared pie plate.

2. In a blender or using an immersion/stick blender, blend together milk, flour, brown sugar, eggs and vanilla and almond extracts until smooth. Pour batter over fruit. Sprinkle with cinnamon.

3. Bake in preheated oven for 50 to 60 minutes or until puffed and golden and set in the center. Let cool for 20 minutes before serving.

Jam Berry Crumble Pie

Serves 8 to 12

- Preheat oven to 350°F (180°C)
- 9-inch (23 cm) deep-dish glass pie plate, greased

This pie is so simple, yet is absolutely delish! It's almost like a jam-filled bar but baked in a pie plate for a unique new twist. You can serve it topped with a scoop of ice cream or just simply give it a quick dusting of confectioner's sugar. However you top it, this pie's great.

> **Tip**
> This pie is best served the day that it's made.

1½ cups	all-purpose flour	375 mL
1½ cups	old-fashioned rolled oats	375 mL
¾ cup	packed brown sugar	175 mL
1 tsp	ground cinnamon	5 mL
¾ cup	butter or margarine, melted	175 mL
¾ cup	thick jam or berry preserves	175 mL
	Freshly grated nutmeg	

1. In a large bowl, stir together flour, rolled oats, brown sugar and cinnamon. Add butter, stirring well.

2. Press half of the mixture into prepared pie plate. Spread preserves evenly over top. Sprinkle remaining oat mixture over preserves, gently pressing. Sprinkle top with grated nutmeg.

3. Bake in preheated oven for 25 to 35 minutes or until golden brown. Let cool completely on a wire rack before serving.

Plum Galette

Serves 6 to 8

● Preheat oven to
425°F (220°C)

This recipe was generously
shared with me by
Jennifer MacKenzie,
co-owner of the gourmet
food shop and café In a
Nuttshell and Nuttshell
Next Door in Lakefield,
Ontario. Jennifer's plum
galette is incredibly
delicious, rich with the
flavors of plums and
brown sugar. It's a
fabulous dessert to serve
to company.

Tips

Prune plums tend to be
sweet and tart. This
filling is a little on the
tart side but it goes
nicely with the
sweetness of the crust.
If you prefer a sweeter
filling, add 1 to 2 tbsp
(15 to 25 mL) more
packed brown sugar.

If you have small prune
plums, use 18 to 24 and
cut in half.

Variation

To use black plums
instead of prune plums,
use 6 black plums and
cut each into 8 slices.
Increase flour to $\frac{1}{3}$ cup
(75 mL).

1	recipe Small-Batch All-Purpose Buttery Pastry Dough, chilled (see recipe, page 180)	1
$\frac{1}{3}$ cup	packed brown sugar	75 mL
$\frac{1}{4}$ cup	all-purpose flour	50 mL
12	large prune (blue) plums, pitted and quartered (about 4 cups/1 L)	12
1 tbsp	butter, melted	15 mL
$\frac{1}{2}$ tsp	vanilla extract	2 mL
	Cream or milk	

1. On a large piece of parchment paper lightly dusted with flour, roll out dough into a 14-inch (35 cm) circle, dusting parchment and dough as necessary to keep the dough from sticking. Slide parchment and dough onto a baking sheet.

2. In a bowl, combine brown sugar and flour. Sprinkle about half in a circle in the center of the dough, leaving a 3-inch (7.5 cm) border. Arrange plums on top of sugar mixture, mounding slightly in the center.

3. Stir butter and vanilla into remaining sugar mixture. Crumble between fingers and sprinkle evenly over plums.

4. Gently fold up edge of dough toward center over plums, pleating as necessary, leaving about 4 inches (10 cm) in the center exposed. Brush dough with cream, sealing well at pleats.

5. Bake in bottom third of preheated oven for 20 minutes. Reduce heat to 375°F (190°C) and continue baking for about 30 minutes more or until crust is golden brown and juices are bubbling and thickened. Let cool on baking sheet on a wire rack for about 1 hour before serving.

Pear and Almond Galette

Serves 8

- Preheat oven to 400°F (200°C)
- Rimmed baking sheet

Although this dessert sounds fancy, it's really a rustic pear tart. It's not too sweet and makes a perfect ending to a meal. I love this tart's country elegance.

Tips

If you want this tart to be a little sweeter, increase the confectioner's sugar in the Almond Cream Filling by 1 to 2 tbsp (15 to 25 mL). You can also sprinkle more sugar over top of the unbaked tart.

Don't worry if the pears separate. If they do, overlap them slightly for a nice spoke pattern.

2	large firm Bosc pears, peeled, cored and quartered lengthwise	2
¼ cup	granulated sugar	50 mL
1 tbsp	freshly squeezed lemon juice	15 mL
1	recipe All-Purpose Vegan Pastry Dough or Small-Batch All-Purpose Buttery Pastry Dough, chilled (see recipes, pages 182 and 180)	1
1	recipe Almond Cream Filling (see recipe, page 198)	1
	Cream, milk or soy milk	
1½ tbsp	granulated sugar	22 mL
	Confectioner's (icing) sugar, optional	

1. Place pear quarters on their sides. Using a paring knife, carefully cut 4 slices lengthwise through the pear, trying to keep the pear intact at the end (see Tips, left).

2. In a shallow saucepan over medium-high heat, combine 2 cups (500 mL) water and ¼ cup (50 mL) sugar. Bring liquid to a simmer. Reduce heat to medium-low. Carefully add pears and lemon juice to liquid. Cover pan and simmer for 5 minutes or until softened. Uncover and set aside.

3. On a large piece of parchment paper lightly dusted with flour, roll out dough into a 13-inch (32.5 cm) circle, dusting parchment and dough as necessary to keep the dough from sticking. Slide parchment and dough onto baking sheet. Spread almond filling in center of pastry, leaving a 1½-inch (4 cm) border.

4. Remove pears from liquid and blot dry with a paper towel. Discard liquid. Gently fan pear quarters without separating. Starting in the center of the tart, place fanned pears in a circular pattern, forming a circle. Separate remaining pears into individual slices and place in a circular pattern around the circle of fanned pears. (Don't worry if some of the filling shows.) Gently fold up edges of dough about 3 inches (7.5 cm) toward center over pears, pleating as necessary. Brush dough with cream, sealing well at pleats, and sprinkle 1½ tbsp (22 mL) granulated sugar over top.

5. Bake in preheated oven for 30 to 40 minutes or until pastry is nicely golden brown and filling is puffed. Let cool on baking sheet on a wire rack for 30 minutes before serving. If desired, dust cooled tart with confectioner's sugar before serving.

Variation

For a nice finish and a bit of extra flavor, just before serving brush the pears with sieved apricot jam.

Raspberry Clafouti

Serves 8

- Preheat oven to 350°F (180°C)
- 10-inch (25 cm) deep-dish glass pie plate, greased

This recipe is adapted from the *Moosewood Restaurant Book of Desserts*. It is a great dessert that goes together quickly and is perfect in the summertime. I've always adored clafouti, and love that it's like a cross between a custard and a fruit pie.

2 cups	fresh raspberries	500 mL
¾ cup	all-purpose flour	175 mL
½ cup	granulated sugar	125 mL
½ cup	whipping (35%) cream	125 mL
½ cup	whole milk	125 mL
4	eggs	4
½ tsp	almond extract	2 mL

1. Scatter raspberries in bottom of prepared pie plate.
2. In a blender or using an immersion/stick blender, blend together flour, sugar, cream, milk, eggs and almond extract until smooth. Pour batter over raspberries.
3. Bake in preheated oven for 50 to 60 minutes or until puffed and golden and set in the center. Let cool for 20 minutes before serving.

Fresh Berry Pavlova

Serves 8

Here is another version of Pavlova, the light-as-air dessert named after the famed Russian ballerina Anna Pavlova. I love the combination of the crisp, sweet crust with the tang of the lemon and fresh raspberries.

1	recipe Meringue Tart Shell (see recipe, page 194)	1
1¾ cups	whipping (35%) cream	425 mL
⅓ cup	confectioner's (icing) sugar, sifted	75 mL
2 tsp	grated lemon zest	10 mL
½ tsp	pure lemon oil or extract	2 mL
1½ cups	fresh raspberries or blackberries	375 mL

1. Bake meringue shell according to recipe directions. Let cool.
2. In a large bowl, using an electric mixer, beat cream, confectioner's sugar and lemon zest and oil just until soft peaks form.
3. Scoop whipped cream over top of cooled meringue shell, swirling with the back of a spoon. Sprinkle raspberries over whipped cream and serve immediately.

Tip

Don't make this dessert on a rainy or hot, humid day, as the moisture will negatively affect the crispness of the crust.

Savory Pies & Tarts

Biscuit-Topped Beef Pie

Serves 6

- Preheat oven to 400°F (200°C)
- 10-inch (25 cm) deep-dish glass pie plate or baking dish
- Rimmed baking sheet

This is a hearty savory pie, which was shared by cookbook author Judith Finlayson. Not only is it a great cold weather dish, but Judith says it's also particularly popular with teenage boys.

Tip

You can make the filling ahead of time, without adding the beans, and refrigerate for up to 2 days. When you're ready to bake, cook the beans and add them. Reheat on the stovetop or in a microwave before adding the biscuits.

1 tbsp	olive oil	15 mL
1 lb	lean ground beef	500 g
1	onion, finely chopped	1
4	cloves garlic, minced	4
1 tbsp	all-purpose flour	15 mL
½ tsp	dried thyme leaves	2 mL
1 cup	beef stock	250 mL
½ cup	dry white wine	125 mL
2 tbsp	tomato paste	25 mL
1 tbsp	Worcestershire sauce	15 mL
	Salt and freshly ground black pepper	
2 cups	cooked sliced green beans	500 mL

HERBED BISCUIT TOPPING

1½ cups	all-purpose flour (see Tips, right)	375 mL
2 tsp	baking powder	10 mL
¼ tsp	salt	1 mL
2 tbsp	cold butter, cut into small pieces	25 mL
½ cup	cold buttermilk, approx.	125 mL
¼ cup	finely chopped fresh parsley or chives	50 mL

1. In a skillet, heat oil over medium heat for 30 seconds. Add beef and onion and cook, breaking up meat with a spoon, for 5 minutes or until beef is no longer pink. Add garlic, flour and thyme and cook, stirring, for 1 minute. Stir in beef stock, white wine and tomato paste and bring to a boil. Cook, stirring, for 2 minutes or until slightly thickened. Stir in Worcestershire sauce and season to taste with salt and pepper. Stir in beans. Transfer to pie plate. Place on baking sheet.

2. *Herbed Biscuit Topping:* In a food processor fitted with metal blade, pulse flour, baking powder and salt to mix. Add butter, pulsing until mixture resembles coarse meal. Add buttermilk and parsley, pulsing just until mixture starts to come together. If mixture seems too crumbly, add a bit more buttermilk.

3. Divide dough into 6 balls. Flatten each to the size of an average biscuit (about 2 inches/5 cm) and arrange over top of pie. Bake in preheated oven for 20 minutes or until top is golden brown and biscuits are totally cooked through.

Tip

For a more robust and nutritious crust, substitute ¾ cup (175 mL) whole wheat flour for an equal quantity of all-purpose.

Biscuit-Topped Seafood Pie

Serves 6

- 10-inch (25 cm) deep-dish glass pie plate
- Rimmed baking sheet

This recipe from cookbook author Judith Finlayson is a great dish to serve if you're entertaining guests who avoid meat but will eat fish and seafood, or for a special family dinner. Serve it with a tossed green salad or garden–fresh tomatoes drizzled with olive oil. Open a bottle of crisp cold wine. If you are serving guests who particularly like potatoes, try the Seafood Shepherd's Pie (see Variation, page 153).

8 oz	medium shrimp, shells on	250 g
1 cup	dry white wine	250 mL
3 tbsp	butter, divided	45 mL
1 tbsp	olive oil	15 mL
8 oz	white mushrooms, thinly sliced	250 g
2	shallots, minced	2
1 tsp	grated lemon zest	5 mL
1 tbsp	freshly squeezed lemon juice	15 mL
8 oz	scallops, cut into bite-size pieces	250 g
1/4 cup	all-purpose flour	50 mL
1/2 cup	whipping (35%) cream	125 mL
1/4 tsp	cayenne pepper	1 mL
	Salt and freshly ground black pepper	
1 lb	skinless firm white fish fillets, cut into 1-inch (2.5 cm) squares	500 g
1/4 cup	finely chopped fresh parsley	50 mL

TOPPING

1	recipe Herbed Biscuit Topping (see recipe, page 150)	1

1. Peel and devein shrimp, reserving shells. Set shrimp aside in refrigerator.

2. In a saucepan, combine white wine, 1/2 cup (125 mL) water and reserved shrimp shells. Bring to a boil over medium heat. Cover, reduce heat to low and simmer for 15 minutes. Strain, pushing against solids to extract as much liquid as possible. Set liquid aside and discard shells.

3. Meanwhile, preheat oven to 375°F (190°C).

4. In a skillet, melt 1 tbsp (15 mL) of the butter with the oil over medium-high heat. Add mushrooms and shallots and cook, stirring, for 5 minutes or until shallots are softened and mushrooms begin to brown. Stir in lemon zest and juice. Transfer to a bowl and set aside. Add reserved shrimp and scallops to skillet and cook, stirring, for 2 minutes or just until seared (they should not be cooked through). Transfer to bowl with mushrooms and set aside.

5. Reduce heat to low. Melt remaining 2 tbsp (25 mL) butter in skillet. Add flour and cook, whisking, for 5 minutes. Add reserved shrimp liquid, cream, cayenne and any juices that have collected from mushrooms and seared seafood and cook, stirring, for 2 minutes or until thickened. Season to taste with salt and pepper. Stir in reserved mushrooms and seafood, fish and parsley and transfer to pie plate. Place pie plate on baking sheet.

6. *Topping:* Divide biscuit topping into 6 balls. Flatten each to the size of an average biscuit (about 2 inches/5 cm) and arrange over top of pie. Bake in preheated oven for 20 minutes or until top is golden brown and biscuits are totally cooked through.

Variation

Seafood Shepherd's Pie: Instead of a biscuit topping, use garlic mashed potatoes. Bring 3 peeled potatoes and 4 cloves of garlic to a boil in enough water to cover. Reduce heat and simmer for 20 minutes or until tender. Drain and mash or put through a ricer. Stir in 1 tbsp (15 mL) butter, ¼ cup (50 mL) milk and ¼ cup (50 mL) finely chopped green onions. Season to taste with salt and pepper. Spread evenly over top of pie and sprinkle with 2 tbsp (25 mL) Parmesan cheese, if desired. Bake in preheated oven for 35 minutes or until hot and bubbling.

Caramelized Onion, Thyme and Olive Tart

Serves 4

● Baking sheet, lined with parchment paper

This tart recipe is inspired by Nadine Abensur's cookbook *Cranks Fast Food*. She had the brilliant idea of using frozen puff pastry as the base for a savory tart, requiring no special pans or equipment. This is a very delicious and easy tart to make, perfect for summertime entertaining.

Tip

If you have a smaller package of puff pastry, the pastry may be thinner but will still work.

Look for puff pastry made from shortening for a vegan friendly recipe.

This tart is best served within 15 to 20 minutes of baking.

Variation

Omit the olive paste and, if desired, top tart with ¼ cup (50 mL) pitted Kalamata olives before baking.

1 tbsp	olive oil	15 mL
2	large onions, thinly sliced	2
2	cloves garlic, minced	2
1 tsp	dried thyme, approx.	5 mL
1 tsp	granulated sugar	5 mL
½	box (18 oz/540 g) frozen puff pastry, thawed (1 sheet) (see Tips, left)	½
3 to 4 tbsp	prepared olive paste or spread (tapenade)	45 to 60 mL
	Salt and freshly ground black pepper	

1. In a large skillet, heat oil over medium-high heat until hot but not smoking. Reduce heat to medium. Add onions and cook, stirring often, for 10 minutes. Add garlic and 1 tsp (5 mL) thyme and continue cooking, stirring occasionally, until onions are soft. Sprinkle sugar over onions and continue cooking for 20 minutes more or until onions start to caramelize. Remove from heat.

2. Preheat oven to 450°F (230°C).

3. If necessary, on a lightly floured surface, roll out sheet of puff pastry into a 12-inch (30 cm) circle. Place on prepared baking sheet. Using a fork, prick holes all over pastry, leaving a 1-inch (2.5 cm) border. This is important so that the pastry can puff up while baking and form the outer edge of the tart.

4. Spread olive paste evenly over pricked base. Spread cooked onions over olive paste. Sprinkle a pinch of thyme over onions and season with salt and pepper to taste.

5. Bake in preheated oven for 20 to 30 minutes or until edge is nicely browned. Serve immediately.

Crab and Tomato Quiche

Serves 6

- Preheat oven to 375°F (190°C)
- 10-inch (25 cm) deep-dish glass pie plate or fluted metal quiche pan with removable bottom, greased

This recipe from Judith Finlayson is lighter than most quiches, making it a great brunch dish or a nice addition to a buffet. Add a tossed salad to enjoy it as a meal.

1	recipe Quiche Crust (see recipe, page 193), partially baked	1
1 tbsp	olive oil	15 mL
2	shallots, minced	2
8 oz	cooked crabmeat, chopped	250 g
1	can (14 oz/398 mL) diced tomatoes, including juice	1
3	eggs	3
1 cup	whipping (35%) cream	250 mL
¼ cup	finely chopped fresh parsley	50 mL
¼ cup	finely grated Parmesan cheese	50 mL

1. Prebake the crust according to recipe directions. Cook for the minimum amount of time, just until the crust is light golden. You do not want it to be raw but, on the other hand, you don't want it to be overcooked. Let cool in pan on a wire rack for 10 to 15 minutes. Remove weights and foil from crust. If bottom of crust still looks raw, return to oven for 5 to 7 minutes more (without weights). Let cool completely on rack before filling.

2. In a skillet, heat oil over medium heat for 30 seconds. Add shallots and cook, stirring, for 3 minutes or until softened. Add crabmeat and tomatoes with juice and bring to a boil. Set aside.

3. In a bowl, whisk together eggs. Add cream, whisking until smooth. Stir in crabmeat mixture and parsley. Pour into baked crust. Sprinkle Parmesan evenly over top. Bake in preheated oven for 35 minutes or until filling is set and top is nicely browned.

Cheddar, Potato and Thyme Deep-Dish Quiche

Serves 12

- Preheat oven to 375°F (190°C)
- 10-inch (25 cm) deep-dish fluted metal quiche pan with removable bottom, greased
- Rimmed baking sheet

We had friends over one night for dinner, and this quiche was one of their favorites. The combination of Cheddar, potatoes and thyme was rich with flavor and perfect when paired with a simple salad.

1	recipe Quiche Crust (see recipe, page 193), partially baked	1
4 or 5	small red-skinned potatoes (about 12 oz/375 g)	4 or 5
Pinch	salt	Pinch
	Freshly ground black pepper	
1 cup	shredded sharp Cheddar cheese	250 mL
1/3 cup	thinly sliced green onions	75 mL
4	eggs	4
2 cups	whipping (35%) cream	500 mL
1/2 tsp	salt	2 mL
1/4 tsp	dried rosemary, crushed	1 mL
1/4 tsp	dried thyme, crushed	1 mL
1/8 tsp	pimentón (smoked paprika), approx. (see Tip, page 167)	0.5 mL

1. Prebake the crust according to recipe directions. Cook for the minimum amount of time, just until the crust is light golden. You do not want it to be raw but, on the other hand, you don't want it to be overcooked. Let cool in pan on a wire rack for 10 to 15 minutes. Remove weights and foil from crust. If bottom of crust still looks raw, return to oven for 5 to 7 minutes more (without weights). Let cool completely on rack before filling.

2. In a large pot of boiling water, cook potatoes until tender. Drain and let cool. Peel and slice into rounds.

3. Scatter potatoes in bottom of prepared crust. Season with pinch of salt and pepper to taste. Sprinkle cheese and green onions over potatoes.

4. In a bowl, whisk together eggs. Add cream, whisking until smooth. Whisk in 1/2 tsp (2 mL) salt, rosemary, thyme, 1/8 tsp (0.5 mL) pimentón and a few grinds of black pepper. Place prepared crust on rimmed baking sheet and pour egg mixture over cheese, making sure it's evenly distributed. Garnish with pimentón.

5. Reduce oven temperature to 350°F (180°C). Bake for 1 hour and 10 minutes to 1 hour and 25 minutes or until filling is set, top is puffed and a knife inserted into center of quiche comes out clean.

6. Let quiche cool in pan on a wire rack. Place pan on a plate, tray or cardboard round, cover with plastic wrap and refrigerate overnight (see Tip, right). When ready to serve, carefully remove side of pan. You can leave quiche sitting on pan bottom. Slice and serve.

Tip

It's very important for the quiche to be chilled overnight so that it sets up correctly and develops the right texture. If you want to serve the quiche warm or at room temperature, reheat it after chilling.

Chicken Pot Pie with Mushrooms and Leeks

Serves 6

- Preheat oven to 375°F (190°C)
- 10-inch (25 cm) deep-dish glass pie plate or baking dish
- Rimmed baking sheet

Another traditional Sunday dinner, this is comfort food par excellence. But don't think you have to wait for Sunday dinner to prepare it; it's wonderful any day of the week. This rich and savory recipe is from cookbook author Judith Finlayson.

Tip

Leeks can be quite gritty, so be sure to clean them thoroughly before using. Fill a basin full of lukewarm water. Split leeks in half lengthwise and submerge in water, swishing them around to remove all traces of dirt. Transfer to a colander and rinse under cold water. Drain well.

¼ cup	all-purpose flour	50 mL
¼ tsp	cayenne pepper	1 mL
1 lb	skinless boneless chicken breasts, cut into ½-inch (1 cm) cubes	500 g
1 tbsp	oil	15 mL
2 tbsp	butter	25 mL
3	leeks, white part with just a hint of green, thinly sliced (see Tip, left)	3
2	stalks celery, diced	2
2	carrots, peeled and diced	2
8 oz	mushrooms, sliced	250 g
2	cloves garlic, minced	2
2 tsp	dried tarragon	10 mL
½ cup	dry white wine (see Tip, right)	125 mL
1 cup	chicken stock	250 mL
½ cup	whipping (35%) cream	125 mL
¼ cup	finely chopped fresh parsley	50 mL
½	box (18 oz/540 g) frozen puff pastry, thawed (1 sheet) (see Tips, page 154)	½
1	egg yolk	1

1. On a plate or in a plastic bag, combine flour and cayenne. Add chicken and dredge or toss until well coated. Set any excess flour mixture aside.

2. In a skillet, heat oil over medium heat for 30 seconds. Add chicken, in batches, and cook, stirring, for 3 minutes per batch or until lightly browned. (You do not want it to be cooked through.) Remove from pan and set aside.

3. Add butter to pan and reduce heat to low. Add leeks, celery, carrots and mushrooms and stir well. Cover and cook on low for 8 minutes or until leeks are softened. Increase heat to medium. Add garlic and tarragon and stir well. Sprinkle excess flour mixture over vegetables and cook, stirring, for 1 minute. Add wine and bring to a boil. Cook for 3 minutes or until liquid reduces by half. Return chicken to pan. Add chicken stock and cream and cook, stirring, for 2 minutes or until mixture thickens slightly. Stir in parsley and transfer mixture to pie plate.

4. On a lightly floured surface, roll out pastry into a circle about 11 inches (27.5 cm) in diameter and place over pie. Tuck overhang under the edge and flute. Place pie plate on baking sheet.

5. In a small bowl, beat egg yolk with 1 tsp (5 mL) water. Brush crust with egg yolk mixture and pierce with a sharp knife to make several steam vents. Bake in preheated oven for 35 minutes or until top is golden brown.

Tip

The wine lends a pleasant sharpness to the sauce, but if you prefer, substitute ½ cup (125 mL) additional chicken stock.

Coulibiac

Serves 6

- Preheat oven to 375°F (190°C)
- 6 ramekins or small pie plates (about 3½ inches/8.5 cm), lightly greased

The use of salmon places this version of the classic Russian pie firmly in the French tradition. Leeks stand in for traditional shallots, and the use of dill takes it back to its Russian roots. While very tasty, this is quite rich, particularly with the accompanying sauce, so all you'll need is a steamed vegetable, such as green beans or carrots, perhaps followed by a simple green salad to complete the meal. This recipe is from Judith Finlayson.

¾ cup	plain full-fat yogurt	175 mL
¼ cup	whipping (35%) cream	50 mL
¾ cup	long-grain rice	175 mL
2	hard-boiled eggs, chopped	2
	Finely grated zest and juice of 1 lemon	
1 tbsp	butter	15 mL
1 tbsp	olive oil	15 mL
1	large leek (8 oz/250 g), white part only, thinly sliced	1
8 oz	white mushrooms, trimmed and sliced	250 g
1 tbsp	all-purpose flour	15 mL
¼ tsp	cayenne pepper (see Tip, right)	1 mL
	Salt	
¼ cup	finely chopped dill	50 mL
1½	sheets frozen puff pastry (about 12 oz/375 g), thawed	1½
1¼ lbs	salmon fillet, skin removed and cut into 6 equal pieces	625 g
1	egg yolk, beaten	1

DILL SAUCE

½ cup	yogurt mixture (see Step 1)	125 mL
¼ cup	finely chopped fresh dill	50 mL
¼ cup	mayonnaise	50 mL
2 tbsp	drained capers	25 mL
	Salt and freshly ground black pepper	

1. In a measuring cup, combine yogurt and whipping cream. Stir well and refrigerate until ready to use.

2. Cook rice according to package directions or your favorite method. Remove from heat and let cool slightly. Stir in chopped eggs, lemon zest and juice, and ½ cup (125 mL) of the reserved yogurt mixture. Refrigerate remainder of yogurt mixture for Dill Sauce.

3. Meanwhile, in a skillet, melt butter with oil over medium heat. Add leek and mushrooms and cook, stirring, for 6 minutes or until leeks are softened and mushrooms begin to brown. Sprinkle with flour, cayenne and salt to taste and cook, stirring, for 1 minute. Remove from heat and stir in dill. Set aside.

4. Roll out pastry between 2 pieces of waxed or parchment paper to ¼-inch (0.5 cm) thickness. Cut to just fit or slightly larger than tops of ramekins.

5. *Assembly:* Divide rice mixture among ramekins and spread evenly over bottom. Repeat with mushroom mixture. Lay salmon over top. Cover with pastry and flute to fit top of ramekin. With a sharp knife, cut 3 slits in top of each pie. Brush crusts with egg yolk and bake in preheated oven for 35 minutes or until tops are golden.

6. *Dill Sauce:* Meanwhile, in a sauceboat, combine reserved yogurt mixture, dill, mayonnaise and capers. Stir well. Season with salt and pepper to taste and refrigerate until ready to use. Serve alongside hot pies.

Tip

This quantity of cayenne lends a barely perceptible hint of heat to the mixture. Use more if you're a heat seeker. I like to use a larger quantity (about 1 tsp/5 mL) of Aleppo pepper, a medium-heat chili powder from Turkey that is rich and slightly bitter. If you have access to some, give it a try.

Deep-Dish Quiche with Spinach, Feta and Dill

Serves 8

- Preheat oven to 375°F (190°C)
- 10-inch (25 cm) deep-dish fluted metal quiche pan with removable bottom, greased
- Rimmed baking sheet

I love spinach and I love quiche — combined, they equal true love. My stepmother, Ellen, used to make spinach quiche for special occasions when we were growing up, and her quiche was always a favorite of mine. I love it as much now as I did then, especially with a little dill and feta thrown in for good measure.

1	recipe Quiche Crust (see recipe, page 193), partially baked	1
1 cup	crumbled feta cheese	250 mL
⅓ cup	thinly sliced green onions	75 mL
⅓ cup	diced roasted red or yellow peppers	75 mL
	Salt and freshly ground black pepper	
4	eggs	4
2 cups	whipping (35%) cream	500 mL
½ tsp	each salt and dried dillweed	2 mL
	Freshly ground black pepper	
1	bag (1 lb/500 g) frozen chopped spinach, thawed and well drained	1

1. Prebake the crust according to recipe directions. Cook for the minimum amount of time, just until the crust is light golden. You do not want it to be raw but, on the other hand, you don't want it to be overcooked. Let cool in pan on a wire rack for 10 to 15 minutes. Remove weights and foil from crust. If bottom of crust still looks raw, return to oven for 5 to 7 minutes more (without weights). Let cool completely on rack before filling.

2. Scatter feta, green onions and peppers in bottom of crust. Season with salt and pepper to taste.

3. In a large bowl, whisk together eggs. Add cream, whisking until smooth. Add ½ tsp (2 mL) salt, dill and a few grinds of black pepper, whisking well. Add spinach, whisking until mixed.

4. Reduce oven temperature to 350°F (180°C). Place prepared crust on baking sheet and pour egg mixture over peppers, making sure it's evenly distributed. Bake in preheated oven for 1 hour and 10 minutes to 1 hour and 20 minutes or until filling is set, top is puffed and a knife inserted into center of quiche comes out clean.

5. Let quiche cool on rack. Place pan on a plate, cover with plastic wrap and refrigerate overnight. When ready to serve, carefully remove side of pan. You can leave quiche sitting on pan bottom. Slice and serve.

Jamaican Beef Patty Pie

Serves 6

- Preheat oven to 375°F (190°C)
- 9-inch (23 cm) glass pie plate

If you enjoy the spicy flavor of Jamaican beef patties, you'll love this robust pie with a nutritious whole wheat crust from Judith Finlayson.

Variation

Authentic Jamaican-Style Meat Patties: Double the quantity of crust and, instead of rolling out as for pie crust, divide the dough into 24 balls. Roll each ball into a 4-inch (10 cm) round. Place about 3 tbsp (45 mL) filling in the center and brush edges with beaten egg. Fold over into a half-moon shape and crimp edge with a fork. Repeat until all dough is used up. In a small bowl, beat 2 eggs with 2 tsp (10 mL) water. Brush tops of patties with mixture. Bake in preheated oven on greased rimmed baking sheets for 35 minutes or until golden brown.

1 tbsp	vegetable oil	15 mL
1 lb	lean ground beef	500 g
1	onion, finely chopped	1
4	cloves garlic, minced	4
1 tbsp	minced gingerroot	15 mL
1	habañero or Scotch bonnet pepper, seeded and minced	1
2 tsp	curry powder	10 mL
1 tbsp	tomato paste	15 mL
1 cup	cooked green peas	250 mL
	Salt and freshly ground black pepper	
1	recipe Whole Wheat Oil Pastry Dough (see Variation, page 186)	1
1	egg yolk	1

1. In a skillet, heat oil over medium heat for 30 seconds. Add ground beef and onion and cook, stirring, for 5 minutes or until beef is no longer pink. Add garlic, ginger, habañero pepper and curry powder and cook, stirring, for 1 minute. Stir in tomato paste and green peas. Season with salt and pepper to taste. Remove from heat. Let cool.

2. Divide pastry into 2 pieces, one slightly larger than the other. On a lightly floured surface, roll out one piece into a 12-inch (30 cm) circle large enough to fit pie plate, dusting work surface and dough as necessary to keep the dough from sticking (or roll between 2 pieces of waxed or parchment paper). Press dough into prepared pie plate. Place pie plate in freezer or refrigerator for 15 to 20 minutes to chill. Roll out remaining dough for top crust and set aside at room temperature on sheet of parchment paper. Transfer filling to prepared bottom crust. Lightly brush edge with a little water. Place top crust over filling, trimming and fluting edge.

3. In a small bowl, mix egg yolk with 1 tsp (5 mL) water. Brush over top crust. Using a fork, prick holes all over pastry. Bake in preheated oven for 35 minutes or until golden brown. Let stand for 10 minutes before serving.

Quebec-Style Salmon Pie

Serves 6

- Preheat oven to 375°F (190°C)
- 9-inch (23 cm) glass pie plate

This is another delicious recipe from Judith Finlayson. It's a variation on tourtière, a Quebec meat pie, but made with salmon. It was inspired by a recipe in Julian Armstrong's book, *A Taste of Quebec*. Use the All-Purpose Buttery Pastry Dough with added pepper and made with whole wheat flour (see Tips, below). It's almost a meal in itself. Steamed green beans or broccoli are all you need to complete the meal.

Tips

When making this pie, be sure to omit the sugar from the crust recipe.

Add 1 tsp (5 mL) freshly ground black pepper to the flour for the crust. This adds a pleasant zing to the pie.

For added robustness, when making the crust, substitute up to 1½ cups (375 mL) whole wheat pastry flour for the all-purpose.

1	recipe All-Purpose Buttery Pastry Dough, chilled (see recipe, page 179, and Tips, left)	1
2	potatoes (about 8 oz/250 g total)	2
2 tbsp	butter	25 mL
1	onion, finely chopped	1
2 tsp	herbes de Provence	10 mL
1 tsp	celery seed	5 mL
¼ tsp	cayenne pepper, optional (see Tip, right)	1 mL
	Salt and freshly ground black pepper	
1 lb	salmon fillets, skin removed and chopped into bite-size pieces	500 g
1¼ cups	milk	300 mL
2 tbsp	finely chopped fresh parsley	25 mL
1	egg yolk	1

1. Divide pastry dough into 2 pieces, one slightly larger than the other. On a lightly floured surface, roll out larger piece of dough into a circle large enough to fit pie plate, dusting work surface and dough as necessary to keep the dough from sticking (or roll between 2 pieces of waxed or parchment paper). Press dough into prepared pie plate. Place pie plate in freezer or refrigerator for 15 to 20 minutes to chill while you prepare the filling. Roll out remaining dough for top crust and set aside at room temperature on sheet of parchment paper.

2. In a pot of boiling water, cook unpeeled potatoes until barely tender. Drain, rinse well under cold running water and set aside until cool enough to handle. Peel off skins. Using a box grater, grate coarsely and set aside.

3. In a skillet, melt butter over medium heat. Add onion and cook, stirring, for 3 minutes or until softened. Add herbes de Provence, celery seed, cayenne, if using, and salt and pepper to taste. Cook, stirring, for 1 minute. Remove from heat. Stir in salmon, milk, parsley and reserved potatoes.

4. Transfer salmon mixture to prepared bottom crust. Lightly brush edge with a little water. Place top crust over filling, trimming and fluting edge.

5. In a small bowl, beat egg yolk with 1 tsp (5 mL) water. Brush crust with mixture and pierce with a sharp knife to make several steam vents. Bake in preheated oven for 50 minutes or until crust is nicely browned.

Tip

The cayenne adds a pleasant nip to the salmon mixture, but if you're heat-averse, omit it.

Quiche Lorraine

Serves 6

- Preheat oven to 375°F (190°C)
- 10-inch (25 cm) deep-dish pie plate or fluted metal quiche pan with removable bottom, greased

Quiche Lorraine is considered a classic, and for good reason — it's rich, delicious and easy to make. It's perfect for a buffet, brunch or dinner. This recipe is from cookbook author Judith Finlayson.

Tips

Using this quantity of eggs produces a slightly soft quiche, which some people prefer. If you like a firmer version, add 1 more egg to the mixture.

The sprinkling of Parmesan, while not traditional, does produce a nicely browned top.

1	recipe Quiche Crust (see recipe, page 193), partially baked	1
6 oz	chunk smoked bacon, trimmed of rind and diced into ¼-inch (0.5 cm) pieces	175 g
1 tbsp	butter	15 mL
2 tbsp	minced onion	25 mL
4	eggs, beaten (see Tips, left)	4
2 cups	table (18%) cream	500 mL
4 oz	Gruyère cheese, diced	125 g
	Salt and freshly ground black pepper	
	Freshly grated nutmeg	
2 tbsp	freshly grated Parmesan cheese, optional	25 mL

1. Prebake the crust according to recipe directions. Cook for the minimum amount of time, just until the crust is light golden. You do not want it to be raw, but on the other hand, you don't want it to be overcooked.

2. In a pot of boiling water, blanch bacon for 5 minutes. Drain and pat dry.

3. In a skillet, melt butter over medium heat. Add blanched bacon and onion and cook, stirring, until bacon is lightly browned. Transfer to a strainer placed over a bowl and allow fat to drain off, pressing with a spoon to extract as much as possible. Arrange bacon mixture over bottom of cooked crust.

4. In a bowl, whisk together eggs. Add cream, whisking until smooth. Stir in cheese. Season with salt and pepper, to taste, and nutmeg. Pour into crust over bacon mixture. Sprinkle with Parmesan, if using. Bake in preheated oven for 45 minutes or until filling is set and top is lightly browned.

Corn, Green Onion and Cheddar Quiche

Serves 8

- Preheat oven to 350°F (180°C)
- 9-inch (23 cm) deep-dish glass pie plate, greased
- Rimmed baking sheet

This quiche was a favorite that my husband and I prepared regularly at our bakery and catering company in Boise, Idaho. It was very popular for breakfast and brunch, but it's just as wonderful served with soup or salad for dinner. The Southwestern flavors are wonderful together.

Tip

Look for smoked paprika online and in well-stocked grocery and gourmet stores. This spice will change your life. It's that good!

1	recipe Small-Batch All-Purpose Buttery Pastry Dough, chilled (see Variation, page 180), unbaked	1
1½ cups	frozen corn kernels, thawed and drained	375 mL
3	green onions, thinly sliced	3
1 cup	lightly packed shredded pepper Jack cheese	250 mL
¼ tsp	salt, approx.	1 mL
3	eggs	3
1½ cups	whipping (35%) cream	375 mL
	Freshly ground black pepper	
1 tsp	Dijon mustard	5 mL
¼ tsp	pimentón (smoked paprika) (see Tip, left)	1 mL

1. On a lightly floured surface, roll out dough into a circle large enough to fit pie plate, dusting work surface and dough as necessary to keep the dough from sticking (or roll between 2 pieces of waxed or parchment paper). Press dough into prepared pie plate. Place pie plate in freezer or refrigerator for 15 to 20 minutes to chill while you prepare the filling. Evenly scatter corn, green onions and cheese in bottom of crust. Sprinkle with a pinch of salt.

2. In a large bowl, whisk together eggs. Add cream, whisking until smooth. Add ¼ tsp (1 mL) salt, a few grinds of black pepper, mustard and pimentón, whisking well.

3. Place prepared crust on baking sheet and pour egg mixture over filling, making sure it's evenly distributed. Bake quiche in preheated oven for 55 minutes or until filling is set, top is puffed and a knife inserted into center of quiche comes out clean.

4. Let quiche cool in pan on a wire rack, cover with plastic wrap and refrigerate overnight (see Tip, page 157).

Roasted Pepper and Artichoke Quiche

Serves 8

- Preheat oven to 350°F (180°C)
- 9-inch (23 cm) deep-dish glass pie plate, greased
- Rimmed baking sheet

When my husband and I had our bakery, quiche was an extremely popular item. We were constantly striving to come up with new combinations, although almost everything tastes wonderful when combined with cheese and cream. This recipe is very quick to prepare if you use a frozen pie shell.

Tips

For the artichokes, you'll need about half of a 13-oz (370 mL) can.

For the roasted red peppers, you'll need about half of a 12-oz (340 mL) jar.

1	9-inch (23 cm) store-bought frozen deep-dish pie crust or Small-Batch All-Purpose Buttery Pastry Dough, chilled (see Variation, page 180)	1
¾ cup	shredded 4-cheese blend	175 mL
½ cup	packed canned drained artichoke hearts, patted dry	125 mL
½ cup	drained jarred roasted bell peppers, patted dry	125 mL
3	eggs	3
1½ cups	whipping (35%) cream	375 mL
½ tsp	salt, approx.	2 mL
2	cloves garlic, minced	2
	Freshly ground black pepper	

1. If using pastry dough, on a lightly floured surface, roll out dough into a circle large enough to fit pie plate, dusting work surface and dough as necessary to keep the dough from sticking (or roll between 2 pieces of waxed or parchment paper). Press dough into prepared pie plate. Place pie plate in freezer or refrigerator for 15 to 20 minutes to chill.

2. Scatter cheese in bottom of crust. Coarsely chop artichoke hearts and peppers and sprinkle them evenly over cheese. Sprinkle with a pinch of salt.

3. In a bowl, whisk together eggs. Add cream, whisking until smooth. Add ½ tsp (2 mL) salt, garlic and a few grinds of black pepper, whisking well.

4. Place prepared crust on a baking sheet and pour egg mixture over peppers, making sure it's evenly distributed. Bake in preheated oven for 55 minutes or until filling is set, top is puffed and a knife inserted into center of quiche comes out clean.

5. Let quiche cool in pan on a wire rack, cover with plastic wrap and refrigerate overnight (see Tip, page 157).

Roasted Tomato, Pesto and Green Bean Tart

Serves 4

- Preheat oven to 450°F (230°C)
- Baking sheet, lined with parchment paper

I came up with this tart idea one afternoon when I needed to make a quick and easy dinner and had some beautiful green beans and tomatoes from the farmer's market. I flipped through Nadine Abensur's cookbook *Cranks Fast Food* and loved the idea of using frozen puff pastry as the base for the tart. The combination of flavors in this tart is absolutely delicious.

Tip

This tart is best served within 15 to 20 minutes of baking.

Variation

Substitute sun-dried tomato pesto for the basil pesto.

5 oz	small thin green beans, such as haricots verts, ends trimmed	150 g
2	cloves garlic, minced, divided	2
1 tbsp	olive oil, divided	15 mL
	Salt and freshly ground black pepper	
1 cup	small grape or cherry tomatoes	250 mL
½	box (18 oz/540 g) frozen puff pastry, thawed (1 sheet) (see Tips, page 170)	½
¼ cup	store-bought basil pesto	50 mL

1. In a large pot of boiling salted water, cook green beans until just tender to the bite. Drain beans in a colander and place in a bowl of ice water until beans are cool. Remove from water and place on paper towels to dry.

2. In a bowl, combine green beans, half of the minced garlic, ½ tbsp (7 mL) olive oil and salt and pepper to taste. Toss to coat beans. In another bowl, gently toss tomatoes with remaining garlic, remaining olive oil, and salt and pepper to taste.

3. If necessary, on a lightly floured surface, roll out pastry into a 12-inch (30 cm) circle. Place on prepared baking sheet. Using a fork, prick holes all over pastry, leaving a 1-inch (2.5 cm) edge. This is important so that the pastry can puff up while baking and form the outer edge of the tart.

4. Spread pesto evenly over pricked base. Spread half of the green bean mixture over pesto. Place tomatoes over green beans, packing them in as much as you can.

5. Bake in preheated oven for 20 minutes or until tomatoes have begun blistering and bursting. Carefully remove tart from oven and top with remaining green beans. Return to oven and continue baking for 5 to 10 minutes more or until edges are nicely browned. Remove tart from oven, sprinkle with a pinch of salt and freshly ground pepper and serve.

Steak and Mushroom Pie

Serves 6

- Preheat oven to 375°F (190°C)
- 10-inch (25 cm) deep-dish glass pie plate or baking dish
- Rimmed baking sheet

This pie from Judith Finlayson is a real favorite for a chilly day. Judith likes to serve it for Sunday dinner with a tossed green salad or with a bowl of steaming garlic mashed potatoes.

Tips

Use cremini mushrooms in this pie, as they have a robust flavor that works well with the other ingredients.

If you happen to have fresh thyme, substitute it for the dried version. Use 1 tbsp (15 mL) leaves and add along with the parsley.

If you have a smaller package of puff pastry, the pastry may be thinner but will still work.

¼ cup	all-purpose flour	50 mL
1 tsp	salt	5 mL
1 tsp	cracked black peppercorns, divided	5 mL
¼ tsp	cayenne pepper	1 mL
1½ lbs	beef sirloin, cubed (½-inch/1 cm cubes)	750 g
2 tbsp	butter, divided	25 mL
1 tbsp	olive oil, approx.	15 mL
1 lb	sliced mushrooms (see Tips, left)	500 g
½ cup	diced shallots	125 mL
½ tsp	dried thyme leaves (see Tips, left)	2 mL
1 tbsp	brandy or cognac, optional	15 mL
2 cups	beef stock	500 mL
2 tbsp	finely chopped fresh parsley	25 mL
1 tbsp	Worcestershire sauce	15 mL
½	box (18 oz/540 g) frozen puff pastry, thawed (1 sheet) (see Tips, left)	½
1	egg yolk	1

1. In a resealable plastic bag, combine flour, salt, ½ tsp (2 mL) of the peppercorns and cayenne. Add beef and toss until well coated. Reserve excess flour mixture and set aside.

2. In a skillet, heat 1 tbsp (15 mL) of the butter and oil over medium-high heat for 30 seconds. Add beef, in batches, and cook, stirring, for 4 minutes per batch or just until browned, adding more oil if necessary. Transfer to a plate. Add remaining butter to pan and add mushrooms. Cook, stirring, for 5 minutes or until mushrooms start to brown. Remove with a slotted spoon and set aside.

3. Add shallots to pan, adding a bit more oil if necessary, and cook, stirring, for 5 minutes or just until they begin to turn golden. Add thyme and remaining ½ tsp (2 mL) peppercorns and cook, stirring, for 1 minute. Add reserved flour mixture and cook, stirring, for 1 minute. Add brandy, if using, and cook until it evaporates. Add stock and bring to a boil, scraping up bits stuck to pan. Return beef and mushrooms to pan and stir well. Remove from heat and stir in parsley and Worcestershire sauce. Transfer to pie plate.

4. On a lightly floured surface, roll out pastry into a circle about 11 inches (27.5 cm) in diameter and place over pie. Tuck overhang under the edge and flute. Place pie on baking sheet.

5. In a small bowl, beat egg yolk with 1 tsp (5 mL) water. Brush pastry with mixture and, using a sharp knife, cut 3 vents in the top to allow steam to escape. Bake in preheated oven for 35 minutes or until mixture is hot and bubbling and top is golden brown.

Tip
You can make the filling ahead and refrigerate it for up to 2 days. Add about 10 minutes to the baking time and, if necessary, cover the top of the pie with foil if it is browning too much.

Tourtière

Serves 6

- 10-inch (25 cm) deep-dish pie plate

This meat pie is a tradition in Quebec, where it is often served on Christmas Eve. It is rich and dense, and is excellent served with a chutney or relish. This recipe is from cookbook author Judith Finlayson, who always serves it on Christmas Eve accompanied by a salad of baby greens and preceded by champagne and oysters.

CRUST

2½ cups	all-purpose flour	625 mL
1 tbsp	fresh thyme leaves or 1 tsp (5 mL) dried	15 mL
½ tsp	salt	2 mL
½ cup	non-hydrogenated shortening, cubed	125 mL
¼ cup	cold butter, cut into small pieces	50 mL
¼ cup	ice water	50 mL

FILLING

2	potatoes	2
4 oz	salt pork, diced	125 g
3	onions, finely chopped	3
12 oz	ground pork	375 g
12 oz	ground beef	375 g
2	cloves garlic, minced	2
1 tbsp	minced gingerroot	15 mL
1 tsp	ground cinnamon	5 mL
½ tsp	cracked black peppercorns	2 mL
1	can (14 oz/398 mL) diced tomatoes, drained	1
	Chutney or relish	

1. *Crust:* In a food processor, pulse together flour, thyme and salt to blend. Add shortening and butter and pulse until mixture resembles large-flake oatmeal. Sprinkle ice water over top and pulse just to blend. Transfer dough to a clean surface and knead well until dough holds together. Divide pastry dough into 2 pieces, one slightly larger than the other. Shape each into a ball, press flat into a disk, wrap in plastic and refrigerate for 1 hour.

2. *Filling:* In a large pot of boiling water, cook unpeeled potatoes until barely tender. Drain, rinse well under cold water and set aside until cool enough to handle. Peel off skins. Using a box grater, grate coarsely and set aside.

3. Meanwhile, in a large skillet over medium-high heat, cook salt pork, stirring, for 7 minutes or until it browns and renders its fat. Add onions, pork and beef and cook, stirring, for 5 minutes or until onions are softened and meat is browned. Add garlic, ginger, cinnamon and peppercorns and stir well. Stir in tomatoes and grated potatoes. Reduce heat to low and simmer for 45 minutes or until mixture is cooked and flavors have melded. Let cool.

4. On a lightly floured surface, roll out larger piece of dough into a circle large enough to fit pie plate, dusting work surface and dough as necessary to keep the dough from sticking (or roll between 2 pieces of waxed or parchment paper). Press dough into prepared pie plate. Place pie plate in freezer or refrigerator for 15 to 20 minutes to chill. Roll out remaining dough for top crust and set aside at room temperature on sheet of parchment paper.

5. Preheat oven to 425°F (220°C). Transfer meat mixture to prepared bottom crust. Lightly brush edge with a little water. Place top crust over filling, trimming and fluting edge. Pierce with a sharp knife to make several steam vents.

6. Bake in preheated oven for 15 minutes. Reduce heat to 350°F (180°C) and bake for 30 minutes more or until crust is golden. Let cool for about 20 minutes before serving. Serve with relish or chutney.

Tip
You can make the pie and freeze it for up to 1 month before baking. Thaw in the refrigerator and bake as directed.

Sun-Dried Tomato and Feta Quiche

Serves 8

- Preheat oven to 350°F (180°C)
- 9-inch (23 cm) deep-dish glass pie plate, greased
- Rimmed baking sheet

When you want to make a quiche, but don't want to spend hours in the kitchen preparing it, this is a perfect recipe. You can use a frozen prepared shell and simply layer in the rest of your ingredients.

1	9-inch (23 cm) store-bought frozen pie crust or Small-Batch All-Purpose Buttery Pastry Dough, chilled (see Variation, page 180)	1
6 oz	feta cheese, crumbled (about 1 rounded cup/250 mL)	175 g
2	green onions, thinly sliced	2
½ cup	diced oil-packed sun-dried tomatoes, drained and patted dry	125 mL
2 tbsp	pine nuts, lightly toasted	25 mL
½ tsp	salt, approx.	2 mL
3	eggs	3
1½ cups	whipping (35%) cream	375 mL
	Freshly ground black pepper	

1. If using pastry dough, on a lightly floured surface, roll out dough into a circle large enough to fit pie plate, dusting work surface and dough as necessary to keep the dough from sticking (or roll between 2 pieces of waxed or parchment paper). Press dough into prepared pie plate. Place pie plate in freezer or refrigerator for 15 to 20 minutes to chill.

2. Scatter cheese in bottom of crust. Sprinkle green onions, tomatoes and pine nuts evenly over cheese. Sprinkle with a pinch of salt.

3. In a bowl, whisk together eggs. Add cream, whisking until smooth. Add ½ tsp (2 mL) salt and a few grinds of black pepper, whisking well.

4. Place pie plate on baking sheet and pour egg mixture over tomatoes, making sure it's evenly distributed. Bake in preheated oven for 55 minutes or until filling is set, top is puffed and a knife inserted into center of quiche comes out clean.

5. Let quiche cool in pan on a wire rack, cover with plastic wrap and refrigerate overnight (see Tip, page 157).

Vegetarian Pot Pie with Biscuit Top

Serves 8

- Preheat oven to 400°F (200°F)
- 12-inch (30 cm) cast-iron skillet or 10-inch (25 cm) deep-dish glass or ceramic plate, greased

My kids love pot pie so much that they will devour the entire dish. Fortunately, pot pies aren't hard to throw together and are even easier with a biscuit top. Besides being scrumptious, this version is lower in fat than a traditional pot pie.

Tips

It's important to make sure that the filling is hot when assembling the pot pie, because otherwise the biscuit topping tends to be a little raw underneath.

Vegetarian chicken-style strips are often found in the freezer section or in the produce section with the veggie burgers.

Variation

Substitute a pastry or puff pastry crust for the biscuit dough.

5	small red-skinned potatoes (about 1 lb/500 g)	5
1	bag (10 oz/300 g) frozen broccoli florets, thawed, chopped if large (about 3 cups/750 mL)	1
2 cups	refrigerated or frozen vegetarian chicken-style strips, thawed (and cooked if necessary) (see Tips, left) or an additional 2 cups (500 mL) vegetables or seitan	500 mL
¾ cup	frozen peas, thawed	175 mL
1	recipe Vegetarian Gravy (see recipe, page 176)	1
1 tbsp	dry sherry, optional	15 mL
2	cloves garlic, minced	2
½ tsp	dried thyme leaves	2 mL
½ tsp	dried sage, crumbled	2 mL
	Salt and freshly ground pepper	
1	recipe Buttermilk Biscuit Crust made with 1¼ cups (300 mL) buttermilk (see recipe, page 196)	1

1. In a large pot of boiling water, cook potatoes for 20 to 25 minutes or until tender. Drain and let cool to the touch. Peel potatoes and cut into pieces.

2. In a large bowl, combine potatoes, broccoli, vegetarian chicken, peas and hot gravy. Add sherry, garlic, thyme, sage, and salt and pepper to taste. You want the mixture to be hot. If it's not, heat in microwave oven for 2 minutes or until hot to the touch.

3. Scoop vegetable mixture into skillet or dish, smoothing top. Drop scoops of biscuit dough over filling, covering pie (it's okay if not every spot of filling is covered). Bake in preheated oven for 35 to 45 minutes or until biscuit topping is golden brown and cooked through.

Vegetarian Gravy

Makes about 2½ cups (625 mL)

This is a delicious gravy for savory pies. Although chickpea flour may seem like an odd ingredient, it's absolutely delicious and adds great flavor and some nutrition, as well.

¼ cup	all-purpose flour	50 mL
¼ cup	chickpea flour (garbanzo bean flour)	50 mL
1	large vegetable bouillon cube, crumbled	1
¼ cup	milk or plain unsweetened soy milk, optional	50 mL
1 tsp	dried parsley	5 mL
	Salt and freshly ground pepper	
Pinch	white pepper, optional	Pinch

> **Tip**
> Although the milk is optional, is does add a nice creaminess to the gravy.
>
> **Variation**
> Add 1 tsp (5 mL) dried dill to the gravy.

1. In a saucepan over medium heat, combine all-purpose and chickpea flours and toast just until fragrant. Remove saucepan from heat. Whisk in 2½ cups (625 mL) water. Using an immersion blender or transferring to an upright blender, blend mixture until smooth. Add bouillon cube and blend until smooth.

2. Return to saucepan, if necessary. Return saucepan to medium heat. Whisk in milk, if using, and parsley, whisking until smooth. Season with salt and black pepper to taste, and white pepper, if using. Reduce heat and boil gently, whisking constantly, for 10 minutes or until mixture is very thick and bubbling. Use gravy in recipes as needed.

Crusts

To roll out dough

Double-crust pie: On a lightly floured surface, roll out larger piece of dough into a circle large enough to fit pie plate, dusting work surface and dough as necessary to keep the dough from sticking (or roll between 2 pieces of waxed or parchment paper). Press dough into prepared pie plate. Place pie plate in freezer for 1 hour to chill while you prepare the filling. Roll out remaining dough for top crust and set aside at room temperature on sheet of parchment paper until ready to use.

Single-crust pie: Roll out dough as above. Press pastry into a 9-inch (23 cm) glass pie plate, trimming dough even along edge, leaving about a ½-inch (1 cm) overhang. Pinch to form a decorative edge. Prick the prepared crust in several places with a fork. Place pie plate in freezer or refrigerator for up to 1 hour until cold and firm.

To partially bake crust

Preheat oven to 375°F (190°C). Line the chilled crust with parchment paper or foil and a layer of dried beans or pie weights to weigh it down. Bake for 20 to 25 minutes or until the shell is golden brown and the bottom is no longer moist. Keep an eye on your shell as it's baking (preferably without opening the oven too much) and look for visual signs of doneness. If you use a glass pie plate, you can look at the bottom to check that all of the moisture has baked out of the crust. Proceed with filling according to recipe directions.

When prebaking the crust, you can use dried beans, rice or a double layer of foil, smoothly pressed onto bottom and up side of crust, in place of commercial pie weights. The added weight prevents air bubbles from forming in the crust and supports the side of the crust as it bakes.

To fully prebake the crust

Preheat oven to 375°F (190°C). Line the chilled crust with parchment paper or foil and a layer of dried beans or pie weights to weigh it down. Bake for 20 to 25 minutes or until the shell is golden brown and the bottom is no longer moist. If you use a glass pie plate, you can look at the bottom to check that all of the moisture has baked out of the crust. Remove paper and weights. Return crust to oven and bake for 5 minutes more or just until lightly browned.

Hand-mix method for dough

Any of the recipes that use a food processor can be done the old-fashioned way, by hand. Here is the basic technique:

In a large bowl, combine dry ingredients. Using a pastry blender or 2 knives, cut butter and/or shortening (as called for) into flour mixture. Add liquid ingredients, mixing with a fork just until it comes together and forms a mass. Gather dough into a ball or 2 balls as directed.

All-Purpose Buttery Pastry Dough

Makes enough dough for one 9-inch (23 cm) double-crust pie or two 9-inch (23 cm) single-crust pies

- One or two 9-inch (23 cm) glass pie plates, greased

This recipe is a larger version of the Small-Batch All-Purpose Buttery Pastry Dough (see recipe, page 180). When you want to make a double-crust pie or lots of turnovers, this is the recipe for you. It's easy to make, buttery and delicious!

3 cups	all-purpose flour	750 mL
¼ cup	granulated sugar	50 mL
½ tsp	salt	2 mL
1 cup	cold butter, cut into small pieces	250 mL
6 to 8 tbsp	ice water	90 to 120 mL

1. In a food processor fitted with metal blade, pulse flour, sugar and salt until mixed. Add butter, pulsing until mixture resembles coarse meal.

2. Add 6 tbsp (90 mL) ice water to flour mixture, pulsing until moist clumps form, stopping to test the dough with fingertips to see if it's moist enough to hold together. If dough is too dry, add 1 to 2 tbsp (15 to 25 mL) more ice water as needed. Remove blade and divide dough into 2 pieces, one slightly larger than the other if making a double-crust pie or equal-sized for 2 single-crust pies, flattening each into a disk. Wrap in plastic and refrigerate for 15 to 20 minutes.

3. For rolling and prebaking instructions, see page 178.

Tip

To chill butter, cut into pieces with a knife and place on a small plate. Place in freezer for 15 minutes or until very cold. Use immediately from freezer in recipe.

Variations

Savory Crust: Omit the sugar in this recipe and use it to make the pies in the Savory Pies & Tarts chapter.

Vegan-Friendly Crust: Substitute vegan margarine for the butter. Do not use a lower-fat variety. A brand I like is Earth Balance.

Small-Batch All-Purpose Buttery Pastry Dough

Makes enough dough for one 9-inch (23 cm) single-crust pie

- 9-inch (23 cm) pie plate, greased

This recipe is adapted from a pie crust in the classic *Moosewood Cookbook*. It is rich and flaky and delish! It's one of my husband's favorites, and the one that he reaches for when making pastries.

Tip

To chill butter, cut into pieces with a knife and place on a small plate. Place in freezer for 15 minutes or until very cold. Use immediately from freezer in recipe.

Variation

Savory Crust: Omit the sugar in this recipe and use it to make the pies in the Savory Pies & Tarts chapter.

1 1/2 cups	all-purpose flour	375 mL
2 tbsp	granulated sugar	25 mL
1/4 tsp	salt	1 mL
1/2 cup	cold butter, cut into small pieces	125 mL
3 to 5 tbsp	ice water	45 to 75 mL

1. In a food processor fitted with metal blade, pulse flour, sugar and salt until mixed. Add butter, pulsing until mixture resembles coarse meal.

2. Add 3 tbsp (45 mL) ice water to flour mixture, pulsing until moist clumps form, stopping to the test dough with fingertips to see if it's moist enough to hold together. If dough is too dry, add 1 to 2 tbsp (15 to 25 mL) more ice water as needed. Remove blade and gather dough into a ball, flattening into a disk. Wrap in plastic wrap and refrigerate for at least 30 minutes.

3. For rolling and prebaking instructions, see page 178.

Buttery Pie Pastry Dough

Makes enough dough for one 9-inch (23 cm) double-crust pie or two 9-inch (23 cm) single-crust pies

- One or two 9-inch (23 cm) glass pie plates, greased

This recipe is an adaptation of a recipe that I developed for *Bon Appétit* magazine. Just a small amount of baking powder helps give a little boost to this buttery and delicious crust.

Tips

Don't forget to use a light touch when pulsing your dough in the processor.

To chill butter, cut into pieces with a knife and place on a small plate. Place in freezer for 15 minutes or until very cold. Use immediately from freezer in recipe.

Variation

Light Peppery Crust: Add about 1 tsp (5 mL) freshly ground black pepper to the flour. The pepper crust can work with a sweet or savory filling.

3 cups	all-purpose flour	750 mL
3 tbsp	granulated sugar	45 mL
½ tsp	salt	2 mL
¼ tsp	baking powder	1 mL
1 cup	cold butter, cut into small pieces	250 mL
6 to 8 tbsp	ice water	90 to 120 mL
2 tsp	cider vinegar	10 mL

1. In a food processor fitted with metal blade, pulse flour, sugar, salt and baking powder until mixed. Add butter, pulsing until mixture resembles coarse meal.

2. Add 6 tbsp (90 mL) ice water and vinegar to flour mixture, pulsing until moist clumps form, stopping to test the dough with fingertips to see if it's moist enough to hold together. If dough is too dry, add 1 to 2 tbsp (15 to 25 mL) more ice water as needed. Remove blade and divide dough into 2 pieces, one slightly larger than the other if making a double-crust pie or equal-sized for 2 single-crust pies, flattening each into a disk. Wrap in plastic wrap and refrigerate for 15 to 20 minutes.

3. For rolling and prebaking instructions, see page 178.

All-Purpose Vegan Pastry Dough

Makes enough dough for one 9-inch (23 cm) single-crust pie

- 9-inch (23 cm) glass pie plate, greased

This makes a great all-purpose flaky pastry, perfect for filling with luscious summer fruit. It's an old-school recipe, probably similar to the one that your grandmother made. The pastry dough is great for filled pies and prebaked crusts, especially if you want to eliminate dairy from the dessert.

Tips

I like to use a non-hydrogenated vegetable shortening, as it's a much healthier choice.

Variations

Savory Crust: Omit the sugar in this recipe and use it to make the pies in the Savory Pies & Tarts chapter.

Savory Herbed Crust: Omit the sugar and add 2 to 3 tsp (10 to 15 mL) dried herbs, such as dried dill, or a combination of mixed dried herbs, such as parsley, dill and marjoram.

1½ cups	all-purpose flour	375 mL
1 tbsp	confectioner's (icing) sugar	15 mL
¼ tsp	salt	1 mL
½ cup	cold vegetable shortening	125 mL
3 to 5 tbsp	ice water	45 to 75 mL

1. In a food processor fitted with metal blade, pulse flour, sugar and salt until mixed. Add shortening, pulsing until mixture resembles coarse meal.

2. Add 3 tbsp (45 mL) ice water to flour mixture, pulsing until moist clumps form, stopping to test the dough with fingertips to see if it's moist enough to hold together. If dough is too dry, add 1 to 2 tbsp (15 to 25 mL) more ice water as needed. Remove blade and gather dough into a ball, flattening into a disk. Wrap in plastic wrap and refrigerate for 15 to 20 minutes.

3. For rolling and prebaking instructions, see page 178.

Large-Batch All-Purpose Vegan Pastry Dough

Makes enough dough for one 9-inch (23 cm) double-crust pie or two 9-inch (23 cm) single-crust pies

- One or two 9-inch (23 cm) glass pie plates, greased

If you've been looking for a flaky pastry that doesn't include butter, eggs or dairy, stop right here. This recipe makes a very flaky pastry, which will work well with a sweet or savory pie.

3 cups	all-purpose flour	750 mL
2 tbsp	confectioner's (icing) sugar	25 mL
½ tsp	salt	2 mL
1 cup	cold vegetable shortening	250 mL
6 to 8 tbsp	ice water	90 to 120 mL

1. In a food processor fitted with metal blade, pulse flour, sugar and salt until mixed. Add shortening, pulsing until mixture resembles coarse meal.

2. Add 6 tbsp (90 mL) ice water to flour mixture, pulsing until moist clumps form, stopping to test the dough with fingertips to see if it's moist enough to hold together. If dough is too dry, add 1 to 2 tbsp (15 to 25 mL) more ice water as needed. Remove blade and divide dough into 2 pieces, one slightly larger than the other if making a double-crust pie or equal-sized for making 2 single-crust pies, flattening each into a disk. Wrap in plastic wrap and refrigerate for at least 30 minutes.

3. For rolling and prebaking instructions, see page 178.

Tips

I like to use a non-hydrogenated vegetable shortening, as it's a much healthier choice, although some purists feel that the hydrogenated version makes a somewhat flakier pastry.

Variations

Savory Crust: Omit the sugar in this recipe and use it to make the pies in the Savory Pies & Tarts chapter.

Almond-Scented Crust: Add 1 tsp (5 mL) pure almond extract along with the ice water.

Sour Cream Pie Pastry Dough

**Makes enough
dough for one
9-inch (23 cm)
double-crust pie or
two 9-inch (23 cm)
single-crust pies**

- One or two 9-inch
  (23 cm) glass pie
  plates, greased

Diane Morgan graciously
shared this recipe with me.
Diane pairs this rich and
flaky crust with berries for
her famous Thanksgiving
Cranberry Blueberry Pie
(see recipe, page 39). This
crust is also wonderful
paired with just about any
other filling you choose.

2½ cups	all-purpose flour	625 mL
2 tsp	granulated sugar	10 mL
1 tsp	salt	5 mL
½ cup	cold butter, cut into small pieces	125 mL
½ cup	cold vegetable shortening	125 mL
⅓ cup	sour cream	75 mL
2 tbsp	ice water	25 mL

1. In a food processor fitted with metal blade, combine
   flour, sugar and salt. Add butter and shortening, pulsing
   until mixture resembles coarse meal.

2. Add sour cream and ice water to flour mixture, pulsing
   until a ball of dough begins to form. Do not
   overprocess. Remove blade and gather dough into
   2 balls, one slightly larger than the other if making a
   double-crust pie or equal-sized for 2 single-crust pies,
   flattening each into a disk. Wrap in plastic wrap and
   refrigerate for at least 30 minutes or overnight.

3. For rolling and prebaking instructions, see page 178.

Tip

To chill butter and
shortening for this
recipe, cut butter into
pieces with a knife and
place on a small plate.
Place shortening on
another plate and place
plates in freezer for
15 minutes or until very
cold. Once shortening
is cold, you can cut or
chop it into pieces. Use
immediately from
freezer in recipe.

Sweet Oil Pastry Dough

**Makes enough
dough for two
9-inch (23 cm)
single-crust pies**

- Two 9-inch (23 cm)
glass pie plates,
greased

This is an easy crust recipe
to throw together quickly,
without the need to cut in
butter or chill any of the
ingredients. In fact, it's a
one-bowl wonder. This is a
perfect recipe to use with
a pie press (see page 8),
although you might need
to add a touch more liquid
to press properly.

> **Tips**
> Use a light-flavored oil,
> such as canola oil. Olive
> oil would not make a
> good replacement
> unless you're making
> a savory pie.
>
> The dough should be
> pressed into the pan
> right after making. It
> shouldn't sit around or
> be chilled first.
>
> This soft-textured dough
> doesn't work well for
> a prebaked crust. It
> is best used for a pie
> that requires an
> unbaked crust.

2¼ cups	all-purpose flour	550 mL
1 tbsp	granulated sugar	15 mL
¼ tsp	salt	1 mL
½ cup	vegetable oil (see Tips, left)	125 mL
4 to 6 tbsp	orange juice, milk or soy milk	60 to 90 mL

1. In a large bowl, mix together flour, sugar and salt. Add oil and 4 tbsp (60 mL) orange juice, stirring with a fork until flour is evenly moistened. If mixture is still too dry to work with your hands, add 1 to 2 tbsp (15 to 25 mL) more orange juice until moist clumps form. Divide dough in half.

2. With your hands, press half of the dough evenly on the bottom and up the side of each pie plate. With the tines of a fork, score the edge of pastry.

3. Fill and bake according to recipe directions (see Tips, left).

Whole Wheat Oil Pastry Dough

Makes enough dough for one 9-inch (23 cm) double-crust pie or two 9-inch (23 cm) single-crust pies

- One or two 9-inch (23 cm) glass pie plates, greased

This recipe is adapted from the *Bob's Red Mill Baking Book* by John Ettinger. The folks at Bob's Red Mill have a fantastic line of whole-grain flours, which I love. So when I was in need of a great whole-grain crust, I decided to go straight to the source.

Tips

For easier rolling, use a silicone mat and rolling pin. The combination of silicone surfaces makes it possible to use very little flour when rolling dough.

This soft-textured dough doesn't work well for a prebaked crust. It is best used for a pie that requires an unbaked crust.

Variation

Savory Crust: Omit the sugar.

1 cup	whole wheat pastry flour	250 mL
1 cup	all-purpose flour	250 mL
2 tbsp	granulated sugar	25 mL
¼ tsp	salt	1 mL
½ cup	cold vegetable oil (see Tips, page 185)	125 mL
¼ cup	cold milk or soy milk, approx.	50 mL

1. In a large bowl, combine pastry flour, all-purpose flour, sugar and salt, mixing well. Add oil and milk, stirring just until combined. If dough is too dry and crumbly, add 1 to 2 tsp (5 to 10 mL) more milk. Press mixture into 2 balls, one slightly larger than the other if making a double-crust pie or equal-sized for 2 single-crust pies, flattening each into a disk. Do not chill.

2. For rolling instructions, see page 178.

The Best Tart Dough

Makes enough dough for one 9-inch (23 cm) or 10-inch (25 cm) tart

- 9- or 10-inch (23 or 25 cm) metal fluted tart pan with removable bottom, greased

This has been one of my tried-and-true tart crusts over the years.

1½ cups	all-purpose flour	375 mL
¼ cup	granulated sugar	50 mL
Pinch	salt	Pinch
½ cup	cold butter, cut into pieces	125 mL
4 to 5 tbsp	cold whipping (35%) cream	60 to 75 mL
1½ tsp	vanilla extract	7 mL

1. In a food processor, pulse flour, sugar and salt until mixed. Add butter, pulsing until mixture resembles coarse meal with a few pea-size butter lumps. Add 4 tbsp (60 mL) cream and vanilla, pulsing until dough just forms a ball, stopping to test the dough with fingertips to see if it's moist enough to hold together. If dough is too dry, add remaining 1 tbsp (15 mL) cream as needed until dough just comes together into a ball. Do not overprocess or pastry will be tough. Remove blade and gather dough into a ball.

2. Press dough into prepared pan, making the side a little thicker than the bottom. At this point, depending on the tart recipe, you can either prebake the shell or fill and bake it according to the recipe.

3. To prebake the tart shell: Using a fork, lightly prick a few small holes in bottom of crust. Place tart pan on a flat plate or cardboard round and freeze until cold and firm, about 30 minutes. Remove plate or cardboard round. Line pan with a piece of parchment paper and fill with pie weights, rice or beans.

4. Meanwhile, preheat oven to 375°F (190°C).

5. For a partially baked shell: Bake in preheated oven for 10 minutes. Remove pie weights and parchment and bake for 10 minutes more or until pastry is golden. If bottom of crust still looks raw, return to oven for 5 to 7 minutes more. Fill and bake according to recipe.

6. For a fully baked shell: Bake in preheated oven for 15 minutes. Remove pie weights and parchment and bake for 15 to 20 minutes more or until pastry is golden brown and baked through. Let tart shell cool completely on rack before filling. Once tart is cooled and filled, remove shell from tart pan.

Variation

Tartlets: Instead of making one large tart, this recipe will fill about twenty-four 2½-inch (6 cm) fluted tartlet tins. Divide tart dough into 1-tbsp (15 mL) balls and press into greased tartlet tins or 30 mini muffin cups. If using metal tartlet tins, place on a baking sheet lined with parchment paper. Using a fork, lightly prick a few small holes on bottoms. Place in freezer for 30 minutes. Bake in preheated 375°F (190°C) oven for 20 to 25 minutes or until light golden. Let cool slightly in pans on a wire rack. Gently turn tart shells over and unmold. Turn right side up and let cool completely.

Sweet Tart Dough

**Makes about
19 tartlets**

● Mini muffin pans,
each cup about 1½ to
2 inches (4 to 5 cm)
in diameter, greased

● 3-inch (7.5 cm) round
or fluted cookie cutter,
or slightly larger
diameter than cup

This is a quick and easy
recipe when you want to
make a rolled dough for
tarts. Since the dough
needs to chill for an hour
or so, you can make it a
couple of days ahead and
keep it in the refrigerator.
That way, when you're
ready to make tarts, you're
already halfway there!

1 cup	all-purpose flour	250 mL
2 tbsp	confectioner's (icing) sugar	25 mL
Pinch	salt	Pinch
½ cup	cold butter, cut into small pieces	125 mL
2 to 3 tbsp	ice water, approx.	25 to 45 mL

1. In a food processor fitted with metal blade, pulse flour, sugar and salt until mixed. Add butter, pulsing until mixture resembles coarse meal.

2. Add 2 tbsp (25 mL) ice water to flour mixture, pulsing until moist clumps form, stopping to test dough with fingertips to see if it's moist enough to hold together. If dough is too dry, add up to 1 tbsp (15 mL) more ice water as needed. Remove blade and gather dough into a ball, flattening into a disk. Wrap in plastic wrap and refrigerate for at least 30 minutes or for up to 2 days.

3. On a lightly floured surface, roll out dough to about ⅛-inch (0.25 cm) thickness, dusting work surface and dough as necessary to keep the dough from sticking. Cut the dough into rounds with cookie cutter. Press rounds into prepared mini muffin pans. Prebake the shells or fill them and bake according to the recipe.

4. To prebake shells: Using a fork or toothpick, lightly prick a few small holes on bottoms of pastry. Place in freezer for 20 to 30 minutes or until cold and firm. Meanwhile, preheat oven to 425°F (220°C). Bake in preheated oven for 10 to 15 minutes or until shells are golden brown. If tarts start to puff when baking, gently prick dough with a toothpick or fork. Let tartlet shells cool in pan on rack for 10 minutes. Gently turn the pan over and unmold. Turn right side up and let cool completely on a wire rack.

Tips

To chill butter, cut into pieces with a knife and place on a small plate. Place in freezer for 15 minutes or until very cold. Use immediately from freezer in recipe.

These flaky tarts might not look picture-perfect after baking, so just top with a dollop of lemon curd or lemon cream and a tiny bit of whipped cream and they'll look fantastic.

Variation

Savory Tarts: Reduce sugar to 1 tbsp (15 mL).

Vegan Buttery Sweet Tart Dough

Makes enough dough for one 10-inch (25 cm) tart

- 10-inch (25 cm) metal tart pan with removable bottom, greased

Whether you're allergic to dairy, are vegan or just want to make a dairy-free dough, this is a great recipe. It's very easy to make, especially if you have a food processor.

Tip
Not all sugar is necessarily vegan, but organic sugar and beet sugar generally are.

Variation
Tartlets: Instead of making one large tart, this recipe will fill about twenty-one 2½ inch (6 cm) fluted tartlet tins (see Variation, page 187).

1½ cups	all-purpose flour	375 mL
2 tbsp	granulated sugar	25 mL
½ cup	cold hard vegan margarine, cut into small pieces	125 mL
2 to 3 tbsp	soy milk	25 to 45 mL

1. In a food processor fitted with metal blade pulse together flour and sugar until mixed. Add margarine, pulsing until mixture is crumbly. Add 2 tbsp (25 mL) soy milk, pulsing again until mixture just comes together, stopping to test dough with fingertips to see if it's moist enough to hold together. If dough is too dry, add 1 tbsp (15 mL) more soy milk as needed.

2. Press dough into prepared pan, making the side a little thicker than the bottom. Prebake the shell or fill and bake it according to the recipe.

3. To prebake the tart shell: Using a fork, lightly prick a few small holes in bottom of crust. Place tart pan on a flat plate or cardboard round and freeze until cold and firm, about 30 minutes. Remove plate or cardboard round from bottom of pan. Line pan with a piece of parchment paper and fill with pie weights, rice or beans.

4. Meanwhile, preheat oven to 375°F (190°C).

5. For a partially baked shell: Bake in preheated oven for 10 minutes. Remove pie weights and parchment and bake for 10 minutes more or until pastry is golden. If bottom of crust still looks raw, return to oven for 5 to 7 minutes more. Fill and bake according to recipe.

6. For a fully baked shell: Bake in preheated oven for 15 minutes. Remove pie weights and parchment and bake for 15 minutes more or until pastry is golden brown and baked through. Let tart shell cool completely in pan on rack before filling. Once tart is cooled and filled, remove shell from tart pan.

Oil Tart Dough

Makes enough for one 9-inch (23 cm) tart or about fifteen 2½-inch (6 cm) tartlets

- 9-inch (23 cm) metal tart pan with removable bottom or fifteen 2½-inch (6 cm) tartlet pans, greased
- Preheat oven to 425°F (220°C)

This is a very easy tart dough, which can easily be mixed in a bowl. I also love the fact that I usually have all of the ingredients on hand.

1½ cups	all-purpose flour	375 mL
2 tbsp	granulated sugar	25 mL
¼ tsp	salt	1 mL
½ cup	cold vegetable oil (see Tips, left)	125 mL
1 to 2 tbsp	cold milk or soy milk	15 to 25 mL

1. In a large bowl, combine flour, sugar and salt. Pour in oil and 1 tbsp (15 mL) of the milk and mix just until blended and dough comes together. Test dough with fingertips to see if it's moist enough to hold together. If dough is too dry, add 1 tbsp (15 mL) more milk as needed.

2. For a large tart: Press dough into prepared tart pan. Using a fork, lightly prick a few small holes in bottom of crust. Bake in preheated oven for 25 minutes or until golden brown. If the crust starts to puff when baking, gently prick with a fork. Let tart shell cool completely in pan on rack before filling. Once tart is cooled and filled, remove shell from tart pan. Be careful, as the crust is particularly delicate.

3. For tartlets: Press rounded tablespoonful (15 mL) of dough into bottoms and up sides of prepared tartlet pans. Using a fork or toothpick, lightly prick a few small holes in bottom of pastry. Bake in preheated oven for 12 to 15 minutes or until golden brown. If tarts start to puff when baking, gently prick dough with a toothpick or fork. Let tartlet shells cool in pan on rack for 10 minutes. Gently turn the tart shells over and unmold. Turn right side up and let cool completely on a wire rack.

Tips

Chill oil in the freezer for about 30 minutes, or until very cold and thickened to ensure a flaky crust.

Don't refrigerate this dough before pressing into pan. It needs to be used right away.

This crust is best used as a fully baked shell rather than adding the filling to the raw shell.

Mini Butter Tart Dough

Makes about 44 small tarts

- Two 24-cup mini-muffin pans (see Tip, page 192), greased

Here's a nice, buttery tart dough that makes for very easy miniature tarts. The recipe is adapted from one by Donna Hay, whose magazines and books are filled with mouthwatering recipes and photos. To save time, I often press the dough into the muffin tins the day before I need them and refrigerate until I'm ready to bake.

2 cups	all-purpose flour	500 mL
3 tbsp	granulated sugar	45 mL
Pinch	salt	Pinch
½ cup + 2 tbsp	cold unsalted butter, cut into small pieces	150 mL
5 to 6 tbsp	ice water	75 to 90 mL

1. In a food processor fitted with metal blade, pulse flour, sugar and salt until mixed. Add butter, pulsing until mixture resembles coarse meal.

2. Add 5 tbsp (75 mL) ice water to flour mixture, pulsing until moist clumps form, stopping to test dough with fingertips to see if it's moist enough to hold together. If dough is too dry, add 1 tbsp (15 mL) more ice water as needed. Remove blade and gather dough into a ball, flattening into a disk. Wrap in plastic wrap and refrigerate for at least 30 minutes.

3. Scoop balls of dough and press into cups of prepared muffin pans. Depending on the size of the pans, it may make more or fewer tarts. Prebake the shells or fill and bake them according to the recipe.

4. To prebake mini tart shells: Preheat oven to 375°F (190°C). Using a toothpick, lightly prick the bottoms of the shells. Place pans in freezer for 15 to 30 minutes or until cold and firm. Bake in preheated oven for 20 to 30 minutes or until crusts are light golden brown.

Tip
The cups in each muffin pan should be 1½ to 2 inches (4 to 5 cm) in diameter.

Variations
Savory Tarts: Omit the sugar and add ½ tsp (2 mL) freshly ground black pepper or ½ to 1 tsp (2 to 5 mL) dried dill to the flour.

Slightly Spiced Sweet Tarts: Add ½ tsp (2 mL) ground nutmeg to the flour.

Small-Batch Mini Tart Dough

Makes about 22 small tarts

- Preheat oven to 375°F (190°C)
- One 24-cup mini muffin pan (see Tip, below), greased

This is a smaller version of the Mini Butter Tart Dough Recipe (see recipe, page 191), because not everyone wants to make a huge batch of tarts. My mom always appreciates a small recipe, one that she can throw together quickly.

1 cup	all-purpose flour	250 mL
2 tbsp	granulated sugar	25 mL
Pinch	salt	Pinch
5 tbsp	cold butter, cut into small pieces	75 mL
2 to 3 tbsp	ice water	25 to 45 mL

1. In a food processor fitted with metal blade, pulse flour, sugar and salt until mixed. Add butter, pulsing until mixture resembles coarse meal.

2. Add 2 tbsp (25 mL) ice water to flour mixture, pulsing until moist clumps form, stopping to test dough with fingertips to see if it's moist enough to hold together. If dough is too dry, add 1 tbsp (15 mL) more ice water as needed. Remove blade and gather dough into a ball, flattening into a disk. Wrap in plastic wrap and refrigerate for at least 30 minutes.

3. Scoop balls of dough and press into cups of prepared muffin pan. Depending on the size of the pan, it may make more or fewer tarts. Prebake the shells or fill and bake them according to the recipe.

4. For prebaking instructions, see page 178.

Tip
The cups in each muffin pan should be 1½ to 2 inches (4 to 5 cm) in diameter. To make the process go more quickly, I like to take small scoops of the dough and press them into the prepared pans with a wooden or plastic tart tamper. These tampers can be found at kitchen stores or online.

Variation
Savory Tarts: Omit the sugar and add ½ tsp (2 mL) freshly ground black pepper or ½ to 1 tsp (2 to 5 mL) dried dill to the flour.

Mini Milk Chocolate Caramel Tarts with Sea Salt (page 108)
Overleaf: Chocolate Chip Brownie Tart (page 112)

Quiche Crust

Makes enough dough for one 10-inch (25 cm) deep-dish quiche

- Preheat oven to 375°F (190°C)
- 10-inch (25 cm) deep-dish fluted metal quiche pan with removable bottom, greased

I have been making this quiche crust recipe for years. Quiches were a staple of our business when my husband and I had our catering company. Although this recipe may look complicated, it's very simple to make and will impress even the most critical quiche connoisseur.

> **Tips**
>
> If using salted butter, reduce amount of salt to 1 small pinch.
>
> To chill butter, cut into pieces with a knife and place on a small plate. Place in freezer for 15 minutes or until very cold. Use immediately from freezer in recipe.

2 cups	all-purpose flour	500 mL
½ tsp	salt	2 mL
¾ cup	cold butter, cut into small pieces	175 mL
4 to 5 tbsp	cold whipping (35%) cream	60 to 75 mL

1. In a food processor, pulse flour and salt until mixed. Add butter, pulsing until mixture resembles coarse meal with some pea-size butter lumps. Add 4 tbsp (60 mL) cream, pulsing just until dough forms a ball, stopping to test the dough with fingertips to see if it's moist enough to hold together. If dough is too dry, add 1 tbsp (15 mL) more cream, pulsing just until dough comes together into a ball. Remove blade and gather dough into a ball.

2. Press dough into prepared pan, making the side a little thicker than the bottom. Using a fork, lightly prick a few small holes in bottom of crust. Cover with plastic wrap and place tart pan on a flat plate or cardboard round. Place in freezer for 30 minutes or until cold and firm. Prebake the crust or fill and bake according to the recipe.

3. To prebake crust: Preheat oven to 375°F (190°C). Remove plastic wrap from tart pan and remove plate or cardboard round from bottom of pan. Line with a piece of parchment paper and fill with pie weights or beans. Bake in preheated oven for 20 to 35 minutes or just until light golden brown. Let cool in pan on a wire rack for 10 to 15 minutes. Remove weights and parchment from crust. If bottom of crust still looks raw, return to oven for 5 to 7 minutes more (without weights or parchment paper). Let cool completely on a wire rack before filling. Once tart is filled and baked, push up bottom of tart pan to release crust.

Strawberry Rhubarb Crisp (page 133)
Overleaf: Rum Pecan Pie (page 118)

Meringue Tart Shell

Makes 1 shell

- Preheat oven to 350°F (180°C)
- Baking sheet, lined with parchment paper

This deliciously light and airy crust is used as the base for a Pavlova. You can also use the meringue to form mini shells as well.

Tip

Don't make this shell on a rainy or hot, humid day. The moisture in the air will keep the shell from getting crisp and drying out.

4	egg whites	4
1 tsp	white balsamic vinegar	5 mL
1 cup	granulated sugar	250 mL
1 tbsp	cornstarch	15 mL

1. Draw an 8-inch (20 cm) circle in the center of parchment paper with a dark pen. Flip the parchment paper over so that the circle can be seen but the ink won't come into contact with the egg white mixture. Set aside.

2. In a clean large bowl, using an electric mixer, beat egg whites on medium speed just until white and beginning to hold their shape. Beat in vinegar. Increase speed to medium-high and gradually add sugar, beating until meringue forms stiff glossy peaks. Sprinkle in cornstarch and beat just until mixed. Spoon or pipe mixture onto prepared baking sheet inside the circle, shaping it like a nest with a slightly raised edge.

3. Bake in preheated oven for 5 minutes. Reduce temperature to 250°F (120°C) and continue baking for 1 hour more. Without opening oven door, turn oven off and let meringue stand in oven for 40 minutes. Remove from oven and let cool completely on a wire rack.

4. Top cooled shell with desired fillings.

Cookie Crumb Crust

Makes one 9-inch (23 cm) crust

- 9-inch (23 cm) glass pie plate, greased

Here's the quintessential cookie crumb crust. It's perfect filled with a creamy mousse filling, scoops of cold ice cream or a pastry cream. The best part about the crust is that there's no baking required!

| 25 | chocolate or vanilla sandwich cookies with a cream filling | 25 |
| ¼ cup | butter or margarine, melted | 50 mL |

1. In a food processor fitted with metal blade, pulse cookies until finely ground. Add butter and process until mixture resembles wet sand.

2. Transfer crumb mixture to prepared pie plate, pressing into bottom and up side of pan.

3. Chill crust until firm. Fill with prepared or cooked filling or, alternatively, bake crust in preheated 350°F (180°C) oven for 10 to 15 minutes or until crust is set and fragrant.

Graham Cracker Crust

Makes one 9-inch (23 cm) crust

- 9-inch (23 cm) pie plate, greased

When you mention Key lime pie, this is the buttery crust that usually comes to mind. This crust is quick to make, is a perfect shell for creamy fillings and has a wonderfully buttery taste.

10	whole graham crackers, ground (about 1⅓ cups/325 mL crumbs)	10
5 tbsp	butter or margarine, melted	75 mL
3 tbsp	packed light brown sugar	45 mL

1. In a large bowl, combine graham cracker crumbs, butter and brown sugar, mixing well.

2. Transfer crumb mixture to prepared pie plate, pressing into bottom and up side of pan.

3. Chill crust until firm. Fill with prepared filling or, alternatively, bake crust in preheated 350°F (180°C) oven for 10 minutes or until crust is set and fragrant.

Variation
Spiced Crust: Add ¼ to ½ tsp (1 to 2 mL) ground ginger or cinnamon to the crumb mixture.

Toasted Coconut Crust

Makes one 9-inch (23 cm) crust

- 9-inch (23 cm) pie plate, greased

Coconut crusts make me think of Hawaii, where I had one of the most wonderful coconut pies ever. The toasty coconut crust was filled with lusciously rich coconut custard. Paradise!

3 cups	sweetened flaked coconut	750 mL
6 tbsp	butter or margarine, melted	90 mL

1. In a large skillet over medium heat, combine coconut and butter. Cook, stirring constantly, until butter is melted and coconut is light golden brown. If butter or coconut starts to burn or get too brown, reduce heat.

2. Scoop hot coconut mixture into prepared pie plate, evenly pressing mixture into plate.

3. Let crust cool completely in pan on a wire rack. Transfer to the refrigerator and chill for at least 30 minutes or for up to 8 hours.

Buttermilk Biscuit Crust

Makes enough batter to top one 10-inch (25 cm) deep-dish pie

A biscuit topping makes a wonderful top crust for a pie. It's simple to make, delicious and much lower in fat than a traditional pastry crust. My kids love it when I top pot pies with this biscuit crust.

Variation
Vegan Biscuit Crust: Use vegan margarine and substitute 1 cup (250 mL) plain soy milk plus 1½ tsp (7 mL) cider vinegar for the buttermilk.

3 cups	all-purpose flour	750 mL
1 tbsp	baking powder	15 mL
1½ tsp	granulated sugar	7 mL
½ tsp	salt	2 mL
¼ cup	cold butter or margarine, cut into pieces (see Tips, page 193)	50 mL
1 cup	buttermilk	250 mL

1. In a food processor fitted with metal blade, pulse flour, baking powder, sugar and salt until mixed. Add butter, pulsing until mixture resembles coarse meal. Add buttermilk, pulsing until mixture starts to come together.

2. Place scoops of biscuit batter on top of unbaked pie. (You want to cover the pie, but leave a little room for the biscuits to expand while baking.) Bake according to recipe directions.

Fillings

Almond Cream Filling

Makes enough for 1 large tart or 8 turnovers

In the very first restaurant that I worked in, we made wonderful little fruit tarts that had a lovely baked almond filling under the fruit. It's very easy to prepare, especially now that you can find ground almond meal or flour in many markets. This is adapted from a Bob's Red Mill recipe.

½ cup	confectioner's (icing) sugar, sifted	125 mL
¼ cup	butter, softened	50 mL
¾ cup	almond meal (flour)	175 mL
1 tbsp	all-purpose flour	15 mL
1	egg	1
½ tsp	pure almond extract	2 mL

1. In a large bowl or bowl of a stand mixer fitted with paddle attachment, combine confectioner's sugar and butter, beating until light and fluffy. Add almond meal and flour, beating well. Add egg and almond extract, beating until smooth.

2. *Serving suggestion:* Spread filling in unbaked turnovers or tart or tartlet shells as directed in recipe.

VEGAN FRIENDLY

Blackberry Filling

Makes about 4 cups (1 L)

My brother has always adored Blackberry Skillet Crumble (see recipe, page 122), so when he comes to visit I try to bake him one. The great thing about this filling is that you can use fresh or frozen berries, depending on the season. Once you've made the filling, the possibilities are endless.

4 cups	fresh blackberries or boysenberries	1 L
¾ cup	granulated sugar	175 mL
¼ cup	cornstarch	50 mL

1. In a large saucepan over medium heat, combine blackberries, sugar and ¼ cup (50 mL) water. Bring to a simmer, without stirring to avoid mashing berries.

2. In a small bowl, whisk together cornstarch and 3 tbsp (45 mL) water until smooth. Stir cornstarch mixture into hot berries and simmer, stirring carefully, until thick and mixture is glossy. The mixture can be thinned slightly, if desired, when making a pie or crisp (see Tip, page 199). Let mixture cool.

3. *Serving suggestions:* Use filling for a single- or double-crust pie, crisp, crumble or cobbler. The filling can also be used for tarts or sandwiched between pastry dough to make turnovers.

Blueberry Pie Filling

Makes about 1½ cups (375 mL)

This is a great master recipe for blueberry filling. Not only can you make this delectable filling year-round with frozen berries, but you can also use it for pies, tarts, crumbles and hand pies, and as a topping for cheesecake. You've got to love a multipurpose recipe!

2 cups	frozen blueberries	500 mL
⅓ cup	granulated sugar, or to taste	75 mL
2 tbsp	cornstarch	25 mL
1 tbsp	freshly squeezed lemon juice	15 mL
Pinch	ground nutmeg	Pinch

1. In a large saucepan over medium heat, combine blueberries, sugar and ¼ cup (50 mL) water. Bring mixture to a simmer, stirring gently to avoid mashing the berries.

2. In a small bowl, whisk together cornstarch and 3 tbsp (45 mL) water until smooth. Stir cornstarch mixture into hot berries and simmer, stirring carefully, until juices are thickened and glossy.

3. Remove saucepan from heat. Stir in lemon juice and nutmeg. Let cool or use warm.

4. *Serving suggestion:* Use cool or warm filling in baked and cooled tart shells or sandwiched between pastry dough for turnovers.

Tip

If using this filling for a 9-inch (23 cm) pie, double the recipe. After cooking, if filling seems a bit too thick for your liking, add 1 or 2 tbsp (15 or 25 mL) water, liqueur or red wine, or as needed, and stir until it is the desired consistency.

Variation

For a blueberry rose flavor, add 1 tsp (5 mL) rose water (or to taste) along with the lemon juice.

Brown Sugar Caramel Tart Filling

Makes about 1¾ cups (425 mL)

This is, hands down, one awesome recipe for caramel. I don't remember where the recipe originated, but it's one that I've used for many years — all the way back to my bakery days.

Tip
If light (white) corn syrup is unavailable, you can substitute golden.

1⅓ cups	packed light brown sugar	325 mL
6 tbsp	light (white) corn syrup (see Tip, left)	90 mL
5 tbsp	butter	75 mL
½ tsp	salt	2 mL
6 tbsp	whipping (35%) cream	90 mL

1. In a heavy saucepan over medium heat, combine brown sugar, corn syrup, butter and salt. Cook, stirring constantly, until sugar dissolves. Increase heat to high and boil, without stirring, for 2 minutes or until large bubbles form.

2. Remove saucepan from heat and stir in cream. Let caramel cool for 5 minutes.

3. *Serving suggestion:* Spoon caramel into baked tart shells. Make sure not to leave the caramel for any longer than 5 minutes before filling tart shells, as it will become very thick and hard to scoop.

Cheesecake Mousse Filling

Makes about 2½ cups (625 mL)

Sometimes all you need for an out-of-this-world tart or pie is a fluffy mousse filling and some fresh berries. This filling is truly ethereal, with the light flavor of cheesecake and the fluffy texture of whipped cream.

8 oz	cream cheese, softened	250 g
1 cup	confectioner's (icing) sugar, sifted	250 mL
1 tbsp	gold rum, optional	15 mL
1¼ cups	whipping (35%) cream	300 mL

1. In a bowl of large stand mixer fitted with whisk attachment, whip cream cheese until smooth. Add confectioner's sugar, whipping until creamy and smooth. With machine on low speed, slowly add rum, if using, and cream in a steady stream. Whisk mixture on high speed until soft peaks form.

2. *Serving suggestion:* Swirl mousse into baked and cooled pie or tart shells and top with fresh berries.

Cherry Pie Filling

Makes about 3½ cups (875 mL)

This is the filling to use for cherry pie, which is every bit as American as apple pie and just as delicious. There are endless uses for this pie filling, from tarts and pies to crisps and turnovers.

1	jar (24.7 oz/740 mL) sour cherries in light syrup (not cherry pie filling) (see Tips, left)	1
½ cup	granulated sugar, or to taste	125 mL
3 tbsp	cornstarch	45 mL
¼ tsp	pure almond extract	1 mL

1. In a large saucepan over medium heat, combine cherries with syrup and sugar. Bring mixture to a simmer, stirring continuously.

2. In a small cup, mix together cornstarch and 2 tbsp (25 mL) water. Add cornstarch mixture to saucepan, stirring well. Continue cooking cherry mixture, stirring continuously, until thickened and juices are glossy.

3. Remove saucepan from heat. Stir in almond extract. Let cool or use warm.

4. *Serving suggestions:* Use cool or warm filling for a single- or double-crust pie. The filling can also be used for tarts or sandwiched between pastry dough for turnovers.

Tips

If a jar of cherries is not available, use 2 cans (each 14 oz/398 mL). You should have about 3½ cups (875 mL) with juice.

Recipe can be cut in half for small tarts or turnovers. Use 3 to 4 tbsp (45 to 60 mL) granulated sugar, or to taste. You may need to reduce the heat when cooking in Step 2 to prevent burning when making a smaller batch.

If using the filling for a pie or crisp, if it is a bit thicker than you want, you can add a tablespoon or two (15 or 25 mL) of water, liqueur or red wine as needed.

Variation

Cherry Berry Filling: Add 1 cup (250 mL) fresh or frozen berries along with the cherries.

Dairy-Free Chocolate Mousse Tart Filling

Makes about 2 cups (500 mL)

Even if you're not a big fan of tofu, don't overlook this recipe. Tofu makes an amazingly delicious and quick chocolate mousse, perfect as a base for buttery tarts. If you don't tell anyone there's tofu in this recipe, no one will ever know.

1	box (12.3 oz/340 g) extra-firm or firm silken tofu	1
1 cup	confectioner's (icing) sugar	250 mL
4 oz	bittersweet chocolate, melted	125 g
¼ cup	unsweetened Dutch-process cocoa powder	50 mL
¼ cup	chocolate-flavored soy milk	50 mL
3 tbsp	chocolate-flavored liqueur or rum	45 mL

1. In a food processor fitted with metal blade or blender, blend together tofu and confectioner's sugar until very smooth and fluffy. (You might have to stop the machine and scrape down the side a couple of times.) Add chocolate and cocoa powder, pulsing or blending until smooth. Add soy milk and liqueur, pulsing or blending until smooth. Refrigerate until ready to use.

2. *Serving suggestion:* Spread mixture into tart shell or shells.

Tip
If making the filling ahead, you may find that it gets very thick after being refrigerated. Simply stir in 1 to 2 tbsp (15 to 25 mL) more chocolate soy milk until mixture is pudding-like and spreadable.

Variation
Substitute an equal amount of additional chocolate-flavored soy milk or coffee for the liqueur.

Dark Chocolate Mousse

**Makes about
5½ cups (1.375 L)**

This mousse makes a great
filling for little tartlet
shells. You can also fill two
prepared cookie crusts or
one 11-inch (27.5 cm)
baked tart shell.

Variation
Substitute 1 tbsp (15 mL)
liqueur, such as
raspberry, chocolate or
coffee, for the vanilla.

8 oz	bittersweet chocolate, chopped	250 g
2½ cups	whipping (35%) cream, divided	625 mL
3 tbsp	superfine sugar	45 mL
2 tsp	vanilla extract	10 mL

1. In a microwave-safe bowl, combine chocolate and
½ cup (125 mL) of the cream. Microwave on High for
60 seconds or until cream is hot and chocolate is soft
and almost melted. Stir until smooth. Let cool slightly.

2. In a bowl, combine remaining 2 cups (500 mL) cream,
sugar and vanilla. Using a hand mixer, whip cream
until soft peaks form. With mixer on low speed, add
melted chocolate, mixing just until smooth.

3. *Serving suggestion:* Scoop mousse into small tartlet
shells. Chill for several hours before serving.

Lemon Curd

**Makes about
1⅓ cups (325 mL)**

This flavorful and tangy
lemon curd recipe is
adapted from *Gourmet*
magazine. Lemon curd can
be very temperamental. It
will curdle easily because
of the egg whites. So here
I've used just the yolks. I
dub this lemon curd
"nectar of the gods."

Tip
If your lemon curd does
lightly curdle, strain the
warm curd into a bowl
to remove lumps.

½ cup	superfine sugar	125 mL
1 tsp	cornstarch	5 mL
2 tsp	finely grated lemon zest	10 mL
½ cup	freshly squeezed lemon juice	125 mL
4	egg yolks, at room temperature (see Tip, left)	4
6 tbsp	cold butter, cut into pieces	90 mL

1. In a heavy-bottomed nonstick saucepan, whisk together
sugar and cornstarch. Whisk in lemon zest and juice
and egg yolks, whisking well. Whisk in butter and cook
over medium-low heat, whisking continuously, for
6 minutes or until thickened to pudding consistency.

2. Scoop lemon curd into a bowl and place a sheet of
plastic wrap directly on the surface to prevent a skin
from forming. Refrigerate for 1 hour or until cold.

3. *Serving suggestion:* Use the chilled lemon curd as a pie
and tart filling.

Raspberry Pie Filling

Makes about 5½ cups (1.375 L)

Cooking your filling before using it in a pie or crisp greatly reduces your baking time. It also ensures that you will have a perfectly thickened filling.

5½ cups	fresh or frozen raspberries, divided	1.375 L
1 cup	granulated sugar	250 mL
¼ cup	cornstarch	50 mL

1. In a large saucepan over medium heat, combine 4 cups (1 L) of the raspberries, sugar and ¼ cup (50 mL) water. Bring mixture to a simmer, without stirring to avoid mashing the berries.

2. In a small bowl, whisk together cornstarch and 3 tbsp (45 mL) water until smooth. Stir cornstarch mixture into hot berries and simmer, stirring carefully, until thick and mixture is glossy.

3. Remove saucepan from heat. Gently stir in remaining 1½ cups (375 mL) raspberries into cooked filling. Let cool.

4. *Serving suggestions:* Use as a filling for a single- or double-crust pie or crisp. The filling can also be used for tarts or sandwiched between pastry dough for turnovers.

Tip
Recipe can be cut in half for tartlets or turnovers.

Variations
Substitute partially thawed frozen mixed berries for the fresh raspberries.

Raspberry Lemon Filling: Add 2 tsp (10 mL) grated lemon zest to the cooked filling.

Strawberry Rhubarb Filling

Makes 2 cups (500 mL)

Although often mistaken for a fruit, rhubarb is a vegetable that some people are unsure of. It resembles red-tinged celery and looks like something that belongs in a salad. Trust me, though, when I say that the flavor is wonderful, especially when combined with sweet strawberries.

Variation
Substitute 2 tsp (10 mL) grated orange zest for the juice.

1 lb	rhubarb, sliced into ½-inch (1 cm) pieces (about 2½ cups/625 mL)	500 g
⅓ cup	granulated sugar, or to taste	75 mL
1 tbsp	orange juice	15 mL
2 cups	fresh strawberries, hulled and sliced	500 mL

1. In a heavy-bottomed saucepan over medium heat, combine rhubarb, sugar and orange juice. Bring mixture to a simmer. Reduce heat to low and simmer, stirring occasionally, for 5 to 10 minutes or until rhubarb is soft.

2. Transfer to a bowl. Add strawberries, stirring until combined. Let mixture cool. Once cool, cover and chill for at least 2 hours.

3. *Serving suggestion:* This filling is fabulous in pies and tarts, and makes a wonderful pancake topping.

Vanilla Pastry Cream

Makes about 1½ cups (375 mL)

Although they take a little extra effort in terms of prep time, custard-filled tarts topped with fresh fruit make a fabulous summer dessert. This custard filling is so good that my daughter prefers to eat it with a spoon.

Tip

Pastry cream will keep, covered, in the refrigerator for up to 2 days.

Variation

For an almond variation, add ½ tsp (2 mL) almond extract (or to taste) instead of the vanilla paste.

⅓ cup	granulated sugar	75 mL
¼ cup	cornstarch	50 mL
Pinch	salt	Pinch
3	egg yolks	3
1 cup	milk	250 mL
½ cup + 3 tbsp	whipping (35%) cream, divided	125 mL + 45 mL
1 tbsp	butter	15 mL
1 tsp	vanilla paste or extract	5 mL

1. In a heavy-bottomed saucepan, whisk together sugar, cornstarch and salt.

2. In a bowl, whisk together egg yolks, milk and ½ cup (125 mL) of the whipping cream until smooth. Add to sugar mixture, whisking well to dissolve sugar and eliminate lumps. Cook over medium heat, whisking constantly, until mixture starts to thicken. Reduce heat to low and continue whisking until cream is very thick, about 10 minutes total. Remove from heat and whisk in butter and vanilla paste. Strain cream mixture through a fine-mesh sieve into a small bowl to remove any bits of cooked egg.

3. Fill a slightly larger bowl with ice and place bowl of custard on top. Whisk pastry cream until cool. Remove bowl of custard and dry bottom and side with a towel so that no moisture touches custard. Whisk in remaining 3 tbsp (45 mL) of whipping cream.

4. Place a piece of plastic wrap directly onto surface of pastry cream to prevent a skin from forming and refrigerate until ready to use.

5. *Serving suggestion:* Spread custard in bottom of baked and cooled tart shells.

Ice Cream Pies
& Toppings

Chocolate Chip Mocha Tarts

Makes about 19 mini tarts or 9 regular tarts

- Preheat oven to 350°F (180°C)
- Mini muffin pan or standard-size muffin pan, greased

I usually have a roll or two of homemade chocolate chip cookie dough in my freezer. I found that it makes great tart crusts for recipes like this. It's a fun recipe to make with kids, as they find them not only delicious but "fancy," too.

1	roll (1 lb/500 g) store-bought or homemade chocolate chip cookie dough	1
1 pint	coffee ice cream	500 mL
	Miniature semisweet chocolate chips	
	Whipped cream, optional	

1. Remove cookie dough from freezer or refrigerator (if frozen, let stand at room temperature until slightly softened). Cut dough into ¼-inch (0.5 cm) slices for mini muffin pan or ½-inch (1 cm) slices for regular muffin pan and press into prepared muffin cups. Bake in preheated oven for 10 minutes for small tarts, 12 to 14 minutes for large tarts, or until puffed and golden brown. Let cool in pan for 5 minutes before removing to a wire rack to cool completely.

2. Place a scoop of ice cream on top of cookie tart and sprinkle with miniature chocolate chips. If desired, garnish with whipped cream before serving.

Tip

You can also freeze the cooled and filled tarts for up to 2 weeks. Remove the tarts from the freezer up to 1 hour before serving. Fill with ice cream and serve. Just make sure to store them in a resealable freezer bag.

Frozen Caramel Almond Pie

Serves 8

- 9-inch (23 cm)
  deep-dish glass pie
  plate, greased

Ice creams are super-easy
to make and utterly
delicious to eat. My son
absolutely adores this pie,
requesting it for dessert
whenever he can.

Tips

Substitute a store-
bought graham or
chocolate crumb crust
for the homemade crust.

To toast almonds: Preheat
oven to 350°F (180°C).
Spread nuts on a baking
sheet lined with foil
or parchment paper.
Bake for 5 to 10 minutes
or until light brown
and fragrant.

Variation

Substitute vanilla ice
cream for the dulce
de leche.

20	vanilla sandwich cookies	20
¼ cup	butter, melted	50 mL
1 quart	premium-quality dulce de leche ice cream, softened, divided	1 L
1 cup	store-bought caramel sauce or Rich Caramel Sauce or Chocolate Caramel Sauce (see recipes, pages 237 and 233), divided	250 mL
1½ cups	whipping (35%) cream	375 mL
3 tbsp	confectioner's (icing) sugar, sifted	45 mL
½ tsp	vanilla extract	2 mL
⅓ cup	almonds, toasted and coarsely chopped (see Tips, left)	75 mL

1. In a food processor fitted with metal blade, process cookies until crumbs form. Add butter and process until finely ground. Press onto bottom and up side of prepared pie plate. Freeze for 30 minutes or until firm.

2. Spread half of the ice cream in prepared crust. Drizzle three-quarters of the caramel sauce over ice cream. Return pie to freezer until ice cream firms up a bit. Spread remaining ice cream over pie and return to freezer.

3. In a bowl, using an electric mixer, whip cream, confectioner's sugar and vanilla until soft peaks form.

4. Spread whipped cream over pie and sprinkle with almonds. Return to freezer for several hours or until completely frozen. Drizzle with remaining sauce.

Frozen Chocolate Banana Cream Pie

Serves 8

- 9-inch (23 cm) deep-dish glass pie plate, greased

Ice cream pies are lots of fun to make. I love to whip them up for a cool summer dessert. One of the wonderful things about ice cream pies is that they can be prepared ahead of time.

20	chocolate sandwich cookies	20
¼ cup	butter, melted	50 mL
1 quart	premium-quality chocolate ice cream, softened, divided	1 L
1	large banana, peeled and sliced	1
1 cup	store-bought chocolate fudge sauce or Hot Fudge Sauce, Milk Chocolate Banana Sauce or Chocolate Caramel Sauce (see recipes, pages 235 and 233), divided	250 mL
1½ cups	whipping (35%) cream	375 mL
¼ cup	confectioner's (icing) sugar, sifted	50 mL
½ tsp	vanilla extract	2 mL
⅓ cup	semisweet chocolate chips	75 mL

Tip

Substitute a store-bought chocolate crumb crust for the homemade crust.

Variation

Substitute vanilla ice cream for the chocolate.

1. In a food processor fitted with metal blade, process cookies until crumbs form. Add butter and process until finely ground and clumps start to form. Press onto bottom and up side of prepared pie plate. Freeze for 30 minutes or until firm.

2. Spread half of the ice cream in prepared crust. Place banana slices in a single layer over ice cream. Drizzle three-quarters of the fudge sauce over bananas. Return pie to freezer until ice cream firms up a bit. Spread remaining ice cream over pie and return to freezer.

3. In a bowl, using an electric mixer, whip cream, confectioner's sugar and vanilla until soft peaks form.

4. Spread whipped cream over pie and sprinkle with chocolate chips. Return to freezer for several hours or until completely frozen. Drizzle with remaining sauce.

Frozen Chocolate Cherry Pie

Serves 8

- 9-inch (23 cm) deep-dish glass pie plate, greased

I've always been a huge ice cream fan, which is probably the reason why I love ice cream pies so much. One of my first jobs as a teenager was working in an ice cream parlor, and let me just say that I had some of the strongest arms in town from scooping. I also learned how to make some outrageous ice cream desserts, like this one!

> **Tip**
> Substitute a store-bought chocolate crumb crust for the homemade crust.

20	chocolate sandwich cookies	20
¼ cup	butter, melted	50 mL
1	recipe Cherry Chocolate Chunk Ice Cream (see recipe, page 214) or 1 quart (1 L) premium-quality cherry vanilla ice cream, softened, divided	1
1 cup	store-bought chocolate fudge sauce or Hot Fudge Sauce (see recipe, page 235), divided	250 mL
1½ cups	whipping (35%) cream	375 mL
¼ cup	confectioner's (icing) sugar, sifted	50 mL
2 tbsp	cherry-flavored liqueur	25 mL
⅓ cup	semisweet chocolate chips	75 mL

1. In a food processor fitted with metal blade, process cookies until crumbs form. Add butter and process until finely ground. Press onto bottom and up side of prepared pie plate. Freeze for 30 minutes or until firm.

2. Spread half of the ice cream in prepared crust. Drizzle three-quarters of the fudge sauce over ice cream. Return pie to freezer until ice cream firms up a bit. Spread remaining ice cream over pie and return to freezer.

3. In a bowl, using an electric mixer, whip cream, confectioner's sugar and cherry liqueur until soft peaks form.

4. Spread whipped cream over pie and sprinkle with chocolate chips. Return to freezer for several hours or until completely frozen. Drizzle with remaining sauce.

Mississippi Mud Pie

Serves 8

- 9-inch (23 cm) deep-dish glass pie plate, greased

Ice cream pies were all the rage for dessert in the '60s and '70s and they've never really gone out of style. Although this dessert is related to the humble ice cream pie, it has been taken up a notch.

20	chocolate sandwich cookies	20
¼ cup	butter, melted	50 mL
1 quart	premium-quality coffee ice cream, softened, divided	1 L
1 cup	store-bought chocolate fudge or caramel sauce or Bourbon Fudge Sauce, Hot Fudge Sauce or Chocolate Caramel Sauce (see recipes, pages 232, 235 and 233)	250 mL
1 cup	semisweet chocolate chips, divided	250 mL
1½ cups	whipping (35%) cream	375 mL
¼ cup	confectioner's (icing) sugar, sifted	50 mL
½ tsp	vanilla extract	2 mL
⅓ cup	almonds, toasted and coarsely chopped (see Tips, page 209)	75 mL

1. In a food processor fitted with metal blade, process cookies until crumbs form. Add butter and process until finely ground. Press onto bottom and up side of prepared pie plate. Freeze for 30 minutes or until firm.

2. Spread half of the ice cream in prepared crust. Drizzle evenly with fudge sauce and sprinkle with half of the chocolate chips. Return to freezer until ice cream firms up a bit. Spread remaining ice cream over pie and return to freezer.

3. In a bowl, using an electric mixer, whip cream, confectioner's sugar and vanilla until soft peaks form.

4. Spread whipped cream over pie and sprinkle with almonds and remaining chocolate chips. Return to freezer for several hours or until completely frozen.

Brown Sugar Cinnamon Ice Cream

**Makes about
4 cups (1 L)**

• Ice cream maker

If you want to top your
homemade peach or
blueberry pie with an
amazing ice cream, this
is it. The rich flavor of
brown sugar, with a hint
of cinnamon, makes this
one special ice cream.

1½ cups	whipping (35%) cream	375 mL
1½ cups	milk (not low-fat or nonfat)	375 mL
¾ cup	light brown sugar	175 mL
1 tsp	vanilla extract	5 mL
½ tsp	ground cinnamon	2 mL

1. In a bowl, whisk together cream, milk, brown sugar, vanilla and cinnamon until smooth and sugar is dissolved.

2. Transfer mixture to ice cream maker and freeze according to manufacturer's directions. Homemade ice cream will be somewhat softer in texture than store-bought. Serve immediately or freeze in an airtight container (for storage info, see Tip, page 217). This ice cream is best served the same day that it is made.

Coconut Sorbet

**Makes about
5 cups (1.25 L)**

• Ice cream maker

This sorbet will transport
you to the tropical paradise
of your choice.

Tip
Coconut milk can sizes
vary. You'll need one
19-oz (540 mL) can or
two 14-oz (398 mL) cans
(you won't use the entire
contents of the two cans).
Whisk before measuring
and refrigerate or freeze
any extra for another use.

2⅓ cups	coconut milk (see Tip, left)	575 mL
½ cup	granulated or superfine sugar	125 mL
2 tsp	coconut-flavored or light rum	10 mL

1. In a saucepan over medium-high heat, combine coconut milk, ½ cup (125 mL) water and sugar. Bring to a simmer, stirring occasionally, and simmer for 5 minutes. Remove from heat and stir in coconut rum. Pour mixture into a bowl or pitcher and refrigerate until chilled.

2. Transfer mixture to ice cream maker and freeze according to manufacturer's directions. Serve immediately or freeze in an airtight container (for storage info, see Tip, page 217). This sorbet is best served the same day that it is made.

Cherry Chocolate Chunk Ice Cream

Makes about 4 cups (1 L)

• Ice cream maker

Here's another super-quick, ultra-delicious ice cream. No need to run down to your local ice cream parlor; impress your friends with your own gourmet-savvy ice cream.

Tip
This is fabulous garnished with toasted chopped almonds.

Variations
The almond extract can be omitted.

Omit almond extract and add an additional 1 tsp (5 mL) vanilla extract.

Bittersweet chocolate can be substituted for the semisweet chocolate.

½ cup	dried pitted cherries, coarsely chopped	125 mL
2 tbsp	cherry-flavored liqueur or dark rum	25 mL
2 cups	whipping (35%) cream	500 mL
1 cup	milk (not low-fat or nonfat)	250 mL
½ cup	granulated or superfine sugar	125 mL
1 tsp	vanilla extract	5 mL
½ tsp	almond extract	2 mL
½ cup	coarsely chopped semisweet chocolate	125 mL

1. In a microwave-safe bowl, mix together dried cherries and liqueur. Microwave on High for 20 to 30 seconds or until cherries are very warm. Set cherries aside to absorb liqueur.

2. In a bowl, whisk together cream, milk, sugar and vanilla and almond extracts until smooth and sugar is dissolved.

3. Transfer mixture to ice cream maker and freeze according to manufacturer's directions. Without stopping machine, when ice cream is thick, add reserved cherries with any remaining liqueur and chocolate. Continue freezing according to manufacturer's directions. Homemade ice cream will be somewhat softer in texture than store-bought. Serve immediately or freeze in an airtight container (for storage info, see Tip, page 217). This ice cream is best served the same day that it is made.

Coffee Ice Cream

Makes about 4 cups (1 L)

- Ice cream maker

This is a fun way to top your pies. It's simple. Just scoop some homemade ice cream onto your fresh baked pies.

Variation

For a chocolate chip version, add ½ cup (125 mL) miniature semisweet chocolate chips when the ice cream is almost finished churning. This way, the chocolate chips will be nicely incorporated throughout the ice cream.

1½ cups	milk (not low-fat or nonfat), divided	375 mL
¼ cup	ground dark roast coffee	50 mL
1 tbsp	instant coffee granules	15 mL
1¾ cups	whipping (35%) cream	425 mL
½ cup	granulated or superfine sugar	125 mL
1 tsp	vanilla paste or extract	5 mL

1. In a small heavy-bottomed saucepan over medium heat, combine ½ cup (125 mL) of the milk and ground and instant coffees. Bring mixture to a simmer. Set aside and let cool.

2. In a bowl, whisk together cream, remaining 1 cup (250 mL) milk, sugar and vanilla until smooth and sugar is dissolved. Strain cooled coffee mixture into cream mixture, whisking well.

3. Transfer mixture to ice cream maker and freeze according to manufacturer's directions. Homemade ice cream will be somewhat softer in texture than store-bought. Serve immediately or freeze in an airtight container (for storage info, see Tip, page 217). This ice cream is best served the same day that it is made.

Dark Chocolate Sorbet

**Makes about
4 cups (1 L)**

- Ice cream maker

I fell in love with sorbet
on my first trip to France,
right out of high school.
I loved the way sorbets
burst with flavor yet
aren't overly rich, as they
contain no cream. I still
adore sorbets today,
especially this one.

2½ cups	boiling water	625 mL
1 cup	unsweetened Dutch-process cocoa powder	250 mL
¾ cup	granulated sugar	175 mL
3 oz	unsweetened chocolate, chopped	90 g
2 tbsp	dark rum	25 mL

1. In a bowl, whisk together boiling water, cocoa powder
   and sugar. Whisk in chocolate and rum until smooth
   and sugar is dissolved. Refrigerate mixture until chilled.

2. Transfer mixture to ice cream maker and freeze
   according to manufacturer's directions. Serve
   immediately or freeze in an airtight container (for
   storage info, see Tip, page 217). This sorbet is best
   served the same day that it is made.

Eggnog Ice Cream

**Makes about
5 cups (1.25 L)**

- Ice cream maker

Here's a richly spiced ice
cream topping for all of
your holiday pies. All I can
say about this pie topper is
more, more, more! Eggnog
is readily available in
supermarkets around the
winter holiday season.

1¾ cups	whipping (35%) cream	425 mL
1¾ cups	eggnog (not low-fat)	425 mL
½ cup	granulated or superfine sugar	125 mL
1 to 2 tbsp	dark rum	15 to 25 mL
1 tsp	ground nutmeg	5 mL

1. In a large bowl or measuring cup, whisk together cream,
   eggnog, sugar, 1 tbsp (15 mL) rum and nutmeg until
   smooth and sugar is dissolved. If you desire a stronger
   rum flavor, add an additional 1 tbsp (15 mL) dark rum.

2. Transfer mixture to ice cream maker and freeze
   according to manufacturer's directions. Homemade
   ice cream will be somewhat softer in texture than
   store-bought. Serve immediately or freeze in an airtight
   container (for storage info, see Tip, page 217). This ice
   cream is best served the same day that it is made.

Frozen Cappuccino

Makes about 5 cups (1.25 L)

- Ice cream maker

This is one of my favorite sorbets. It was inspired by a sorbet that my mother was raving about. I never did get to taste her sorbet but developed this one based on her description. It is truly heavenly.

1 cup	unsweetened Dutch-process cocoa powder, sifted	250 mL
¾ cup	granulated or superfine sugar	175 mL
½ tsp	ground cinnamon	2 mL
2 cups	freshly brewed hot coffee	500 mL
½ cup	semisweet chocolate chips	125 mL
½ cup	whipping (35%) cream	125 mL
1 tbsp	dark rum	15 mL
1 tsp	lightly packed finely grated orange zest	5 mL
1 tsp	vanilla extract	5 mL

Tip

Even though this ice cream is best served the day that it is made, the best way to store any leftover ice cream is to pack it in a plastic container, press a piece of plastic wrap onto the surface, cover with a tight-fitting plastic lid and freeze. This helps prevent freezer burn.

1. In a bowl, whisk together cocoa powder, sugar and cinnamon.

2. In a large bowl, combine coffee, chocolate chips, cream, rum, orange zest and vanilla. Whisk in cocoa mixture until smooth. Refrigerate mixture until cold.

3. Transfer to ice cream maker and freeze according to manufacturer's directions. Serve immediately or freeze in an airtight container (for storage info, see Tip, left). This sorbet is best served the same day that it is made.

Frozen Raspberry Chocolate Cream

Makes about 4 cups (1 L)

- Ice cream maker

This ice cream is too delicious for words. It's creamy and full-flavored without being too rich. If you prepare the raspberry chocolate sauce ahead of time (up to 2 days ahead), you can freeze this dreamy dessert just prior to serving.

1	recipe Raspberry Chocolate Sauce (see recipe, page 236)	1
1 cup	whipping (35%) cream	250 mL
¼ cup	granulated or superfine sugar	50 mL

1. In a bowl, whisk together raspberry chocolate sauce, cream and sugar until smooth and sugar is dissolved.

2. Transfer mixture to ice cream maker and freeze according to manufacturer's directions. Homemade ice cream will be somewhat softer in texture than store-bought. Serve immediately or freeze in an airtight container (for storage info, see Tip, page 217). This ice cream is best served the same day that it is made.

Frozen Raspberry Cream

Makes about 5 cups (1.25 L)

- Ice cream maker

This ice cream is always a hit, especially when served with little lemon tarts or lemon pie. The flavor of the raspberries is really bright but mellowed by the softness of the cream.

3 cups	fresh or frozen raspberries	750 mL
1¼ cups	granulated or superfine sugar, divided	300 mL
1¼ cups	whipping (35%) cream	300 mL
1 tbsp	freshly squeezed lemon juice	15 mL

1. In a blender, combine raspberries and half of the sugar, blending until smooth. Strain mixture into measuring cup or bowl. (You should have about 1½ cups/375 mL purée.) Whisk in remaining sugar, cream and lemon juice until sugar is dissolved.

2. Transfer mixture to ice cream maker and freeze according to manufacturer's directions. Homemade ice cream will be somewhat softer in texture than store-bought. Serve immediately or freeze in an airtight container (for storage info, see Tip, page 217). This ice cream is best served the same day that it is made.

Green Tea Ice Cream

Makes about 4 cups (1 L)

- Ice cream maker

Green tea ice cream is delicious, a must-try if you've never had the pleasure. Look for matcha (green tea powder) in tea shops or well-stocked health food or grocery stores.

1½ cups	milk (not low-fat or nonfat), divided	375 mL
1 tbsp	matcha (green tea powder)	15 mL
1½ cups	whipping (35%) cream	375 mL
¾ cup	granulated or superfine sugar	175 mL

1. In a small microwave-safe bowl, microwave ½ cup (125 mL) of the milk on High for 1 minute or until steamy. Whisk in matcha until smooth. Let mixture cool.

2. In a bowl, whisk together cooled green tea mixture, cream, remaining 1 cup (250 mL) milk and sugar until smooth and sugar is dissolved.

3. Transfer mixture to ice cream maker and freeze according to manufacturer's directions. Homemade ice cream will be somewhat softer in texture than store-bought. Serve immediately or freeze in an airtight container (for storage info, see Tip, page 217). This ice cream is best served the same day that it is made.

Honey Vanilla Ice Cream

Makes about 4 cups (1 L)

- Ice cream maker

This honey-and-cream combo is what heavenly dreams are made of. It's really amazing scooped on top of just about any pie you can imagine.

1½ cups	whipping (35%) cream	375 mL
1½ cups	milk (not low-fat or nonfat)	375 mL
½ cup	liquid honey	125 mL
2 tsp	vanilla paste or extract	10 mL

1. In a bowl, whisk together cream, milk, honey and vanilla until smooth.

2. Transfer mixture to ice cream maker and freeze according to manufacturer's directions. Homemade ice cream will be somewhat softer in texture than store-bought. Serve immediately or freeze in an airtight container (for storage info, see Tip, page 217). This ice cream is best served the same day that it is made.

Lemon Ice Milk

Makes about 4 cups (1 L)

- Ice cream maker

This fabulous lemon ice cream recipe was shared with me by Lois Schnitzer. Lois says that she's made this frozen dessert for years and that it's a family favorite. It's incredibly delicious served with both pies and tarts, or eaten with a spoon.

2 cups	milk (not low-fat or nonfat)	500 mL
1 cup	superfine sugar	250 mL
1 tsp	grated lemon zest	5 mL
½ cup	strained freshly squeezed lemon juice	125 mL

1. In a large bowl, whisk together milk and sugar until sugar is dissolved. Transfer to ice cream maker and freeze according to manufacturer's directions until it stiffens considerably. Add lemon zest and juice. Continue to churn until ice milk is really thick.

2. Serve immediately or freeze in an airtight plastic container. This ice milk is best served the same day that it is made.

VEGAN FRIENDLY

Mai Tai Sorbet

Makes about 4 cups (1 L)

- Ice cream maker

Sorbets are really fun, because you can take all of the flavors of your favorite drink and put them into a frozen treat. The best part is the look on your guests' faces when you serve Key lime pie (see White Chocolate Key Lime Pie, page 58) with a side of Mai Tai Sorbet.

1 cup	pineapple juice	250 mL
1 cup	guava nectar	250 mL
1 cup	passion fruit nectar	250 mL
½ cup	superfine sugar	125 mL
3 tbsp	dark rum	45 mL
2½ tbsp	grenadine	32 mL
2 tbsp	freshly squeezed lime juice	25 mL

1. In a large bowl, whisk together pineapple juice, guava nectar, passion fruit nectar, sugar, rum, grenadine and lime juice until sugar is dissolved.

2. Transfer mixture to ice cream maker and freeze according to manufacturer's directions. Serve immediately or freeze in an airtight container (for storage info, see Tip, page 217). This sorbet is best served the same day that it is made.

Maple Ice Cream

Makes about
4 cups (1 L)

- Ice cream maker

Maple syrup plus brown sugar plus cream equals one fantastic way to top a slice of pie! I think that this recipe will forever be on my Thanksgiving dessert menu.

1½ cups	whipping (35%) cream	375 mL
1½ cups	whole milk	375 mL
½ cup	packed brown sugar	125 mL
¼ cup	pure maple syrup	50 mL
1 tsp	maple extract	5 mL

1. In a bowl, whisk together cream, milk, brown sugar, and maple syrup and extract until smooth and sugar is dissolved.

2. Transfer mixture to ice cream maker and freeze according to manufacturer's directions. Homemade ice cream will be somewhat softer in texture than store-bought. Serve immediately or freeze in an airtight container (for storage info, see Tip, page 217). This ice cream is best served the same day that it is made.

Mocha Frozen Yogurt

Makes about
4½ cups (1.125 L)

- Ice cream maker

This frozen dessert is devilishly delicious. It's decadent, with a deep chocolate flavor and a nice tang from the yogurt. It's also a great way to satisfy your chocolate tooth while getting a hefty dose of calcium.

1 cup	whipping (35%) cream	250 mL
½ cup	malted milk powder	125 mL
4 oz	unsweetened chocolate, chopped	125 g
2 cups	plain yogurt (not nonfat)	500 mL
1 cup	granulated or superfine sugar	250 mL

1. In a microwave-safe bowl, microwave cream on High for about 1 minute or until steamy.

2. Whisk in malted milk powder and chocolate until smooth. Whisk in yogurt and sugar.

3. Transfer mixture to ice cream maker and freeze according to manufacturer's directions. Homemade frozen yogurt will be somewhat softer in texture than store-bought. Serve immediately or freeze in an airtight container (for storage info, see Tip, page 217). This frozen yogurt is best served the same day that it is made.

Mocha Ice

Makes about 3 cups (750 mL)

- 2 plastic ice cube trays

This is a great treat to serve atop a piece of chocolate pie when you want something delicious but light. You can top this with a dollop of whipped cream or serve it alongside a scoop of vanilla ice cream. Basically, any way you serve it, it's delicious!

Tips

To make strong brewed coffee, use a heaping 2 tbsp (25 mL) finely ground coffee, such as espresso roast, French roast or Sumatra, for every 6 oz (175 mL) water.

If you want to make this dessert ahead of time, place frozen cubes in a resealable plastic bag. They will keep, frozen, for up to 2 days. Remove from freezer and process right before serving.

Variation

This is fabulous drizzled with chocolate sauce.

2 cups	freshly brewed hot strong coffee (see Tips, left)	500 mL
⅓ cup	packed light brown sugar	75 mL
¼ cup	unsweetened Dutch-process cocoa powder, sifted	50 mL
2 oz	bittersweet chocolate, chopped (see Tips, page 232)	60 g
3 tbsp	granulated or superfine sugar	45 mL
½ tsp	ground cinnamon	2 mL
1 tbsp	dark rum	15 mL

1. Place coffee in a bowl. Whisk in brown sugar, cocoa powder, chocolate, sugar, cinnamon and rum until smooth and sugar is dissolved.

2. Transfer mixture to ice cube trays. Freeze overnight or until solid.

3. In a food processor fitted with metal blade, add frozen cubes and pulse until finely chopped with a texture like snow. Serve immediately or freeze in an airtight container until ready to serve.

Orange Vanilla Ice Cream

**Makes about
4 cups (1 L)**

- Ice cream maker

Remember those
wonderful Creamsicle
ice cream bars when
we were kids? This ice
cream — with its luscious
flavors of vanilla and
orange — will bring you
back to that time.

Tip
This is fabulous
garnished with toasted
chopped almonds.

1 cup	whipping (35%) cream	250 mL
1 cup	milk (not low-fat or nonfat)	250 mL
1 tsp	grated orange zest	5 mL
1 cup	freshly squeezed orange juice	250 mL
¾ cup	granulated or superfine sugar	175 mL
1 tsp	vanilla extract	5 mL
½ tsp	orange oil	2 mL

1. In a bowl, whisk together cream, milk, orange zest and juice, sugar, vanilla and orange oil until smooth and sugar is dissolved.

2. Transfer mixture to ice cream maker and freeze according to manufacturer's directions. Homemade ice cream will be somewhat softer in texture than store-bought. Serve immediately or freeze in an airtight container (for storage info, see Tip, page 217). This ice cream is best served the same day that it is made.

Peppermint Stick Gelato

**Makes about
4 cups (1 L)**

- Ice cream maker

The flavors in this ice
cream are downright
refreshing on a hot
summer day. Even better,
it pairs beautifully with a
chocolate tart or pie and
will have your guests
screaming for more.

1¼ cups	whipping (35%) cream	300 mL
1¼ cups	milk (not low-fat or nonfat)	300 mL
½ cup	superfine sugar	125 mL
½ cup	crushed peppermint candies or candy canes	125 mL
¼ tsp	peppermint extract	1 mL

1. In a bowl, whisk together cream, milk, sugar, peppermint candies and extract until combined and sugar is dissolved.

2. Transfer mixture to ice cream maker and freeze according to manufacturer's directions. Homemade gelato will be somewhat softer in texture than store-bought. Serve immediately or freeze in an airtight container (for storage info, see Tip, page 217). This gelato is best served the same day that it is made.

Pumpkin Ice Cream

Makes about 4 cups (1 L)

• Ice cream maker

Imagine a velvety slice of pumpkin pie with a big scoop of ice cream. Now picture those flavors swirled together and frozen, then scooped atop a slice of pumpkin pie. You've got the best flavors of autumn rolled into one dessert.

Tip

If you enjoy pumpkin desserts but can only purchase canned pumpkin in the fall, stock up on extra. That way, you can enjoy the luscious flavors of fall all year long.

Variation

For an extra-delicious treat, add ½ cup (125 mL) coarsely chopped candied ginger bits or finely chopped semisweet chocolate to the ice cream mixture once it is thick.

1½ cups	whipping (35%) cream	375 mL
1¼ cups	pumpkin purée (not pie filling) (see Tip, left and page 59)	300 mL
1 cup	milk (not low-fat or nonfat)	250 mL
¾ cup	granulated or superfine sugar	175 mL
1 tsp	ground cinnamon	5 mL
1 tsp	ground allspice	5 mL
1 tsp	ground ginger	5 mL

1. In a saucepan over medium heat, whisk together cream, pumpkin, milk, sugar, cinnamon, allspice and ginger. Bring to a simmer, whisking continuously.

2. Strain mixture into a bowl. Let cool until lukewarm, then cover and refrigerate until chilled.

3. Transfer mixture to ice cream maker and freeze according to manufacturer's directions. Homemade ice cream will be somewhat softer in texture than store-bought. Serve immediately or freeze in an airtight container (for storage info, see Tip, page 217). This ice cream is best served the same day that it is made.

Pear and Almond Galette (page 146)
Overleaf: Tourtière (page 172)

Vanilla Rose Ice Cream

Makes about 4 cups (1 L)

- Ice cream maker

This is a lovely ice cream, with a whisper of the floral flavors of rose and vanilla. It makes a wonderful addition to freshly baked berry pies and tarts.

Tip

If you desire a sweeter ice cream, add more sugar to taste.

1½ cups	whipping (35%) cream	375 mL
1½ cups	milk (not low-fat or nonfat)	375 mL
½ cup	superfine or granulated sugar	125 mL
4 tsp	rose water	20 mL
1 tsp	vanilla paste or extract	5 mL

1. In a large bowl or measuring cup, whisk together cream, milk, sugar, rose water and vanilla until sugar is dissolved.

2. Transfer mixture to ice cream maker and freeze according to manufacturer's directions. Homemade ice cream will be somewhat softer in texture than store-bought. Serve immediately or freeze in an airtight container (for storage info, see Tip, page 217). This ice cream is best served the same day that it is made.

Rum Raisin Ice Cream

Makes about 4 cups (1 L)

• Ice cream maker

There's something so heavenly about rum raisin ice cream. It has such a rich spiced flavor that I can't ever get enough. Try this ice cream paired with your favorite pie. You can't go wrong.

> **Tip**
> If you desire a sweeter ice cream, add more sugar to taste.

½ cup	raisins	125 mL
6 tbsp	dark rum, divided	90 mL
1¾ cups	whipping (35%) cream	425 mL
1¾ cups	milk (not low-fat or nonfat)	425 mL
⅔ cup	granulated or superfine sugar	150 mL
2½ tsp	rum extract	12 mL

1. In a small microwave-safe bowl, combine raisins and 4 tbsp (50 mL) of the rum. Microwave mixture on High for four 20-second intervals or until raisins are hot and have soaked up most of the rum. Set aside for at least 1 hour to absorb remaining rum.

2. In a large bowl or measuring cup, whisk together cream, milk, sugar and rum extract until sugar is dissolved.

3. Transfer mixture to ice cream maker and freeze according to manufacturer's directions. When ice cream is about three-quarters of the way frozen, add raisin mixture. Continue freezing according to manufacturer's directions.

4. Stir remaining 2 tbsp (25 mL) dark rum into ice cream and pack mixture into an airtight freezer container. Place a piece of plastic wrap on the surface of the ice cream. Place in freezer for several hours before serving. Homemade ice cream will be somewhat softer in texture than store-bought. Serve immediately or freeze in an airtight container (for storage information, see Tip, page 217). This ice cream is best served the same day that it is made.

Spumoni

Makes about
6 cups (1.5 L)

- Ice cream maker

Spumoni instantly brings me back to my childhood. My grandmother would take my brother and me out for pizza at our favorite Italian restaurant. As long as we were good and ate our dinner, we knew that we would be rewarded with a frosty scoop of this delicious ice cream.

Tip
If you desire a sweeter ice cream, add more sugar to taste.

Variation
You can substitute frozen sweet cherries for the fresh. Alternatively, you can also use maraschino cherries.

2 cups	milk (not low-fat or nonfat)	500 mL
2 cups	whipping (35%) cream	500 mL
2/3 cup	superfine or granulated sugar	150 mL
2 tbsp	orange-flavored liqueur	25 mL
2 tsp	vanilla extract	10 mL
1/2 tsp	almond extract	2 mL
1/2 tsp	orange extract	2 mL
2/3 cup	Bing or other sweet cherries, chopped	150 mL
1/3 cup	toasted almonds, coarsely chopped	75 mL
1/3 cup	toasted pistachios, chopped	75 mL
2 1/2 oz	bittersweet chocolate, chopped (see Tips, page 232)	75 g

1. In a large bowl or measuring cup, whisk together milk, cream, sugar, liqueur and vanilla, almond and orange extracts until sugar is dissolved.

2. Transfer mixture to ice cream maker and freeze according to manufacturer's directions. When ice cream is about three-quarters of the way frozen, add cherries, almonds, pistachios and chocolate. Continue freezing according to manufacturer's directions. Homemade ice cream will be somewhat softer in texture than store-bought. Serve immediately or freeze in an airtight container (for storage info, see Tip, page 217). This ice cream is best served the same day that it is made.

Tiramisu Ice Cream

Makes about 4 cups (1 L)

- Ice cream maker

Here you have all of the great flavors of an Italian tiramisu whipped together into a creamy ice cream. This ice cream would be fabulous with almost any freshly baked pie.

2 tbsp	coffee-flavored liqueur	25 mL
1 tbsp	instant coffee granules	15 mL
1 cup	whipping (35%) cream	250 mL
½ cup	granulated or superfine sugar	125 mL
8 oz	cream cheese, softened	250 g
1 cup	milk (not low-fat or nonfat)	250 mL

1. In a small bowl, stir together coffee liqueur and instant coffee.

2. In a food processor fitted with metal blade, pulse cream, sugar and cream cheese until smooth, scraping down side of bowl as necessary. Add milk and coffee mixture, pulsing until smooth.

3. Transfer mixture to ice cream maker and freeze according to manufacturer's directions. Homemade ice cream will be somewhat softer in texture than store-bought. Serve immediately or freeze in an airtight container (for storage info, see Tip, page 217). This ice cream is best served the same day that it is made.

Vanilla Bean Ice Cream

Makes 4 cups (1 L)

- Ice cream maker

I think that vanilla often gets a bad rap as being boring. I wholeheartedly disagree, especially when it comes to homemade vanilla ice cream. Besides having a creamy flavor, this ice cream gets a nice zing from vanilla paste. Have you ever seen anyone turn down a scoop of vanilla ice cream on a slice of pie? I sure haven't!

1½ cups	whipping (35%) cream	375 mL
1½ cups	milk (not low-fat or nonfat)	375 mL
½ cup	granulated or superfine sugar	125 mL
1 tsp	vanilla paste or extract	5 mL

1. In a bowl, whisk together cream, milk, sugar and vanilla paste until smooth and sugar is dissolved.

2. Transfer mixture to ice cream maker and freeze according to manufacturer's directions. Homemade ice cream will be somewhat softer in texture than store-bought. Serve immediately or freeze in an airtight container (for storage info, see Tip, page 217). This ice cream is best served the same day that it is made.

Variations

For a chocolate chip version, add ½ cup (125 mL) miniature semisweet chocolate chips when the ice cream is thick.

For a fruit version, add 1 cup (250 mL) chopped peeled pitted fresh peaches, nectarines or strawberries. If you want chunks of fruit throughout the ice cream, add them halfway through churning, when the ice cream has thickened somewhat. Otherwise, the fruit can be added with the milk, which will give the ice cream more of a fruit flavor throughout.

White Chocolate Cheesecake Ice Cream

Makes about 4 cups (1 L)

- Ice cream maker

The luscious combination of white chocolate and cream cheese makes this ice cream both incredibly decadent and delicious. Try serving it the next time you have pie for dessert. You will be amazed at the moans of delight coming from your guests.

> **Variation**
>
> Substitute chopped bittersweet chocolate for the chopped white chocolate.

1 cup	whipping (35%) cream	250 mL
3 oz	white chocolate, chopped	90 g
8 oz	cream cheese, softened	250 g
⅔ cup	superfine sugar	150 mL
1 cup	milk (not low-fat or nonfat)	250 mL

1. In a microwave-safe bowl, microwave cream on High for about 1 minute or until steamy. Remove from microwave and add chopped white chocolate, stirring until smooth.

2. In a food processor fitted with metal blade, blend cream cheese and sugar. Add milk and blend until smooth. Add white chocolate mixture and blend again until mixture is smooth.

3. Transfer mixture to ice cream maker and freeze according to manufacturer's directions. Homemade ice cream will be somewhat softer in texture than store-bought. Serve immediately or freeze in an airtight container (for storage info, see Tip, page 217). This ice cream is best served the same day that it is made.

Sauces, Creams, Glazes & Toppings

Bourbon Fudge Sauce

Makes 1⅓ cups (325 mL)

When you're in the mood for a grown-up dark chocolate sauce, this is it. It is beyond delish! Don't be surprised if this sauce brings on marriage proposals.

¾ cup	whipping (35%) cream	175 mL
6 oz	bittersweet chocolate, chopped (see Tips, left)	175 g
2 tbsp	bourbon	25 mL

1. In a saucepan, bring cream to a boil over medium heat. Remove from heat. Add chocolate and bourbon and whisk until melted and smooth. Let cool for 5 minutes before serving. Store in a glass jar in the refrigerator. Reheat in the microwave as needed.

Tips

Bittersweet chocolate, also known as dark chocolate, must have at least 35% chocolate liquor, but many brands now go beyond that, up to 90%. When I use dark chocolate in my baking, I often reach for a 70% bar. If you like a sweeter chocolate, use semisweet, which has a less-intense chocolate flavor than bittersweet. For a darker, more-intense chocolate flavor, reach for one of the darker, higher percentage bars.

Let sauce thicken for 5 minutes before using.

Variation

Omit the bourbon for a G rating and add 2 tsp (10 mL) vanilla extract.

Chocolate Caramel Sauce

Makes about 1½ cups (375 mL)

This decadent sauce goes together lickety-split. Beginning to end, it takes 5 minutes to prepare (quicker than running to the neighbors' to borrow a cup of sugar).

Tips

Omit salt if using salted butter.

Store extra sauce in the refrigerator for up to 1 month. You'll need to warm it to soften it after it's been refrigerated.

Serve this sauce warm for a fun fondue.

Serve sauce with tarts or pies. It makes a wonderful addition to a fresh berry or chocolate tart.

¼ cup	butter	50 mL
¾ cup	packed light brown sugar	175 mL
⅓ cup	light (white) corn syrup	75 mL
¼ tsp	salt	1 mL
½ cup	whipping (35%) cream	125 mL
⅓ cup	semisweet chocolate chips	75 mL

1. In a saucepan, melt butter over medium heat. Add brown sugar, corn syrup and salt. Increase heat to medium-high and bring to a boil, stirring constantly. Once boiling, it will look like bubbling lava. Boil for 1 minute.

2. Remove from heat and whisk in cream. Add chocolate chips and whisk until melted and smooth. The sauce will look like it's separating but will smooth out after a minute or so of whisking. The sauce will thicken as it cools. Serve warm.

Chocolate Merlot Sauce

Makes about 1⅓ cups (325 mL)

This is an outrageous and mouthwatering sauce. Complex and simple at the same time, it takes only a couple of minutes to prepare. Drizzle this sauce over tarts or pies for a very special dessert.

1 cup	semisweet chocolate chips	250 mL
½ cup	Merlot or Cabernet Sauvignon wine	125 mL
⅓ cup	light (white) corn syrup	75 mL

1. In a saucepan, combine chocolate chips, wine and corn syrup. Cook over medium heat, whisking constantly, just until chocolate is melted.

2. Remove from heat and whisk until smooth. Let cool slightly.

Chocolate Toffee Sauce

Makes about 1½ cups (375 mL)

This recipe was adapted from a tried-and-true toffee sauce recipe by Jill Dupleix. I've added a hint of chocolate, but you can certainly omit it for a non-chocolate version.

Tip
This sauce keeps, covered, in the refrigerator for up to 2 days.

Variation
Omit the chocolate from the recipe for a plain toffee sauce, which is incredible spooned or drizzled over apple pie.

1 cup	whipping (35%) cream	250 mL
¾ cup	packed light brown sugar	175 mL
2 tbsp	light (white) corn syrup	25 mL
2 tbsp	butter	25 mL
1 oz	unsweetened chocolate, chopped	30 g
1 tsp	vanilla extract	5 mL

1. In a heavy saucepan, whisk together cream, brown sugar, corn syrup and butter. Butter will be lumpy, but don't worry.

2. Place saucepan over medium heat and bring to a simmer, whisking continuously. If mixture starts to boil rapidly, you can reduce heat in order to maintain a simmer. Simmer for 5 minutes. Remove from heat. Add chocolate and vanilla and whisk until melted and smooth. Spoon hot sauce over pies or tarts as desired.

Hot Fudge Sauce

**Makes about
1¼ cups (300 mL)**

My friend Tamara gave
me this recipe years ago.
I'm not sure where she
found it, but I do know
that it's delicious beyond
words and obscenely
fantastic drizzled over
pies, ice cream and just
about anything else you
can sink your teeth into.

½ cup	packed light brown sugar	125 mL
½ cup	whipping (35%) cream	125 mL
¼ cup	salted butter	50 mL
½ cup	unsweetened Dutch-process cocoa powder, sifted	125 mL
1 tbsp	dark rum	15 mL

1. In a heavy saucepan, whisk together brown sugar, cream and butter. Bring to a simmer over medium-high heat, whisking occasionally. Reduce heat to medium-low and whisk in cocoa powder, whisking continuously.

2. Remove from heat and whisk in rum. Let cool until thickened. Fudge sauce will become very thick as it cools. Spoon over pies or tarts.

Milk Chocolate Banana Sauce

**Makes 1¼ cups
(300 mL)**

Something about the
flavor of bananas
caramelized in butter
and brown sugar and
then mixed with a touch
of cream and milk
chocolate is utterly
irresistible to me. Needless
to say, I can again forgo
the ice cream altogether
and eat this sauce with a
spoon. Dieters, beware!
But it's also unbelievably
good served with
chocolate or banana pies
or tarts.

2 tbsp	salted butter	25 mL
¼ cup	packed light brown sugar	50 mL
1	large banana, sliced	1
¾ cup	whipping (35%) cream	175 mL
2 oz	milk chocolate, chopped	60 g

1. In a nonstick skillet, melt butter over medium-high heat. Stir in brown sugar and cook until melted.

2. Add sliced bananas and continue to cook, stirring often, until the bananas are soft and caramelized (the butter-sugar mixture will thicken). Stir in cream and cook, stirring continuously, for 2 to 3 minutes or until sauce is smooth and thickened.

3. Remove from heat. Add chopped chocolate and stir until melted and smooth. Serve immediately.

Raspberry Chocolate Sauce

**Makes scant
2 cups (500 mL)**

Raspberry sauce is a great way to fancy-up a dessert. It goes beautifully with homemade tarts, especially those of the chocolate variety.

1	package (12 oz/375 g) unsweetened frozen raspberries, thawed (about 3 cups/750 mL)	1
½ cup	superfine sugar, or to taste	125 mL
3 oz	bittersweet chocolate, chopped (see Tips, page 232)	90 g

1. In a food processor fitted with metal blade, combine raspberries, sugar and ½ cup (125 mL) water. Process until blended and smooth.

2. In a fine-mesh sieve set over a small saucepan, strain raspberry mixture, discarding seeds.

3. Bring mixture to a simmer over medium heat, stirring occasionally. Remove from heat. Add chocolate and stir until melted and smooth. Serve warm or let cool, cover and refrigerate for up to 2 days and serve cold.

Tips

If you prefer a more-pronounced chocolate flavor, add an additional 1 oz (30 g) chocolate.

If you prefer the sauce a bit sweeter, you can add additional sugar to taste. If you prefer your sauce a bit tangier, reduce the sugar to taste.

Raspberry Sauce

**Makes scant
2 cups (500 mL)**

Raspberry sauce is wonderful served with a slice of lemon pie, chocolate tart or mixed berry pie. After tasting this sauce, you'll wonder how you ever served pie without it.

1	package (12 oz/375 g) unsweetened frozen raspberries, thawed	1
⅓ cup	superfine sugar, or to taste	75 mL
2 tsp	grated lemon zest, optional	10 mL

1. In a food processor fitted with metal blade, combine raspberries, ½ cup (125 mL) water and sugar. Process until blended and smooth.

2. In a fine-mesh sieve set over a bowl, strain mixture, discarding seeds. Add lemon zest, if using. Serve immediately or cover and refrigerate for up to 2 days.

Rich Caramel Sauce

**Makes about
1½ cups (375 mL)**

This decadent sauce goes
together in a snap.
Beginning to end, this
sauce takes 5 minutes
to prepare (quicker
than finding your keys
to run to the store). Let
me just say that caramel
sauce drizzled over pies
and tarts is amazing!

¼ cup	butter	50 mL
¾ cup	packed light brown sugar	175 mL
⅓ cup	light (white) corn syrup	75 mL
¼ tsp	salt	1 mL
⅓ cup	whipping (35%) cream	75 mL

1. In a saucepan, melt butter over medium heat. Add
   brown sugar, corn syrup and salt. Increase heat to
   medium-high and bring to a boil, stirring continuously.
   Once boiling, it will look like bubbling lava. Boil for
   1 minute.
2. Remove from heat and whisk in cream. The sauce might
   look like it's separating but will smooth out after a
   minute or so of whisking. Sauce will thicken
   up a lot as it cools.

Sticky Chocolate Raisin Sauce

**Makes about
1⅓ cups (325 mL)**

This sauce is soooo good
that I could almost forgo
the pie and ice cream
altogether and eat it with
a spoon. It's almost like
candy: sweet, chocolaty,
sticky and chewy. This
sauce is what dreams are
made of!

6 tbsp	salted butter	90 mL
1 cup	packed light brown sugar	250 mL
⅓ cup	unsweetened Dutch-process cocoa powder, sifted	75 mL
⅓ cup	raisins	75 mL
⅓ cup	whipping (35%) cream	75 mL
2 tbsp	light (white) corn syrup	25 mL

1. In a saucepan, melt butter over medium heat. Whisk in
   brown sugar, cocoa powder, raisins, cream and corn
   syrup. Bring mixture to a boil. Reduce heat and simmer,
   stirring, for 3 minutes. Serve warm.

Variation
You can omit the raisins
altogether or substitute
dried cherries for them.

White Chocolate Sauce

**Makes about
1¼ cups (300 mL)**

This is a most delicious, mouthwatering, silky sauce that tastes as amazing on ice cream as it does drizzled over chocolate tarts.

¾ cup	whipping (35%) cream	175 mL
5 oz	white chocolate, chopped	150 g

1. In a microwave-safe bowl, microwave cream on High for 1 minute or until steaming. Add white chocolate and whisk until melted and smooth.
2. Let mixture stand for 10 minutes to thicken slightly before serving. This sauce can be cooled, covered and refrigerated for up to 2 days.

Lemon Cream

**Makes about
2 cups (500 mL)**

Hello! Calling all lemon lovers. This ethereal, cloud-like topping is heavenly atop a pie. It's also fabulous spooned into little baked and cooled tart shells and topped with a sprinkling of fresh raspberries or blueberries.

⅔ cup	whipping (35%) cream	150 mL
3 tbsp	confectioner's (icing) sugar, sifted	45 mL
1 tsp	grated lemon zest	5 mL
½ cup	Lemon Curd (see recipe, page 203) or store-bought	125 mL

1. In a bowl, using an electric mixer, whip cream, confectioner's sugar and lemon zest just until soft peaks form.
2. Gently fold lemon curd into whipped cream. Use immediately or cover and refrigerate for up to 2 hours.

Lemon-Scented Whipped Cream

**Makes about
2 cups (500 mL)**

OK, can life get much better than freshly baked pie with fluffy whipped cream? Not much, as far as I'm concerned. So when you need a flavored topping, this lemon cream is just the thing.

Tip
This is fantastic served on top of freshly baked berry pie.

1 cup	whipping (35%) cream	250 mL
1/3 cup	confectioner's (icing) sugar, sifted	75 mL
2 tsp	finely grated lemon zest	10 mL
1/4 tsp	lemon oil	1 mL

1. In a bowl, using an electric mixer, whip cream, confectioner's sugar and lemon zest until blended. Add lemon oil and whip until soft peaks form. Do not overbeat.

2. Use immediately or cover and refrigerate for up to 2 hours.

Whipped Coffee Cream

**Makes about
2 cups (500 mL)**

If you want to take your chocolate pies and tarts to the next level, then this whipped coffee cream is just the ticket.

Tip
If making ahead, cover and refrigerate until ready to serve, for up to 2 hours.

1 cup	whipping (35%) cream	250 mL
1/3 cup	confectioner's (icing) sugar, sifted	75 mL
1 tsp	instant espresso powder	5 mL

1. In a bowl, using an electric mixer, whip cream, confectioner's sugar and instant espresso powder until soft peaks form.

2. Use immediately or cover and refrigerate for up to 2 hours.

Almond Glaze

Makes enough for 4 large hand pies or one 9-inch (23 cm) pie

Sometimes the smallest touch can turn a dessert into something unexpected. This glaze has the power to do just that when drizzled over a freshly baked peach pie, berry pie, tart or crumble.

1 cup	confectioner's (icing) sugar, sifted	250 mL
1½ tbsp	milk or soy milk, approx.	22 mL
½ tsp	almond extract	2 mL

1. In a bowl, using an electric mixer, beat together confectioner's sugar, milk and almond extract until smooth. If you prefer a thinner glaze, you can add another ½ tsp (2 mL) or so of milk.

2. Spread or drizzle over pie. This glaze needs to be made just before using, as it hardens quickly.

Cinnamon Glaze

Makes enough for 4 large hand pies or one 9-inch (23 cm) pie

Here's another recipe that will surprise and delight, especially when drizzled over freshly baked hand pies. Please don't stop at hand pies, though. Imagine the possibilities with a cinnamon-glazed apple or boysenberry pie.

1 cup	confectioner's (icing) sugar	250 mL
1½ tbsp	milk or soy milk, approx.	22 mL
¼ tsp	ground cinnamon	1 mL

1. In a bowl, using an electric mixer, beat together confectioner's sugar, milk and cinnamon until smooth. If you prefer a thinner glaze, you can add another ½ tsp (2 mL) or so of milk.

2. Spread or drizzle over pie. This glaze needs to be made just before using, as it will harden quickly.

Tip

This recipe can be doubled if you're planning to use it to cover several pies.

Lemon Glaze

Makes enough for 4 large hand pies or one 9-inch (23 cm) pie

Tangy and tart, this lemon glaze is easy to make. The lemon zest kicks up the flavor of the pie and makes for an elegant-looking garnish.

1 cup	confectioner's (icing) sugar, sifted	250 mL
1½ tbsp	freshly squeezed lemon juice, approx.	22 mL
1 tsp	grated lemon zest	5 mL

1. In a bowl, using an electric mixer, beat together confectioner's sugar, lemon juice and zest until smooth. If you prefer a thinner glaze, you can add another ½ tsp (2 mL) or so of lemon juice.

2. Spread or drizzle over pie. This glaze needs to be made just before using, as it hardens quickly.

Variation
Substitute orange zest and juice for the lemon.

Rich Rum Glaze

Makes enough for 4 large hand pies or one 9-inch (23 cm) pie

Try a drizzle of this over your next apple pie. This glaze adds an extra dimension to the humble pie. Besides, you can't go wrong with the rich flavor of rum.

1 cup	confectioner's (icing) sugar, sifted	250 mL
1½ to 2 tbsp	dark rum	22 to 25 mL

1. In a bowl, using an electric mixer, beat together confectioner's sugar and 1½ tbsp (22 mL) rum until smooth. If you prefer a thinner glaze, you can gradually add remaining rum.

2. Spread or drizzle over pie. This glaze needs to be made just before using, as it hardens quickly.

Tip
This recipe can be doubled if you're planning to use it to cover several pies.

Vanilla Bean Glaze

Makes enough for 4 large hand pies or one 9-inch (23 cm) pie

I love to take desserts to the extreme from time to time, transforming the ordinary into the extraordinary. This Vanilla Bean Glaze is just the ticket. Once you've bitten into a freshly baked pie that's been drizzled with this sweet vanilla glaze, you'll never want to go back to an ordinary pie again.

1 cup	confectioner's (icing) sugar	250 mL
1½ tbsp	milk or soy milk, approx.	22 mL
1 tsp	vanilla paste or extract	5 mL

1. In a bowl, using an electric mixer, beat together confectioner's sugar, milk and vanilla paste until smooth. If you prefer a thinner glaze, you can add another ½ tsp (2 mL) or so of milk.

2. Spread or drizzle over pie. This glaze needs to be made just before using, as it hardens quickly.

Rose Cassis Whipped Topping

Makes about 2 cups (500 mL)

There's something so exotic about rose water, especially in freshly whipped cream. I also love it combined with crème de cassis, as the cassis helps soften its floral flavor.

1 cup	whipping (35%) cream	250 mL
⅓ cup	confectioner's (icing) sugar	75 mL
¼ cup	crème de cassis	50 mL
1 tsp	rose water	5 mL

1. In a bowl, using an electric mixer, whip cream, confectioner's sugar, cassis and rose water until soft peaks form. Do not overbeat.

2. Use immediately or cover and refrigerate for up to 2 hours.

> **Tip**
> If making ahead, cover and refrigerate until ready to serve, for up to 2 hours.

Sherry Cream Topping

**Makes about
2 cups (500 mL)**

I love to serve softly
whipped cream with
many of my homemade
pies. This sherry cream is
divine and goes with
many different pies and
tarts, from pumpkin to
apple to chocolate. Of
course, like many things,
it's also equally good eaten
straight from a spoon.

1 cup	whipping (35%) cream	250 mL
1/3 cup	confectioner's (icing) sugar, sifted	75 mL
2 tbsp	cream sherry	25 mL

1. In a bowl, using an electric mixer, whip cream, confectioner's sugar and sherry until soft peaks form. Do not overbeat.

2. Use immediately or cover and refrigerate for up to 2 hours.

Whipped Almond Topping

**Makes about
2 cups (500 mL)**

A cloud-like topping of
whipped cream is a fun
way to top your pie. You
can alter the flavor of the
whipped cream by using
different flavored syrups. I
love this almond-flavored
cream atop almost any
variety of home-baked pie.

1 cup	whipping (35%) cream	250 mL
1/4 cup	confectioner's (icing) sugar, sifted	50 mL
2 tbsp	almond-flavored syrup	25 mL

1. In a bowl, using an electric mixer, whip cream, confectioner's sugar and almond syrup until soft peaks form. Do not overbeat.

2. Use immediately or cover and refrigerate for up to 2 hours.

Tips

Sprinkle fresh berries or
sliced almonds over the
whipped cream when
serving with pie.

If making ahead, cover
and refrigerate until
ready to serve, for up to
2 hours.

Raspberry Whipped Topping

**Makes about
2 cups (500 mL)**

This delicious whipped topping has a beautiful pink tint to it because of the color of the raspberry liqueur. I love to serve this whipped cream with little fruit tarts for afternoon tea, as it makes a lovely presentation.

1 cup	whipping (35%) cream	250 mL
⅓ cup	confectioner's (icing) sugar, sifted	75 mL
¼ cup	raspberry-flavored liqueur or Framboise	50 mL

1. In a bowl, using an electric mixer, whip cream, confectioner's sugar and liqueur and until soft peaks form. Do not overbeat.

2. Use immediately or cover and refrigerate for up to 2 hours.

> **Tip**
> If making ahead, cover and refrigerate until ready to serve, for up to 2 hours.

Whipped Eggnog Spice Topping

**Makes about
2 cups (500 mL)**

The flavors of eggnog are always fall favorites, and this spiced whipped cream is no exception. It's fun to serve flavored whipped cream with pie, especially when the rich flavors of nutmeg and rum complement fall fruits so well.

1 cup	whipping (35%) cream	250 mL
⅓ cup	confectioner's (icing) sugar, sifted	75 mL
3 tbsp	eggnog-flavored syrup	45 mL
1½ tsp	ground nutmeg, preferably freshly grated	7 mL
¾ tsp	rum extract	4 mL

1. In a bowl, using an electric mixer, whip cream, confectioner's sugar, eggnog syrup, nutmeg and rum extract until soft peaks form.

2. Use immediately or cover and refrigerate for up to 2 hours.

Whipped Maple Topping

**Makes about
2 cups (500 mL)**

If you're a maple lover,
then you will flip for this
wonderfully rich whipped
topping. This cream pairs
well with almost any pie,
but just imagine it with
spicy pumpkin or apple.
Simply divine!

1 cup	whipping (35%) cream	250 mL
¼ cup	confectioner's (icing) sugar, sifted	50 mL
2 tbsp	pure maple syrup	25 mL
1½ tsp	maple extract	7 mL

1. In a bowl, using an electric mixer, whip cream, confectioner's sugar, and maple syrup and extract until soft peaks form. Do not overbeat.
2. Use immediately or cover and refrigerate for up to 2 hours.

Whipped Orange Topping

**Makes about
2 cups (500 mL)**

This whipped topping
has a wonderful orange
flavor, the perfect
accompaniment to a nice
big wedge of pie or as a
filling in little baked and
cooled tartlet shells.

1 cup	whipping (35%) cream	250 mL
6 tbsp	confectioner's (icing) sugar, sifted	90 mL
1 tbsp	orange-flavored liqueur	15 mL
¼ tsp	orange oil	1 mL

1. In a bowl, using an electric mixer, whip cream, confectioner's sugar, orange liqueur and orange oil until soft peaks form. Do not overbeat.

Whipped Rum Topping

**Makes about
2 cups (500 mL)**

Here's the perfect partner
for pumpkin pie, but it's
equally delicious with a
berry cobbler. Say goodbye
to boring holiday desserts
and hello to rum whipped
cream. Who could resist?

1 cup	whipping (35%) cream	250 mL
⅓ cup	confectioner's (icing) sugar, sifted	75 mL
1½ tbsp	dark rum	22 mL

1. In a bowl, using an electric mixer, whip cream, confectioner's sugar and rum until soft peaks form. Do not overbeat.
2. Use immediately or cover and refrigerate for up to 2 hours.

Sources

American Almond Products Company, Inc.
www.lovenbake.com
(718) 875-8310
Artisan-quality almond paste, marzipan, poppy seed filling, prune lekvar, sweetened nut pastes and Schmear fillings.

Birds Hill Enterprises
www.birdshillenterprises.com
(204) 669-4320
A Canadian company that manufactures beautiful handmade wooden pie presses in a variety of sizes.

Bob's Red Mill Natural Foods
www.bobsredmill.com
(800) 349-2173
A wonderful source for whole-grain flours, grains and beans.

Boyajian
www.boyajianinc.com
(800) 965-0665 or (781) 828-9966
Fabulous line of pure citrus oils, olive oils and natural flavorings.

Cuisinart
www.cuisinart.com
Manufacturer of small kitchen appliances and cookware, including food processors, mixers and ice cream makers.

Fiesta Products
www.fiestaproducts.com
Manufacturer of Sil-Pin™ silicone rolling pins.

Gardein Protein International
www.gardein.com
Manufacturers of Gardein™ vegetarian meat and chicken substitutes. Gardein™ products are incredibly delicious alternatives to meat.

KitchenAid
www.kitchenaid.com
Manufacturer of both small and large kitchen appliances, including food processors, mixers and ranges.

Le Creuset
www.lecreuset.com
Manufacturer of excellent-quality enameled cast-iron cookware, ceramic pie plates, mixing bowls, silicone spatulas and much more.

Lodge
www.lodgemfg.com
(423) 837-7181
Manufacturer of excellent-quality American-made cast-iron skillets and Dutch ovens.

Nielsen-Massey Vanillas
In the U.S.: (800) 525-PURE; outside the U.S.: (847) 578-1550
www.nielsenmassey.com
Producers of high-quality pure vanilla extracts, pastes, beans and powders, as well as a variety of other pure extracts.

Qualifirst
www.qualifirst.com
(416) 244-1177
Canadian distributor for Boyajian, including citrus oils.

Tersano
www.tersano.com
Manufacturer of the Lotus Sanitizing System. The machine cleans fruits and vegetables without chemicals using ozone technology, eliminating up to 99.9% of bacteria and pesticides on fruits and vegetables.

Wholly Wholesome
www.whollywholesome.com
Manufacturer of excellent-quality organic frozen pie shells and crumb crusts.

Library and Archives Canada Cataloguing in Publication

Hasson, Julie
    The complete book of pies : 200 recipes from sweet to savory / Julie Hasson.

Includes index.
ISBN-13: 978-0-7788-0191-7.--ISBN-10: 0-7788-0191-8

    1. Pies. I. Title.

TX773.H38 2008   641.8'652   C2008-902463-X

Index